FREEDOM
OF
RELIGION
BY INDIVIDUAL CHOICE

SARAH CARPENTER-VASCIK

ISBN   Paperback   978-1-948653-59-6
              Hardback   978-1-948653-60-2
              eBook   978-1-948653-61-9

Greenberry Publishing LLC
20 Atlantic Cir #104 Pittsburg,
CA 94565

www.greenberrypublishing.com

CONTENTS

INTRODUCTION

This is a revised and updated edition of the work I published in 2015, and in light of the changing political environment over the past year, I've wondered if I should have revised the title to "The war against Freedom of Religion by Individual Choice." This work includes many letters written by the Founding Fathers of America, and where possible, I have incorporated the text and syntax of the original documents. Some readers may find this spelling and grammar difficult to read but I felt it necessary to capture the feelings and the mindset of the authors, so please bear with me. They were included here as a reference, should you the reader wish to read the actual documents that are referenced in the text.

I was raised in a pre-Vatican II Roman Catholic family, where my father was Catholic and my mother was Protestant. When I learned this, I was young and naive enough to see no problem with it, such that I remember being very angry and upset at how devastated my father was when he learned in 1951 that the Catholic Church, an institution that had been such a huge part of his life, had summarily ex-communicated him for marrying my mother who was divorced. Both my parents raised and cared for my brother, my sister and I to the best of their ability and to this day, I still don't believe that my father deserved what the church did to him.

I grew up in a time when, like most baby boomers, I accepted the off-the-shelf concept that schools regularly taught, primarily that America was a land of religious liberty, not bound by any one theological belief or idea. This concept really took hold for me during a trip with my father to New York City when I was about 10 years old. One of the things we did that day, was visit the Statue of Liberty and I was quite taken by the inscription on the plaque attached to the pedestal at the base of the statue. In part, it said, "Give us your tired, your poor, your huddled masses, yearning to breathe free..."

This passage is part of a poem written by the American poet Emma Lazarus, entitled "*The New Colossus*". The poem was written in 1883 and donated to an auction of art and literary works to raise funds for the construction of a pedestal for the Statue of Liberty. The poem was then engraved on a bronze plaque and mounted inside the lower level of the pedestal of the statue in 1903. The poem calls us to remember the millions of people who were immigrating to the United States, most of them, including all my grandparents, arriving at Ellis Island at the port of New York at the turn of the 20th century and for them, this was *their first view of America.*

The title and the first two lines refer to the Colossus of Rhodes, one of the Seven Wonders of the Ancient World, and the complete poetic work is presented here:

> Not like the brazen giant of Greek fame,
> With conquering limbs astride from land to land;
> Here at our sea-washed, sunset gates shall stand
> A mighty woman with a torch, whose flame
> Is the imprisoned lightning, and her name
> Mother of Exiles. From her beacon-hand
> Glows world-wide welcome; her mild eyes command
> The air-bridged harbor that twin cities frame.
> "Keep, ancient lands, your storied pomp!" cries she
> With silent lips. "Give me your tired, your poor,
> Your huddled masses yearning to breathe free,
> The wretched refuse of your teeming shore.
> Send these, the homeless, tempest-tost to me,
> I lift my lamp beside the golden door!"

Why do I bring this up? During his first term in office, I wrote a letter to President Barack Obama, challenging him about his position at the time on same sex marriage (at the time, he was not a strong proponent of the idea). In my letter, I tried to address some of the traditional religious concerns he and by extension, others had expressed about the subject, by emphasizing the point that while the early history of America may have been rooted in one religion, by the mid to late 1700s when America became a sovereign nation, its society had become socially, culturally and religiously pluralistic from the influx of immigrants who were fleeing religious persecution in England and Europe.

As it's so clearly stated on the plaque on the base of the Statue of Liberty, our country threw open its doors in the 20th century and the people of the world took us up on our invitation that is so movingly phrased on Miss Liberty's foundation. What I had somehow lost sight of was that the idea for this invitation and its resultant change to our society began much earlier than I had stated in my letter, or that is stated on the plaque.

My point when I wrote the letter to the President (and remains to this day) is that immigration to America brought with it many different cultures, customs and theological beliefs, along *with their many associated understandings and traditions*, all serving to substantially change the basic fabric of a society that originated on our continent in the early 1600s and this is a fluid, *ongoing process*. That being said, again quoting from my letter to the President, I said, "…we as a country should not and cannot hold everyone who lives in America to the same religious, cultural or societal beliefs that began to take root in New England in 1620, yet this continues to be an ongoing struggle that we as a people address somewhere in this country on a daily basis."

If we examine the theology of all of the Founding Fathers, John Jay (one of the country's most celebrated Founders, Jay was America's first Supreme Court Chief Justice and a co-author of the Federalist Papers) might be considered the only 'orthodox Christian', who, as Secretary for Foreign Affairs in Congress, argued, albeit *unsuccessfully,* to exclude Catholics from holding public office. In a letter written on October 12, 1816 by Jay to revolutionary war veteran and Pennsylvania House of Representatives member John Murray, Jay said in part,

> "Providence has given to our people the choice of their rulers, and it is the duty, as well as the privilege and interest, of our Christian nation to select and prefer Christians for their rulers."

The idea of Divine Providence is examined below. Perhaps it may just be that John Jay is who today's Christian leaders have in mind in their lectures about the Founding Fathers, however, as I hope to show, Jay's position was not in the majority.

Conservative Christians offer up the Pilgrims' Puritan theology as a shining example of our nation's "Christian Heritage", but this idea is also not supported by the facts. The Pilgrims weren't the ones who rebelled against England during the Revolutionary War, nor were they the ones who crafted the Constitution that governs our nation. Yes, the Pilgrims fled religious persecution in England in the early 1600s, but they put into place and practiced many oppressive religious policies, beginning shortly after settling in the new world.

The concept of religious freedom is both very simple and very complex; as I pointed out above, it is true that these settlers who first established colonies in the New World had a common and deeply held religious belief, what needs to be remembered is the significant religious paradigm shift between the early 1600s when our country was first settled, and 1789, when America declared itself to be a free and independent nation. Today, we as American citizens need to realize and accept the basic concept of religious freedom in this country; while we are *free to observe our religion*, we are *not free* to force others to observe one set of religious beliefs just because a segment of society holds them to be correct, authentic or true.

A case in point was a man named Roger Williams, founder of the colonial colony of Rhode Island. In 1623, Williams was admitted to Cambridge University and received his Bachelor's Degree in 1627. Ordained as a minister in the Church of England, Williams attended graduate school at Cambridge for a year and a half, and during this time, he became deeply influenced by Puritan ideas, such that his conscience would not let him serve as an Anglican minister. Williams left Cambridge early in 1629 without finishing his graduate degree. He began to openly embrace and express his radical Puritan beliefs in England, with ideas such as the emperor Constantine being a worse enemy to *true Christianity* than Roman Emperor Nero, because Constantine's actions at the Council of Nicaea in 325, corrupted Christianity, and his actions eventually led to the decline and ruin of the Christian Church. Williams eventually ran afoul of the Church of England and, left with few options, he and his wife gave into the religious intolerance under England's King Charles 1 and joined the migration to the New World in December of 1630 to join the "American Experiment" as it was then known.

At the age of 28, Williams arrived in Boston on February of 1631, having accepted a call to serve as pastor of the church in Salem. He had been invited to preach in Boston, but immediately got into trouble when he shared his position that people should be free to worship God as they chose, without fear of punishment *by their government*...this, in the eyes of the church in Boston, *made him a heretic*. Williams served in the position as minister at a church in Salem but his ideas again proved too radical and controversial. He then moved to Plymouth but once more, fell out of favor with the local church. Williams insisted that the government of the colony had no right to set up what he described as, "A civil power and officers to judge the convictions of men's souls..."

His position infuriated New England Puritans who held a fervent belief that a strong local government was vital to enforce Godliness and protect true religion, that being a true religion *as they interpreted and understood it*. The Reverend John Cotton, a preeminent minister and theologian of the Massachusetts Bay Colony (and grandfather of Cotton Mather), preached that it was wrong to practice any religion other than Puritanism, because those who did would be (his words) *helping the devil*. It was believed that because Puritans followed the only true religion, everyone should be forced to worship the same Puritan beliefs, as Cotton said, "Tolerance is liberty to tell lies in the name of the Lord." As it turned out, Cotton Mather, who was the second pastor of the

Boston Church, (the Second Church in Boston, Massachusetts was a Congregational church until 1802 when it became a Unitarian church) was indirectly involved in the decision to banish Roger Williams.

In April of 1634, the magistrates in Boston ordered all bay area residents who were not freemen (freeman is a term that originated in 12ᵗʰ century Europe and was a common English and American Colonial expression in Puritan times. To live in the Bay Colony, a man had to be a member of the Church to be a freeman), to take a 'Resident's Oath', pledging themselves to submit to the orders and dictates of the General Court. On May 14, 1634, the court adopted a *revised* Freeman's Oath, forcing all freemen to *pledge allegiance* to the General Court and its officers, the intent being to put an end to all opposition to the "Holy Commonwealth." *The penalty for refusing to take the oath was banishment from the colony.* A copy of the revised oath is presented here:

Att a Genrall Courte, holden at Boston.

May 14, 1634

It was agreed & ordered, that the former oath of ffreemen shalbe revoked, soe farr as it is dissonant from the oath of ffreemen herevnder written, & that those that receaved the former oath shall stand bound noe further thereby, to any intent or purpose, then this newe oath tyes those that nowe takes ye same.

THE OATII OF FREEMEN

I._ A.B. (Able Bodied), being, by Gods providence, an inhabitant & ffreeman within the jurisdiccon of this comonweale, doe freely acknowledge my selfe to be subiect to the govermt thereof, & therefore doe heere sweare, by the greate & dreadfull name of the eurlyving God, that I wilbe true & faithfull to the same, & will accordingly yeilde assistance & support therevnto, with my pson & estate, as in equity I am bound, & will also truely indeavr to maintaine & preserue all the libertyes & previlidges thereof, submitting my selfe to the wholesome lawes & orders made & established by the same; and furthr, that I will not plott nor practise any evill aginst it, nor consent to any that shall soe doe, but will timely discovery & reveale the same lawfull aucthority nowe here established, for the speedy preventing thereof. Moreouer, I doe solemnly binde myselfe in the sight of God, that when I shalbe called to giue my voice touching any such matter of this state, wherein ffreemen are to deale I will giue my vote & suffrage, as I shall iudge in myne owne conscience may best conduce & tend to the publique weale of the body, without respect of psons, or favr of any man. Soe helpe mee God in the Lord Jesus Christ.

Further, it is agreed that none but the Genall Court hath power to chuse and admitt freemen.

Shortly after Williams returned to Salem in 1635, he was put on trial for his views, convicted of holding 'dangerous opinions' and was sentenced with these words:

"Mr. Roger Williams, one of the elders of the church of Salem hath broached and dyvulged dyvers newe and dangerous opinions against the authoritie of magistrates, as also writt lies of defamacon both of the magistrates & churches here & that before many conviccon & yet maintaineth the same without retraction: it is therefore ordered that the same Mr. Williams shall depart out of this jurisdiction within six weeks nowe nexte ensuing, wch if hee neglect to prforme, it shalbe lawful for the Gour (Governor) and two of the magistrates to send him someplace out of this jurisdiccion, not to returne any more with out license from the court."

Williams was granted time to put his affairs in order, but he continued pontificating and his actions began to test the patience of local authorities who finally ordered his arrest. Fortunately for Williams, he was warned about his pending capture by a friend and supporter. Williams fled in the middle of the night, making his way to an area on the south shore of New England, and when it was safe, he sent for his wife. Once settled, Williams insisted that land he settled on must be purchased from the Indians, rather than seizing it from them without providing compensation. He went on to establish a settlement which he named Providence in deference to the divine assistance he felt had been given to him and other Christians during their flights from persecution. The colony Williams founded was structured around the principles of complete religious toleration and separation of church and state, and would eventually come to be known as Rhode Island.

It was there that Williams started the first Baptist church in America in 1638, but he later left the church as he continued his search for spirituality in different ways. Williams took another radical and courageous step when he stopped preaching to the native American Indians, whom he regarded as friends, after realizing that their form of worship fell *under his standard of religious freedom.*

Williams believed that any state supported religion was most certainly the source and motivation for many acts of persecution and religious war, declaring at one point in a letter to Connecticut Governor Thomas Prence in June of 1670 that;

"*...forced worship stinks in God's nostrils.*" *(Emphasis mine)*

In a pamphlet entitled *A Review of the Correspondence of Messrs. Fuller & Wayland: On the Subject of American Slavery,* (written by Baptist Minister and anti-slavery advocate Cyrus Grosvenor and printed in London in 1652) Williams contributed a discourse in which he expressed his position on religion and government this way;

> "I observe the great and wonderful mistake, both our own and our fathers, as to the civil powers of this world, acting in spiritual matters. I have read [as blessed Latimer once said] the last will and testament of the Lord Jesus over many times, and yet I cannot find by one tittle of that testament that if He had been pleased to have accepted of a temporal crown and government

that ever He would have put forth the least finger of temporal or civil power in the matters of His spiritual affairs and Kingdom. Hence must it lamentably be against the testimony of Christ Jesus for the civil state to impose upon the souls of the people a religion, a worship, a ministry, oaths (in religious and civil affairs), tithes, times, days, marryings, and buryings in holy ground, Jesus never called for the sword of steel to help the sword of spirit."

The 'blessed Latimer' Williams referred to here is Bishop Hugh Latimer, an influential member of the Protestant clergy under England's King Edward. When Mary became Queen of England in 1553, one of her first acts was to imprison members of the clergy who would not convert to Roman Catholicism, including Bishop Latimer. He was one of 238 Protestant clergy who were publicly executed under the Heresy Act during Queen Mary's rule. Historians estimate that about 800 managed to flee to Europe...those who didn't (including Latimer and two other Oxford Martyrs) were burned at the stake.

England had become the prime example of abuse and violence that occurred when the head of the government also served as the head of the state church, and one key player was Oliver Cromwell. In 1628, Cromwell was elected to Parliament and it was about that time that he underwent a spiritual crisis, leading to a religious conversion, from being a conventional, centrist, main-line Protestant to a strong, born-again Puritan. Cromwell believed in 'Providentialism', that is, the belief that God was actively directing the affairs of the world through the actions of His 'chosen people' (that is, the people *God had provided*). During the English Civil Wars, Cromwell believed that he was one of these chosen people. More than that, he was convinced that his military victories were indications of God's approval of his actions, while any defeats were a sign that God was leading him in a different direction.

He was passionately opposed to the Roman Catholic Church, which he saw as denying the primacy of the Bible in favor of Papal authority, which he blamed for much of the tyranny and persecution of Protestants in European countries. Cromwell was also opposed to the more radical religious groups on the Protestant side in the Civil Wars. Although he co-operated with Presbyterians and Quakers, he strongly objected to their authoritarian organization, structure and what he saw as the imposition of their beliefs on other Protestant denominations.

When Cromwell became Lord Protector of the Commonwealth of England, Scotland and Ireland, he began to clamp down on religious communities in England who opposed his religious views. This included Baptists and Quakers, both of whom found themselves forced to begin their own migration to the North American colonies to escape religious discrimination and oppression. Cromwell is seen by some religious historians as 'the Protector of European Protestantism'.

While these events were unfolding in England, a man named John Endecott became the first governor of the Massachusetts Bay Colony. He was a passionate and somewhat confrontational Puritan with strong Separatist attitudes toward the Anglican Church, which put him in conflict with the firmly entrenched views of many of the colony's leaders. In addition, Endecott saw women in church as a *distraction during worship* and asserted that *women should be veiled* any time they attend church, "Furthermore," he stated, "women living in the colony should dress modestly (we're still picking on women) and men should not wear long hair as the Native Indian savages did." During Endecott's time as governor, he issued several judicial decisions that banished individuals who held religious views that again, did not agree with those of the Puritans, such as Baptists and Quakers. So, as these new immigrants who were fleeing England, arrived in Boston in 1656, they themselves forced to flee once again, this time under *Endecott's standing orders*.

Roger Williams' colony quickly became a haven for anyone persecuted for their religious beliefs, including Anabaptists, Quakers and Jews among others, many of whom ultimately became permanent settlers in this new colony. Williams learned the language of his hosts, he compiled a Narragansett language dictionary and several times acted as peacemaker among the Indians.

Endecott later invited Williams to return to Massachusetts, but Williams declined the invitation with the rather caustic reply,

> "I feel safer down here among the Christian savages along Narragansett Bay than I do among the savage Christians of Massachusetts Bay Colony."

In Maryland, the Church of England again was the established church, however, with the large number of Protestants arriving in the colonies, the Catholic community in Maryland began to feel ostracized, so the colony passed the Act of Toleration in 1649. This law granted religious freedom to everyone who believed in the concept of the Holy Trinity, but it also authorized the death penalty for atheists, Jews and those who denied the divinity of Jesus as the Son of God and anyone who spoke against the Virgin Mary could be fined and publically whipped.

Established churches that were legally supported by the government had existed in Europe for a long time, so this was a traditional and familiar idea to settlers in the New World. By way of example, residents of Virginia were required by a law passed in 1611 to attend the state sponsored church, one that was supported with *local taxes*. This was particularly familiar to the settlers who were members of the Church of England.

As the colony grew and expanded over time, both internally and from waves of settlers arriving from all over Europe in the years leading up to the War for Independence, the power of the church in Virginia began to wane, principally under pressure of Virginia's ruling class, including people who occupied positions in Anglican Vestries (the term vestry was used to describe a body of lay church members elected by the congregation or parish to run the secular business of the parish county courts and the government).

In addition, for anyone to hold any office in the colony, the candidate was required to be a member of the Church of England. Almost all governmental affairs were handled by county courts and vestries, while municipal justices held a combination of administrative, judicial and clerical powers that allowed them to pass judgment on a wide number of cases, including absence from Anglican church services, bastardy, adultery and other moral offenses *as defined by church law*. Parish vestries not only levied taxes to pay the clergy and to construct and repair churches, but also funded support for orphans and other members of their parishes who were in need. The General Assembly created new parishes, set ministers' salaries and formulated strict conditions under which dissenters were allowed to practice their religion.

Somewhat paradoxically, by the middle 1700s, while many of the elite upper class in colonial America still supported an established, official church, Virginians began to reject the idea of a centralized church hierarchy because it restricted their ability to oversee the affairs of their church. Virginians began to realize that they were capable, independent leaders, such that by the 1770s, residents of Virginia even rejected a proposal to recruit and install a resident American bishop.

By this time, the Founding Fathers, many of them or their families having immigrated from England, began to recognize the need for a secular government, not because they had any problem with or objection to religion in general, indeed, many themselves admitted holding various religious beliefs as we shall see, but because they witnessed firsthand the immediate effect and long term aftermath of a state sponsored and supported church. These men had also studied and in many cases observed the political and social impact that the collusion between the government and the church created in England, as well as several countries across Europe, as part of their academic education.

As the colonies started to come together in the years leading up to the revolution in America, their discussions on what to do next led to bitter sectarian discord. Heated debates began between those who were advocating for an end to government imposed religious tests for public office, tax appropriations for churches and other forms of support for religion by the state government, and those who still supported the idea. The point here is that those who advocated for change were again, not against religion per se, in point of fact, many were members of the clergy. Their argument? True faith *did not warrant,* nor *did it need* government support.

Respect for religious pluralism gradually became an accepted goal. When Thomas Jefferson agreed to draft the Declaration of Independence for example, he spoke of "unalienable rights *endowed by our Creator.*" These four words were understood to be a generic, conventionally used religious term that all religious groups of the day would respond to, not the narrowly defined "Christian" designation that was intentionally used by nations with national churches.

This concept was of course, not universally accepted. By way of example, the contrarian Founding Father, Luther Martin, a representative from Maryland and a key anti-federalist, felt so strongly that the Constitution violated individual states' rights that he refused to sign the document. After failing to garner enough support for a bill of rights that he and a small group were in favor of, Martin and one other Maryland delegate named John Francis Mercer, who believed that there were weaknesses in the proposed U.S. constitution that did not adequately protect the rights of ordinary citizens from potential government tyranny, actually walked out of the Constitutional Convention in protest. Martin passionately maintained that he and a handful of delegates to the Constitutional Convention were also fighting for formal acknowledgement and recognition of Christianity in the Constitution.

In his address to the Maryland Legislature on November 29, 1797, Martin stated his position about the debate in congress in very fundamental terms;

> "The part of the system that provides that no religious test shall ever be required as a qualification to any public office or public trust under the United States, was adopted by a great majority of the convention, *and without much debate*; however there were some members *so unfashionable* as to think, that a belief *of the existence of a deity*, and *a state of future rewards and punishment* would be some security for the good conduct of our rulers, and that, in a Christian country, it would be *at least decent* to hold out some distinction between the professors of *Christianity* and downright *infidelity or paganism.*" *(Emphasis mine)*

This concept of a formal recognition of Christianity in the Constitution was however, not adopted by the convention. As a result, the Constitution *cedes no authority over religion to the government*. It should be noted that paragraph three of Article VI of the document, which explicitly allows persons of all religious viewpoints to hold public office, was adopted by a *unanimous vote* and is presented here:

> "The Senators and Representatives before mentioned, and the members of the several State Legislatures, and all Executive and Judicial Officers, both of the United States and of the several states shall be bound by Oath or Affirmation, to support the Constitution; *but no religious Test shall ever be required as a Qualification to any Office or public Trust under the United States.*" *(Emphasis mine)*

With the ratification of the First Amendment, Jefferson observed that the American people built, as he phrased it, a "wall of separation between church and state." Hearing this, some pastors who supported the integration of the church and the state became outraged and began preaching intensely powerful sermons, proclaiming that the United States would never succeed and prosper as a nation because its Constitution did not give *special consideration* to Christians and to Christianity. However, other church leaders hailed the rejection of the idea as a new beginning of real freedom, applauding the Constitution and the First Amendment as true *defenders of liberty*.

This being said, we should note that more than a few numbers of several determined Christian groups have fought against this policy of separation of church and state throughout America's history. In the mid-19th century, several attempts were made to add specific references to Christianity to the Constitution. One group, the NRA, (the National Reform Association, *not the gun people*) tried to push a 'Christian Nation' amendment through Congress in 1864, at one point petitioning President Abraham Lincoln to support the amendment by making the following changes to the preamble to the Constitution. The suggested addition is shown in italics;

> "We, the People of the United States, *recognizing the being and attributes of Almighty God, the Divine Authority of the Holy Scriptures, the law of God as the paramount rule, and Jesus, the Messiah, the Saviour and Lord of all,* in order to form a more perfect union…

President Lincoln respectfully responded to their request by saying;

> "The general aspect of your movement I cordially approve. In regard to particulars I must ask time to deliberate, as the work of amending the Constitution should not be done hastily. I will carefully examine your paper in order more fully to comprehend its contents than is possible from merely hearing it read, and will take such action upon it as my responsibility *to our Maker and our country demands.*" *(Emphasis mine)*

The National Reform Association members believed that the Civil War was a *divine punishment for failing to mention God in the Constitution* and they saw the amendment as a way to atone for that omission. Their amendment called for, as the Association expressed it,

> "Humbly acknowledging Almighty God as the source of all authority and power in civil government, the Lord Jesus Christ as the Ruler among the nations, [and] His revealed will as the supreme law of the land, in order to constitute a Christian government."

On February 28, 1872, Missouri Senator Carl Schurz presented petitions with over 10,000 signatures that were allegedly gathered across the nation, "…asking Congress to preserve inviolate the great guarantees of religious liberty, and protesting against an amendment to the Constitution establishing religious tests." Two months later, Massachusetts Senator Charles Sumner introduced a similar petition from 6300 citizens of Boston. Due to a busy congressional schedule, it wasn't until January 7, 1874 that Sumner was able to introduce a second petition which contained 35,179 names (and was over 953 feet long), also asking for a vote on a Christian amendment to the Constitution. On February 18 of that same year, the House Judiciary Committee issued a long awaited report on the Christian Amendment. Representative Benjamin Butler, also from Massachusetts, read the report of the Judiciary Committee and *requested that the Amendment be tabled indefinitely*;

> "That, upon examination even of the meager debates by the fathers of the Republic in the convention which framed the Constitution, they (the committee) find that the subject of this memorial was most fully and carefully considered, and then, in that convention, decided, after grave deliberation that it was inexpedient to put *anything* into the constitution or frame a government *which might be construed to be a reference to any religious creed or doctrine.* And they further find that this decision was accepted by our Christian fathers with such great unanimity that in the amendments which were afterward proposed in order to make the Constitution most acceptable to the nation, none has ever been proposed to the States by which this wise determination of the fathers has been attempted to be changed. Wherefore, your committee reports that it is inexpedient to legislate upon the subject of the above memorial, and ask that they be discharged from further consideration thereof, and that this report, together with the petition, be laid upon the table." *(All emphasis mine)*

Similar theocratic proposals reemerged in Congress sporadically over the years, (see the section in the appendix 'Religious Measures introduced in Congress Since 1888'). As late as 1950, a proposal was introduced in the U.S. Senate that would have added language to the Constitution that "devoutly recognizes the Authority and Law of Jesus Christ, Saviour and Ruler of nations, through whom are bestowed the blessings of liberty." This amendment never made it out of committee and subsequent efforts to revive it in the early 1960s were just as futile.

Unfortunately, the U.S. government has not always complied with its own constitutional principles. Toward the end of the 19th century, several states attempted to promulgate a thinly veiled form of Protestantism, with even the U.S. Supreme Court occasionally falling victim to this mindset. In 1892, with Justice David Brewer declared in his decision in the legal case *Holy Trinity v. United States* that America is "a Christian nation." What needs to be clarified here is that the *Holy Trinity* decision has been deemed an anomaly by most legal experts. It has rarely been cited by other courts, and the designation "Christian nation" actually appeared 'in dicta' (a legal term meaning *the part of a judicial opinion which is more a judge's editorializing and does not directly address the legal specifics of the case.*) The fact is, nobody is sure exactly what Brewer meant by his statement, because in a book he wrote in 1905, Brewer attempted to clarify the statement with the observation (that conveniently gets left out of the discussion) that the United States is a Christian nation in *a cultural sense*, not *a legal one.*

A judicially more accurate assessment of the relationship between religion and government was stated by Justice John Paul Stevens in the 1985 case Wallace v. Jaffree, (an Alabama law that authorized teachers to set aside one minute at the start of each day for a moment of *"meditation or voluntary prayer."*) In a 6 to 3 ruling, Justice Stevens (writing for the majority) commented on the constitutional right of all Americans to choose their own religious belief;

> "At one time it was thought that this right merely proscribed the preference of one Christian sect over another, but would not require equal respect for the conscience of the infidel, the atheist, or the adherent of a non - Christian faith such as Mohammedism or Judaism. But when the underlying principle has been examined in the crucible of litigation, the Court has unambiguously concluded that the individual freedom of conscience protected by the First Amendment embraces the right to select any religious faith *or none at all.*"

In the dissenting opinion, Chief Justice Warren Burger began by pointing out that the statute authorizing a moment of silence at the beginning of a school day which mentions the word "prayer" does not, unconstitutionally promote a religion. He contested the decision, making the point that a school is constitutionally on the same level of government as state and federal legislatures and even the Supreme Court. Thus, the endorsement of a "moment of silence" with an oblique suggestion of prayer is *no less constitutional as is the opening of a Congress or Court session with a prayer by a publicly funded chaplain. (Emphasis mine)*

There are of course, more recent examples of this line of thinking. Several charismatic religious leaders suggested that Hurricane Katrina, (the storm that killed over 1,800 people in August of 2005) was sent as a divine retribution because New Orleans was celebrating a festival of sexual excess and debauchery, (more commonly known as Mardi Gras) or for something the South did or again, for something the United States as a whole did, depending on who's observation or opinion was being voiced.

As we shall see, the Founding Fathers' purpose for the idea of a separation of church and state, *and this is a critical point*, was not to free society from religious influences and expressions of religious faith, but to prevent the state from *interfering with a person's personal, privately held beliefs*. However, as the battle for equal rights for *all Americans* rages on, we often witness the due process of law being bent and twisted to suit the specific beliefs and agendas of a small but very vocal subgroup of this country's larger religious community. As the observation, (correctly or incorrectly) attributed to As Otto Von Bismarck says, "If you like laws and sausages, *you should never watch either one being made." (Emphasis mine)*

Again by way of example, at the time this book was written, seven states still have statutes that *prohibit atheists from holding public office*. (The consensus is that these laws would not be enforceable, because it's a given that they would be held to be unconstitutional if challenged). The (troubling) principle here appears to be that any failure to believe in '*The Almighty*' will somehow make you less capable to govern;

Arkansas: Article 19, Section 1: No person who denies *the being of a God* shall hold any office in the civil departments of this State, nor *be competent to testify as a witness in any Court.*

Maryland: Article 37: That no religious test ought ever to be required as a qualification for any office of profit or trust in this State, *other than a declaration of belief in the existence of God*; nor shall the Legislature prescribe any other oath of office than the oath prescribed by this Constitution.

Mississippi: Article 14, Section 265: No person who denies *the existence of a Supreme Being* shall hold any office in this state.

North Carolina: Article 6, section 8 of the state constitution says: "The following persons shall be disqualified for office: First, any person who shall deny *the being of Almighty God*."

South Carolina: Article 17, Section 4: No person who denies the existence of *a Supreme Being* shall hold any office under this Constitution.

Tennessee: Article 9, Section 2: No person who denies *the being of God, or a future state of rewards and punishments,* shall hold any office in the civil department of this state.

Texas: Article 1, Section 4: No religious test shall ever be required as a qualification to any office, or public trust, in this State; nor shall anyone be excluded from holding office on account of his religious sentiments, *provided he acknowledge the existence of a Supreme Being.*

(All emphasis mine)

Some of you may get frustrated as you read this because I have repeated key points two or three times throughout the work but the question I'm attempting to answer with this work is: Is our *religious freedom* under attack or is it our *religious liberty*, and *NO*-they are *not* the same!

Religious freedom allows us to identify with a personal chosen belief or no belief and religious liberty allows us to openly celebrate our religious beliefs.

Let's take a look at how we got where we are...

A Very Brief History
of Religious Freedom
in America

The process of teaching academic subjects in public schools here in America is unique in the world, in that our nation has become so diverse and because of this, in each state and often in each city, the academic subject matter and content is under tight local control and the curriculum closely scrutinized and monitored. This results in a significant but not readily observable variation in the content from school district to school district, and therein lies the problem, simply stated: students come away with different understandings of the same subject. For pure academic subjects like language and mathematics, this may not be an issue, but for other subjects, this inconsistency can and often does create complications for students as they go out into the world and try to live and function in society. This is especially true with biology, evolution, human sexuality and reproduction, and perhaps most importantly, the huge part both the subject of and the impact that religion played and continues to play in American history.

It is this last aspect that I would like to explore in this work. In the American history textbooks most of us used in school, we learned that the Pilgrims came to America aboard the Mayflower in in 1620, (along with the occasional references of the group who settled in Virginia in 1607) in search of a life where they were free to practice their religion. These early settlers were predominantly Puritans who were fleeing the debris field in the aftermath of the Reformation, where many lost their homes, their possessions, the lives of family members and friends around them and in more than a few cases, Puritans found themselves fleeing for their own lives as well.

As the tiny ship Arbella was making its way across the Atlantic to what would become Massachusetts in 1630, a Puritan named John Winthrop gave a sermon entitled "A model of Christian Charity" in which he told the prospective Massachusetts Bay colonists that their new community would become "a city upon a hill" that would be seen around the world. The phrase was taken from the 5th chapter of the Gospel according to Matthew, where the author says in verse 14,

> [14] Ye are the light of the world. A city that is set on an hill cannot be hid.
>
> *Matthew c 5: v 14 KJV*

The city John Winthrop spoke of would eventually become Boston, Massachusetts and he would go on to become the first governor of the Massachusetts Bay Colony.

From this and other narrations, we were carefully led to believe that America was destine to become a pluralistic melting pot, where everyone would be free to practice and follow his or her own faith, free from any government interference. There is one small problem with this idea; it's a lie, inasmuch as it applied to the early colonies, very much like the story we hear every Christmas, where Joseph and Mary arrive in Bethlehem and have to spend the night in a manger "because there was no room at the Inn". The reality is that there were no such things as Inns (or hotels) during the time of Christ, but *that doesn't matter*. The story resonates with anyone who's had trouble finding accommodations when they travel, just as the story of religious freedom in the early colonies resonates, even though many know deep down from their own religious teaching that, while it's a nice idea, it's *loaded with exceptions and exclusions*.

The facts are that the religious history of the early settlers of this country is replete with exclusivism built around post reformation theology, and the schism, conflict and violence that grew out of the reformation that forced the pilgrims to flee to

America. Two ideas that might help with our understanding of the history of religion in America are first, to define what a 'Christian' is, and the second is to explore a little background on the Pilgrims.

Collectively, many of us call ourselves Christians, but what do we mean by this? Well, the most generally accepted definition of today's Christian is someone who believes in God and is following the teachings of Jesus Christ. National surveys from a few years ago indicate that this group as an aggregate comprises about 75% of the population of the United States and Canada, covering a broad range of what would commonly be referred as *main stream* denominations.

However, if we narrow our definition to just Evangelical and Fundamentalist Protestant denominations, the term Christian becomes limited to those persons who are *born again* or *saved*. Reliable figures for this group can only be estimated because the numbers are quite fluid. Additionally, some churches are difficult to fit into any category, because Pentecostals during the 20th century traversed the middle ground between evangelicals (some of whom doubted the miraculous gifts of the Holy Spirit), and some liberal Protestant groups who tended to doubt the miraculous altogether.

The percentage of U.S. adults who consider themselves Christian in the U.S. population is declining, while those who do not identify with any organized religion is increasing, according to data gathered in an extensive survey by the Pew Research Center in 2014 and published in May of 2015. The survey was entitled America's Changing Religious Landscape, and it looked at the largest denominations in the US, asking 35,000 adults who acknowledged having some religious connection, to indicate what their religious affiliation was. The responses given were that 25.4 % were Evangelical Protestant, 22.8 % had no religious membership, (i.e. 'Nones'), 20.8 % identified as Roman Catholic, 14.7 % considered themselves Mainline Protestant and 5.9 % identified in declining percentages as Jewish (the largest in this group), Muslim, Buddhist, Hindu, UU, Neo-pagan, Druids, Wiccans etc. (The survey has a margin of error of less than +/– 1%. The complete report can be found at http://www.pewforum.org/2015/05/12/americas-changing-religious-landscape/ 9/29/2015).

However, Christians in the 1600 and early 1700s had an much narrower and more sharply defined understanding. French and Spanish settlers who introduced Roman Catholicism into the new world found themselves at odds with Protestant settlers, while many later English immigrants brought with them the religion of the Church of England, a belief that conflicted with the beliefs of Puritans who were already living here. Since there was no state, *much less a state religion*, Protestantism had no central authority, *thus*, the colonies reasoned, they were free to chart their own (often quite convoluted) course in religious beliefs while keeping within what they saw as a specific and clearly defined understanding of *Protestant*. Finally, there were two more groups who were fleeing religious persecution in Europe, followers of the Quaker faith and Jewish immigrants who settled in Rhode Island. Already, as many as 8,000 additional Quakers had settled in Pennsylvania by 1685. Although Quakers may have *appeared* outwardly similar to Puritans in some religious beliefs and practices, they differed greatly over the necessity and purpose of a strict and involuntary religious observance in everyday life. (In the years 1659 to 1661, four of the Society of Friends, Marmaduke Stephenson, William Robinson, William Leddra and Mary Dyer were publicly hanged in Boston for not renouncing their *'monstrous'* Quaker faith).

Now, without delving too deeply into the theology of Puritanism, the Puritan religion came into being and began to evolve in England during the sixteenth century, starting as a movement to reform the Church of England. In its simplest form, Puritanism was structured around the authority and inerrancy of the biblical interpretations of the eminent theologian John Calvin, whose doctrine can best be summed up this way: God had predestined or pre-elected a certain Godly Community that would be saved by His grace, and an ungodly community that would not. Jesus died for the chosen Elect, that is, only those predestined for heaven, and not for everyone, and only God would know who was on the *'A list'*.

Calvin's understanding focused on the nature of *man*, on *free will* and *predestination*. Puritans saw God as a stern and fearsome father figure, basically The God of the Old Testament. Puritan theology became centered around and focused on their God's majesty, righteousness and control of the universe to achieve His ends. Maintaining and directing everything in the universe was God's *Providence*.

The term "Puritan" was first used to ridicule or as a slur by traditional Anglicans, directed at those who were critical of the dogma of the Church of England, because many in the Puritan community expressed their feelings that the church needed to be *purified*. We should pause and note here that much of this theological disruption was brought to a head when Johannes Gutenberg designed and constructed his system of mechanized printing with movable metal type in 1439. His innovation created a proliferation of printed books that were economical for printers to produce and for readers to obtain. This quickly introduced a change in mass communication which transformed the fabric of society, a change in magnitude that has remained unchallenged until the arrival of the internet, over 500 years later. One of the first publications was a series of Bibles in vernacular languages. Once the Bible was printed in languages people could understand, they began to see and perhaps more importantly, to question discrepancies between what the Bible actually said and what they were being told by their religious and (in many cases) political leaders.

With access to a Bible they could read, the Puritans (who saw themselves as "the Godly") believed that the reformation in England *hadn't actually gone far enough*. The Church of England was still tolerating too many practices that were associated with the customs and traditions of the Roman Catholic Church, such as a hierarchical leadership, clerical vestments (more on this in a moment) and the various rituals of the church. The Puritans tended to admire the work of the early church fathers and quoted them frequently in their religious life. One in particular was John Chrysostom, Archbishop of Constantinople, who lived from A.D. 349 to A.D. 407. St. Chrysostom was best known for his denunciation of the abuse of authority by both political as well as ecclesiastical leaders, which may be what drew him to the church. His forthright explanation of the Scripture were more literal, in contrast to the Alexandrian tendency of the time that was more an allegorical interpretation (allegory is something, usually written, that can be interpreted to reveal a hidden moral meaning). This meant that the subjects of St. Chrysostom's texts were practical, serving to explain the Bible's application to everyday life. He also emphasized personal study of the Bible.

St. Chrysostom became a favorite of the Puritans because he spoke out eloquently *against the everyday drama* and other *worldly endeavors*. Puritans readily embraced this view, condemning what they saw as the decadent culture of England, a culture that was quite well known at that time for its risqué plays and the bawdy social life in greater London. The Pilgrims, principally the separatist, Congregationalist Puritans who went to America, who were well known for banning many secular entertainments, such as games of chance, maypoles and various forms of drama from their New England colonies', as all of these activities were perceived as a kind of immorality. The word 'puritan' has taken root in our modern lexicon in variations forms, like "puritanical", defined by Merriam-Webster as "of, relating to, or characterized by a rigid morality". The Oxford Dictionary defines puritanical as "Practicing or affecting strict religious or moral behavior" with a note at the end stating that it (again) is often used as a derogatory term.

While the word Puritan eventually came to identify all manner of conservative religious groups, the term originally referred to just two distinct sects. The first were *separating* Puritans, such as the Plymouth colonists. Separating Puritans believed that true Christians must *separate* themselves from the English church. The second group were *non-separating* Puritans, who believed that reformation would solve the problems with the church, *if it was given enough time*, but not with *separation*. The largest group of Massachusetts colonists were non-separating Puritans and were comprised largely of Congregationalists. They believed that churches should be formed through voluntary compacts. The idea of a compact (or covenant) was central to the Puritans' concept of social, political and religious organization.

Several beliefs (with their sources deeply embedded in Calvinism) distinguished Puritans from other Christian sects. The first was their belief in *predestination*: Puritans held that belief in Jesus and participation in the sacraments could not alone bring about one's salvation. Individuals could not choose salvation, *for that is the privilege of God alone*. All aspects of salvation are established by God's sovereignty, including the choice as to who will be saved and who will receive God's irresistible grace. The Puritans also distinguished between *justification*, or the gift of God's grace given to the elect, and *sanctification*, the pious behavior that purportedly resulted when an individual had been saved and I'll expand on this below.

Also during this time, there was a controversy that is often overlooked in church history. Much of the post-reformation upheaval stemmed from the powerful influences and ceremonial traditions that had evolved in the Roman Catholic Church over the previous 1200 years or so. One way this disagreement manifested itself was the belief held by Protestants that much of the ritual and pageantry during a Roman Catholic mass was again, *not supported in scripture*, and the discussion extended to what clergy wore during the worship service.

The issue became a huge area of dispute in the church is best illustrated by the experiences of John Hooper, an English churchman, Anglican Bishop of Gloucester and Worcester and a proponent of the English Reformation. Hooper became chaplain of the town of Warwick in central England in 1550, having returned to England after being exiled during King Henry's reign. He soon became a leading Protestant reformer in England under the patronage of Edward Seymour, First Duke of Somerset.

When Hooper was invited to give a series of Lenten sermons before the King in February 1550, he spoke out against the 1549 ordinal, (one of the rites when becoming ordained as a bishop). Part of this ceremony was to swear an oath that mentioned "all saints" and required newly elected bishops and those attending the ordination ceremony to wear a cope and surplice, (a surplice is a tunic of white linen or cotton fabric, reaching to the knees or occasionally to the ankles, with wide or moderately wide sleeves, a cope is a heavy, ornate cloak or cape, worn over the surplice. These vestments first appeared in the Roman church during the 4th to 6th centuries.

Hooper's position was that any priestly garb meant to distinguish clergy from laity was not indicated by scripture, therefore these requirements were the *vestiges of Judaism and Roman Catholicism*, which had no biblical justification for *authentic* Christians, since they were not used in the early Christian church, that is, prior to the First Ecumenical Council of Nicaea in A.D. 325. Hooper was martyred during the Marian Persecutions, (individuals who were persecuted and severely oppressed for their religious beliefs during the reign of Queen Mary).

This conflict led to a period of extended confrontation between churches over what vestments various members of the clergy would or would not wear when conducting church services and was eventually referred to as the *vestments controversy* or *vestarian controversy* during the Reformation in Great Britain. Puritans objected to the surplice, because once again, it wasn't mentioned in the Bible and it was something Roman Catholics had worn long before the Reformation, which made it a symbol of idolatrous worship, thus it followed that anyone who wore it was clearly an *idolater*. Eventually, the argument reached a point where some clergy wore full vestments and some *refused to wear any*. As a consequence, many members of the church were ex-communicated and a few were imprisoned for noncompliance, but this did little to end the conflict, much less resolve the theological cacophony. This whole discussion was part of the ongoing tumult over the coalescence of the Roman Catholic Church and the Church of England.

Sadly, John Calvin's extreme hostility to all publicly displayed religious images led to a large amount of historic religious artwork being systematically destroyed by Calvinists in western Europe under the sobriquet of 'idolatry'. Calvin rejected the claim that images and art must be in the church as "books for the unlearned." This, he believed, could only lead to false worship and had no support from Scripture. Calvin's view was that teaching and preaching the word of God and administering sacraments was the correct way to worship God. He fought with the idea that pagans had surrendered to the lure of exaggerated ornamentation of their temples. Calvin believed that true pious beauty was not in decoration or images but in the spiritual word and in unity of the church's believers.

William Laud was an affirmed Arminian (Arminianism is the teaching of salvation in keeping with the Dutch theologian Jacob Arminius, who taught the *rejection of predestination* and *upheld the freedom of the human will*) was appointed by Charles I of England as Archbishop of Canterbury in 1633, during a time when the Church of England began incorporating beliefs that were deeply abhorrent to Puritans, such as a focus on individual acceptance or rejection of grace, the overall toleration of diverse religious beliefs and an acceptance of what was viewed as *high church rituals and symbols*, much of this associated with ideas of the Age of Enlightenment (or the Period of Enlightenment) that was sweeping Europe at the time.

During the period of Archbishop William Laud, the church was embroiled in conflicts with Puritans within the Church of England, including the use of ritual implements prescribed by the *Book of Common Prayer*, published as part of the English Reformation following the break with Rome (the full title of the 1662 Book of Common Prayer is *The Book of Common Prayer and Administration of the Sacraments and other Rites and Ceremonies of the Church according to the use of the Church of England together with the Psalter or Psalms of David pointed as they are to be sung or said in churches and the form and manner of making, ordaining and consecrating of bishops, priests and deacons*). There will be more about William Laud below.

While the conflict surrounding the format of the worship service as set forth in The Book of Common Prayer came down to something as basic as the use of candles during the service, a more extreme example of the war against religious imagery would be the idea of the Calvinist theologian J. I. Packer, (a British-born, Canadian Christian theologian in the low church Anglican and Reformed traditions) who suggested that the simple act of imagining God in our minds could violate the Second Commandment because man would, through his imagination, be *comparing God to human beings*. These ideas and events are but a small sample of the religious and political pressures in place during the time when the Puritans fled Europe for America, some that continue to influence America today.

Something that I became aware of as I researched this work, is that there is an ignored or at least unacknowledged idea present here; if we look at the religious environment in pre-revolutionary America in the years leading up to 1776, when many of the families of the Founding Fathers and the Founding Fathers themselves immigrated and settled here, they must have witnessed firsthand, the influence various religious beliefs had on the lives of the settlers in what was to become America, they must have seen a need to change things and how they needed to be changed. Setting aside the pressures brought to bear on the colonies by Great Britain, the constant squabbling between local churches and municipal authorities over how to govern local communities, how to enact local laws and ordinances and how to fund civic needs that were part of every-day life, the effects of these religious and secular pressures all must have weighed heavily on these men as they struggled to strike a balance when they set about forming a new, national government, something that has never been done before. What would that be like?

DIVINE PROVIDENCE

In Puritan theology, the idea of *divine providence*, (or just *Providence*) originated with John Calvin as God's plan for the world, where every soul that He created is guided by His will, that is, *Providence*. The words 'divine providence' have also been used as a title *for God* and over time, the word providence would have taken on other meanings associated with God Himself and the lot assigned by God. Published in 1828, Noah Webster's *American Dictionary of the English Language*, the word providence has a *secular* explanation:

> "The act of providing or preparing for future use of application,"

and a 2nd, theological definition, presented as:

> "...the care and superintendence which God exercises over his creatures. A belief in Divine Providence, is a source of great consolation to good men. By divine providence is often understood God himself."

As far as the sinful actions of man, (Puritans understood and accepted that there were many) they were thought to occur with God's consent: God does not cause or approve of sin, He only limits, restrains and overrules it *for good*. Puritans further believed that God revealed His will in many ways, certainly through the Bible, but also through natural forces and through law. As the 18th century English poet and hymnist William Cowper, who lived from 1730 to 1800, wrote in his hymn *God moves in a mysterious way*, "God is his own interpreter, and he will make it plain." (This compiled from the 11th chapter of Paul's letter to the Romans.)

The Puritans further understood that *it was their duty* to learn God's will. The New England Puritan theological tradition can be found in devotional practices of St. Augustine, (Augustine was an early Christian theologian whose work was instrumental in the growth and development of Western Christianity and philosophy) who placed faith foremost. To accomplish this, they read the Bible, listened to sermons, studied daily events and analyzed nature for signs. They also paid particular attention to events that were out of the ordinary, like earthquakes and other natural events which they considered *notable providences*. Considerable time was spent reviewing the events in their personal lives and the status of their souls, often recording them in diaries and journals, again looking for patterns and spiritual meanings to guide them.

In general, Puritan theology is built around three main covenants (promises) between God and human beings, as they were recounted in and set forth in the Bible. The principle covenants are listed here:

> Puritans emphasized *the covenant of works*, that is, God's promise to Adam, in return for perfect obedience, man would earn God's reward. The reward in this covenant does not result from grace, it's a debt owed to Adam for keeping his part of the covenant (as recounted in Genesis 18-19). Unfortunately, when Adam failed to keep the covenant and after the fall, the gifts upon which salvation depends were withdrawn and the natural gifts corrupted and defiled.

> *The covenant of grace*, which was the promise of eternal life for all people who have faith in Christ, replacing the Covenant of Works entered into with Adam. It's a covenant that requires an active faith and as such, it tempers the doctrine of predestination. Although God reserves the right to choose the elect, the relationship becomes a contract (or covenant) in which punishment for sins is judged in response to disobedience. Augustine

believed that grace transforms the human will so that it is capable of doing good.

and;

> The *Covenant of Redemption* is the most difficult to understand and accept, because there is no biblical designation for it. The covenant states that the three persons of the Trinity entered into a solemn pact to accomplish the work of redemption this way, the Father promising to give a people to the Son as His inheritance, the Son attempting to complete their redemption and the Spirit covenanting to testify to Christ. The Covenant was assumed to be preexistent to the Covenant of Grace and held that Christ, who freely chose to sacrifice Himself for fallen man, bound God to accept Him as man's representative. Having accepted this pact, God is then committed to carrying out the Covenant of Grace.

These covenants all have their origins in Calvinism and they not only make it clear to every man and woman what their duties are, but they also force men and women to face their (implied) inferiority *because of their corrupt nature*, which makes them unfit and therefore, unable to fulfil their duties to God.

Some other important concepts of Puritanism are:

> *The covenant of glorification* unites the soul with God after death and the elect will form a community of saints.

> *The covenant of Justification* is a conversion or being born again and serves as the mark of election that rehabilitates depraved human nature. However, this conversion does not overcome sin, an individual may lapse into unregenerate (that is non-repentant behavior). To persevere in righteousness is an ability bestowed by by God and is given as He pleases. Natural depravity *is part of man's human nature*, so by association, *every human being is by nature, corrupt and perverted because of the fall of Adam and Eve.*

13

The covenant of Vocation is God's call to social, economic, civil, and religious roles or behavior. Individuals must use their talents, which come from God wholeheartedly in fulfilling a call. *(Emphasis Mine)*

The concept of a covenant also served as a practical means of organizing churches. *Since the state government did not control the church*, the Puritans reasoned, *there must be a different method of establishing authority.* Their idea was that if God's word was to function freely and each member of the church was made to feel that they were an essential part of the church's operation, each congregation *must* be self-sufficient and have all the offices and authority for self-regulation. John Cotton, New England's official apologist (a person who makes an argument in defense of something controversial), termed this form of church government 'Congregational,' meaning all authority would be located within *the individual congregations.* (This system was also referred to as '*the New England Way.*')

In a sermon he gave in Salem in 1636, John Cotton described the basic tenets of this system; people would pledge themselves to each other, swearing to obey the word of God that they might become a self-governing church. Checks and balances in this self-governing model included a requirement that members testify to their *experience of grace*, this to ensure the purity of the church and its members. They also elected their own church officials, this to ensure the fair and equitable distribution of power. The congregants would select a pastor *to preach*, a teacher to *attend to doctrine*, elders to oversee the *acts of spiritual Rule* and a deacon to *manage* the everyday tasks of church organization and *caring* for the poor.

This system of agreed-to covenants drew households to each other, to their church and the church leaders, creating an independent, self-governing congregation. This created a process that led to the organization of whole towns, in each village or town, church members (male members only, if you're wondering) who had to be residents of the town, voted to elect 'selectmen' who would run the daily activities, and town meetings had to be called and a vote taken on any legislative issue. Thus, the supreme authority in both political and religious areas became *God's word*, but the commitments made to the congregation and the community through deliberate compliance with the covenants, ensured good order and a purposeful system of religious and political authority.

It was the position of each church that by centralizing power in the town and defining the institution in terms of local covenants and mutual commitments, any weaknesses caused by *mobility atomism* (a doctrine that attempts to explain complex phenomena in terms of aggregates of fixed parts or classes, in this case, people relocating for various reasons), which could threaten stability in the New World would be significantly reduced, because churches came into being through the process of a well-ordered and structured covenant and individual members could only be released from their pledge *with the consent of the congregation*. But this came with a cost, congregants owning property were required to live within the township or village, and any residents leaving the township or village without this consensus, surrendered not only church membership but also the title to *any property in the town*.

Through measures like these, intended to combine economic and spiritual restraints, New England towns achieved amazingly high levels of commitment and solidity. For the next few decades, most Puritans who immigrated, settled in the New England area and formed individual colonies. Their numbers rose from 17,800 in 1640 to 106,000 by 1700, where the ratio of English settlers to other colonists was thought to be about 20 to 1. But by 1775, estimates are that there were 2.5 million people living in the colonies and the ratio of English settlers to other colonists dropped dramatically, some estimates place the ratio at 3 to 1. Make no mistake, in the early years, religious exclusiveness was the dominant ideology of this society and the spiritual beliefs that Puritans held were very strong. Since they kept God first and foremost in their minds, they felt reassured that He would motivate all of their actions.

It's interesting to contrast the Puritan idea of self-government with the position St. Augustine had with regard to original sin and state government. He based his reasoning on the experience of the government in Rome and the struggles of the fledgling Christian Church, all of which led him to the conclusion that *human beings cannot be trusted to govern themselves*. Augustine's view of Original Sin by definition, created a need for a strong political presence in the world. His reasoning was that a *government*, and by extension, *any law associated with that government*, exists to restrain and control the sinful, who's behavior was caused by the actions of Adam and Eve, again, actions that mankind *brought upon itself*.

Augustine's theory of original sin was politically expedient in that it persuaded many of his contemporaries to accept his idea that *because of original sin*, human beings needed some form of *external civil government*, one that had strong ties to *Christianity and the church*. This would therefore provide a *positive moral compass* that was clearly *understood* to be (obviously) free of any *religious bias*.

Thomas Aquinas was an Italian Dominican Friar, Priest, influential philosopher and theologian who also held a position on the subject. He too believed that the church should justifiably guide the state on secular matters, specifically those relating to *moral legislation* and this may be where the idea of state sponsored religion got its start. Ironically, both of these men were Roman Catholic.

A period called The First Great Awakening began in America about 1730 and continued for the next 20 to 25 years. It was in part, in direct conflict with the teaching of the Period of Enlightenment and one of the principle figures during this time was Jonathan Edwards, a revivalist preacher, philosopher and Protestant theologian. The only son in a family of eleven children, Edwards entered Yale in September, 1716 when he was 12 years old, graduated four years later as class valedictorian and received his Master's degree three years after that. After graduating from Yale, he studied theology, spent a few years preaching in New York City, then spent time tutoring at Yale from 1724 to 1726. In 1727, he became a colleague of his grandfather, Solomon Stoddard, in a ministry in Northampton, Mass.

By this time, Puritan theology emphasized a strict methodology to attain salvation, whereas Stoddard's theological concepts contradicted nearly every established and accepted belief held by his Puritan colleagues. In Stoddard's view, as reflected in his ministry, was an effort to promote the growth of church congregations in a colony of second-generation pilgrims, pilgrims who had become increasingly interested in the political and economic life of the colonies, as opposed to the pure idealism their immigrant parents adhered to over the previous 100 years. Stoddard's concepts of theology were not widely accepted by his fellow clergy or laymen in the larger population centers of New England.

Edwards took sole charge of the congregation after his grandfather's death in 1729 and after he succeeded his grandfather, Edwards repudiated most of his grandfather's views. Stoddard's influence remained dominant in the predominately rural area around Northampton Massachusetts but his parishioners eventually became disillusioned with Edwards' views and he was dismissed from the pulpit.

Edwards, who was undeterred, continued to argue against everything that Covenant Theology had become. *His* message as he saw it was that people needed to get back to *orthodox* Calvinism, that is; those bound by a covenant needed to consider themselves charged with a mission from God. In July of 1732, Edwards preached his 'Public Lecture' in Boston and afterwards, published a copy under the title "God Glorified in the Work of Redemption, by the Greatness of Man's Dependence upon Him, in the Whole of It." This was his first public attack against the perceived threat of Arminianism and the emphasis of his lecture was on God's absolute sovereignty in the work of salvation. Edwards felt that, yes, while it befitted God to have created man without sin, it was because of His 'good pleasure' and 'mere and arbitrary grace' that people were granted the faith necessary to incline him or her toward holiness, and that God might deny this grace without any criticism of His character.

In July of 1741, Edwards accepted an invitation to preach in the neighboring town of Enfield, Connecticut. This was at the height of the Great Awakening and was seen as one of the most intense outpourings of God's Spirit in American history. Despite the fact Edwards had earlier preached his sermon, "Sinners in the Hands of an Angry God" to his own congregation and felt that it evoked little if any reaction, (every minister who preaches, waits for the congregation's 'ah-ha' moment when he or she gives a sermon, just as every preacher has had the occasional sermon die before it reaches the first pew) Edwards felt compelled to deliver it again at Enfield.

His preaching techniques were not overly inspiring, Edward tended to read his sermons in an even tone of voice, albeit with great conviction. He avoided shouting and theatrics, preferring instead to impress his listeners with the power of truth as he saw it, while expressing the desperate need for God. Nothing he said or did when he delivered that sermon could explain what happened when he preached in Enfield. One eyewitness, Stephen Williams, recorded this in his diary;

> "We went over to Enfield where we met dear Mr. Edwards of Northampton who preached a most awakening sermon from these words, Deuteronomy 32:35*, and before the sermon was done there was a great moaning and crying went out through ye whole House…. 'What shall I do to be saved,' 'Oh, I am going to Hell,' 'Oh, what shall I do for Christ,' and so forth. So yet ye minister was obliged to desist, ye shrieks and cry were piercing and amazing."

Williams continued,

> "After some time of waiting the Congregation were still, so yet a prayer was made by Mr. W. and after that we descended from the pulpit and discoursed with the people, some in one place and some in another, and amazing and astonishing ye power of God was seen, and several souls were hopefully wrought upon that night, and oh ye cheerfulness and pleasantness of their countenances."

*To me *belongeth* vengeance, and recompence; their foot shall slide in *due* time: for the day of their calamity *is* at hand, and the things that shall come upon them make haste. *Deuteronomy; c 32: v 35- KJB*

By 1735, the revival had spread across the Connecticut River Valley and reached as far south as New Jersey. However, with success came criticism of the revival, as many New Englanders feared that Edwards had led his flock into fanaticism. By the summer of 1735, his religious fervor took a dark turn when a number in the audience fell under the effects of the revival but not experience conversion, instead becoming convinced that they destined for inevitable damnation. This lead Edwards to write in his journal that some felt the urge (presumably manipulated by Satan) to *take their own lives.* At least two people committed suicide in the depths of their spiritual distress, including someone from his own congregation. This resulting 'suicide craze' (as the locals expressed it) all but ended this first wave of revival.

For the most part, the movement had lost momentum by 1750 but its effect went on to successfully challenge the established authority of the church. As a secondary result, it served to further incite hostility and division between traditionalist Protestants who insisted on the continuing importance of ritual and doctrine, and revivalists who promoted emotional participation. It also brought about a major reshaping of the Congregational and Presbyterian churches as well as the fledgling Dutch and the German Reformed denominations and served to strengthen the small Baptist and Methodist Anglican denominations.

However, this First Great Awakening is believed to have launched the Evangelical Christian movement in America and laid the foundation for the successes of the Second Great Awakening of 1790-1830. By the late 1700s, fewer people attended church services on a regular basis and attendance dropped dramatically. This occurred for several reasons, some believed that God didn't actually play an important role in everyday life, or God was unconcerned with a person's church attendance, rather, God would judge the person on how he or she had lived his or her life on

Earth, while others were just too busy earning a living to have time to worship God. *(Has anything changed?)*

With this weakening of religious convictions, many faiths sponsored religious revivals that emphasized human beings' dependence upon God, beginning as a series of religious revivals that became nation-wide, but mainly focused in the Northeast and the Midwest. This movement served to forever change the religious landscape of the country by attracting hundreds of converts to new Protestant denominations as they promoted the growing idea of individual salvation and free will over the older concept of predestination. By 1800, the fastest growing religions in the country were Evangelical Methodism and Baptists.

The Second Great Awakening marked a important transformation in American religious life. Many early American religious groups that held the Calvinist tradition emphasized the deep depravity of human beings and held that they could only be saved through the grace of God, this new, evangelical movement placed greater emphasis on the ability of human beings to change their situation for the better by underscoring that individuals could assert their free will in choosing to be saved. Better yet, this salvation was open to all human beings, because the Second Great Awakening encompassed a more optimistic view of the human condition. Numerous revivals over the next few decades helped make the United States a much more deeply and solidly Protestant nation than it had been. As a bonus, this great awakening included more public roles for white women and much higher African-American participation in Christianity.

THE BATTLE OVER
OBSERVING CHRISTMAS

In most European countries, the identification and celebration of Christmas as a religious holiday played a central part in the ideological and religious struggle that continued after the Reformation. During this time in history, most Quakers, as well as Anabaptists, Congregational and Presbyterian Puritans regarded the day as an *abomination*, (a word with strong theological meaning and inference) while Anglicans, Lutherans, Dutch Reformed, Roman Catholics and others celebrated the day in a more familiar and traditional manner. When the Church of England advanced the idea that the Feast of the Nativity should be celebrated as a major religious holiday, the Puritans quickly attacked the celebration as *Papist idolatry*.

Open hostility over this one holiday mushroomed when the Puritans came to power in England following the execution of King Charles I. With the Parliamentarian side in England's civil war victorious, Puritan rulers banned Christmas in 1647. Predictably, protests followed with pro-Christmas rioting in several cities. Canterbury was overrun for several weeks with roving bands of rioters who decorated buildings with holly as they shouted royalist slogans. In the face of this, Parliament decided to go further, enacting a law abolishing any observance of Christmas, Easter and Whitsuntide, a the name used in the United Kingdom and Ireland for the Christian festival of Pentecost.

In Great Britain, Beltane was an Anglicized name for the Gaelic May Day festival most commonly held on May 1st or whatever day fell halfway between the spring equinox and the summer solstice. It began as a Gaelic May Day festival in Medieval Ireland, when a sacrifice was made to the god of light or sun god Beil and seen as the time when the sun is fully released from his bondage of winter and able to rule over summer and life once again. References to this event appear in early Irish literature and the day is associated with key events in Irish mythology, (before the introduction of Christianity) so we can begin to understand the objections the Puritans had to these two holidays.

While the Restoration of King Charles II to the throne in 1660 (more on this below) may have ended the ban on observing the holiday, many Calvinist clergymen still disapproved of celebrating Christmas, but the more conservative Puritans, including those in the colonies took their issue with the church one step further. It was widely rumored that the most *wicked and impious activities* were conducted during the celebration of Christmas, and in particular, Cotton Mather, who was one of the most influential colonial religious leaders who's job it was to set the moral tone in the colonies, supported and encouraged this idea. Mather openly condemned these activities in his sermons and in public speeches because as he saw it, the Puritan position was clear; if there was no scriptural justification for the birth of Christ having taken place on *December 25th*, then the selection of the date must have coincided with *the pagan Roman festival of Saturnalia*. He was also influential in the establishment of the court for the Salem witch trials of 1692 and began sounding a call for second and third generation Puritans of parents who had left England for the American colonies to return to *their Puritan theological roots*.

The objection the church had to celebrating Christmas was that is was closely associated to the Roman festival Saturnalia, an ancient Roman festival in honor of the god Saturn. In Roman mythology, Saturn was an agricultural deity who was supposed to have reigned over the earth during the Golden Age, (a period of primordial peace, harmony, stability, and prosperity). The festival was commonly held on December 17, with events lasting through December 23 on the ancient Roman Julian calendar, (introduced by Julius Caesar in 45 BC and commonly used until the late 1500s when countries changed to the Gregorian Calendar we use today.

Some countries, such as Greece and Russia continued to use the old calendar until the early 1900s and the Orthodox church in Russia still uses it, as do some Orthodox churches). The holiday was observed with ritual sacrifices in the Temple of Saturn, in the Roman Forum, followed by a public banquet, by private gift giving and continual carousing and pageantry that suspended established Roman moral standards in society. Gambling and dice-playing, normally prohibited or at least frowned upon in Roman society were permitted for all, including slaves, who were being waited on and served *by their masters*. Because gifts of value would mark social status contrary to the spirit of the season, these were often inexpensive pottery or wax figurines that were specially made for the day, candles or gag gifts and children received toys or trinkets.

Of course, none of this behavior could or would be accepted or tolerated by Puritans, who saw this as a move by the Roman Church to absorb pagans (and their ideology) into Christian community, thereby increasing the size of and enhance the position of the church. This again led many Puritans to the further conclusion that to celebrate a December Christmas was to *defile oneself* by paying homage to a *pagan celebration*.

In the New World, Pilgrims living in Plymouth put their abhorrence of the holiday into practice as early as the winter of 1620 by spending their first Christmas Day in the new world by making the settlement permanent and with other activities that showed their complete contempt for the day. Massachusetts and Connecticut quickly followed the lead of the Plymouth colony by refusing to tolerate *any* observance of the day. The Puritans of New England quickly passed a series of laws that made any observance of Christmas illegal, including a 1659 law in Massachusetts that punished offenders with a fine of *five shillings*, (not a trifling sum in a time when hard currency was relatively scarce). Here is a copy of the actual law:

> For preventing disorders, arising in several places within this jurisdiction by reason of some still observing such festivals as were superstitiously kept in other communities, to the great dishonor of God and offense of others: it is therefore ordered by this court and

23

the authority thereof that whosoever shall be found observing any such day as Christmas or the like, either by forbearing of labor, feasting, or any other way, upon any such account as aforesaid, every such person so offending shall pay for every such offence five shilling as a fine to the county.

From the records of the General Court,
Massachusetts Bay Colony
May 11, 1659

What Puritan theologians could not or would not understand and accept was that as emperor, Constantine, who saw himself as the head of the church, was fighting to protect his church from attacks from numerous heretics who were systematically tearing apart the theology and teachings of early Christian theology in the years after the death of Christ. The emperor's role as head of the church as he saw it, was to enforce doctrine, root out heresy and uphold ecclesiastical unity.

Reconstructing the life and the doctrine of Arius, the Fourth Century Alexandrian Presbyter living in Libya and perhaps the best known heretic, has been a difficult task because most if not all of his work was destroyed when he was condemned as a heretic in A.D. 325. What we do know of Arius's writings comes only from the works of his critics who, during the process of condemning him, revealed a great deal about him. From these sources, we know that somewhere around the year 318, Arius began to preach a doctrine about the Son of God, specifically that the Father's divinity was greater than the Son's. Arius further advanced the idea that the Son of God was a Creature made from nothing, begotten directly of the Eternal God and was therefore, God's First Production, before all ages.

These ideas were all extremely threatening to the Church and the fall-out from them eventually caused the Bishop of Alexandria, Peter I to condemn Arius and *all his teachings*. While Arius was formally excommunicated as a heretic in 320, he had many supporters who worked to get him readmitted into the church. In 324, Constantine's sister along with Arius' close friend Eusebius

Pamphili, a Roman historian, exegete, Christian polemicist and the sitting Bishop of Caesarea, made a concerted effort to have him officially reinstated.

However, Constantine believed that the teachings of Arius and his followers presented such a dangerous threat to the church that in desperation, he convened the First Ecumenical Council of Nicaea, organized to settle what has become known as the Arian controversy. This gathering was the first collaborative effort to attain a consensus in the church through an assembly representing all of Christendom. To accomplish this, Constantine extended an invitation to 1800 bishops, 1000 from churches in the west and 800 from churches in the east. The invitation extended across the entire empire and by most estimates, over 300 bishops from every part of the realm except Britain accepted. Each was granted permission to bring with him, two priests and three deacons (all traveling free of charge).

While some bishops arriving at the conference initially saw Arius' teachings in a positive light, after all his work was reviewed by the entire assembly, the decision was unanimous; the teachings of Arius were declared heretical and in a very real sense, threatening the very salvation of man's soul. Arius was banished from the empire and Constantine issued the following decree against *Arius, his teachings and his followers*;

> "...if any writing composed by Arius should be found, it should be handed over to the flames, so that not only will the wickedness of his teaching be obliterated, but nothing will be left even to remind anyone of him. And I hereby make a public order, that if someone should be discovered to have hidden a writing composed by Arius, and not to have immediately brought it forward and destroyed it by fire, his penalty shall be death. As soon as he is discovered in this offence, he shall be submitted for capital punishment..."

In the end, the Council declared that the Son was "...a true God, co-eternal with the Father and begotten from His same substance", further arguing that such a doctrine best codified the scriptural position of the Son as well as traditional Christian belief about Him, as transmitted down from the Apostles. Under Constantine's pressure, this position was supported by all the bishops in attendance and communicated to all of Christianity as the Nicene Statement. (It should be noted here that Arianism should be clearly distinguished from *"Aryanism"*, which formed the core of Nazi racial ideology during the twentieth century and had nothing whatsoever to do with either Arius or his teachings.)

Now, Constantine may or may not have corrupted the Bible as the Puritans maintained, but his efforts at the Council of Nicaea should not be dismissed out of hand. Again, it's important to understand that the Puritans rejection of the content of the creed and their rejection of not just Christmas, but much of the teaching in the Roman Catholic Church was motivated by their strict understanding and a narrow interpretation of scripture. In a very real sense, the Council of Nicaea produced the first, uniform Christian doctrine that clearly defined the beliefs for the whole of Christianity. Known today as *the Nicene Creed*, it can be difficult for us to reconcile that this objection by the Puritans wasn't about the *content*, they may have had no problem with that, it was about *the origin* of the Creed. *(A copy of the creed is included in the appendix)*.

One final thought is that, as Christianity grew and spread in the years after the Council of Nicaea, the church year was organized to fit within the calendar and December 25th became the day assigned on the official church calendar *to celebrate the birth of Christ*, just as we celebrate the Epiphany, Easter and Pentecost on specific days of the year. December 25th wasn't intended to mark the actual day when Jesus was born into the world but it wound up that way, even though people hear every December 25th, 'today is the birthday of Jesus Christ'. The idea has become firmly fixed in the daily life of Christians.

Okay, why bring all this up? In the early 1680s, King Charles II of England began taking steps to reorganize the colonies in New England. He started by revoking the charter of the Massachusetts Bay Colony in 1684, this after Puritan rulers refused to act when the Crown issued demands for reforms in the colony. The king was trying to streamline the administration of his small colonies and bring them under tighter control of the Crown. Charles II died in 1685 and his successor, *the Roman Catholic James II* continued the process, culminating in the creation of the Dominion of New England, (and was given the official motto; "Never does liberty appear in a more gracious form"). The king then appointing Anglican Sir Edmund Andros to the position of Governor.

Sir Edmund took over as Governor of the Dominion of New England in 1686 when he arrived in Boston on December 20th and he immediately took control. But Andros' tenure was totalitarian and querulous at best and his Anglican views did little to further his cause with the Puritan community. During his time in office, the Crown ordered Boston shops to close on Christmas Day and forced the schoolmaster out of town for a mandatory holiday. Town meetings were outlawed and this left the Dominion without any consent of the governed, responsibility for marriage was removed from the clergy and the Old South Church was appropriated for the use of Anglican services. However, when Andros was overthrown in 1689 and the Puritan Way was restored, it was business as usual, shops remained open on Christmas with goods such as fish, hay and lumber being brought into Boston like any other work day and some merchants set the opening time at 05:00 a.m. so their employees could not attend an early church service and still arrive at work on time.

At its height, the Puritan work ethic was one of the most arduous ever and was comprised of 300 working days compared to the 240 days other cultures had adopted throughout the centuries. Days of rest in New England were few and were generally limited to the Sabbath, election day, Harvard commencement day and periodic days of thanksgiving and humiliation. Scripture did not name any holiday except the Sabbath, they argued, and the very concept of 'holy days' implied that *some days were not holy*. This all caused non-Puritans in New England to bemoan the loss of holidays enjoyed by the working classes in Great Britain and other European countries.

Although Christmas celebrations were no longer illegal by 1681, officials in New England continued to openly discourage gift giving, displays of merriment and even evergreen decoration. The Reverend Increase Mather (yes, that's his name and he was father of Cotton Mather) lamented in 1687,

> "The generality of Christmas-keepers observe that Festival after such a manner as is highly dishonourable to the name of Christ. How few are there comparatively that spend those Holidays (as they are called) after an Holy manner. But they are consumed in Compotations, in Interludes, in playing at Cards, in Revellings, in excess of Wine, in mad Mirth; Will Christ the holy Son of God be pleased with such Services?"

All this activity was still strongly connected to those abhorrent pagan customs and was strictly forbidden in Puritan meeting houses. It continued to be discouraged in most New England homes, to the point where merrymakers were charged with and prosecuted for *disturbing the peace*. (Even after the U.S. Constitution came into effect, the U.S. Senate assembled on Christmas Day in 1797 and the House of Representatives continued to meet on December 25th as late as 1802.)

When the Revolutionary War began, the idea to boycott Christmas rose in popularity when the day again became associated with royalist control and tyranny. After the war, while businesses remained open on Christmas Day and private celebrations were not uncommon, there was no official recognition of Christmas in New England. In fact, no state recognized Christmas as an official holiday until Alabama took the initiative in 1836. President Grant finally made Christmas a federal holiday in 1870, and a year later, New England at last gave up the remnants of its obstinate resistance and opposition to the day.

And yet, New Englanders would not completely let go of the idea. In the late 1870s, classes were still held in Boston public schools on Christmas Day and children who chose to miss school and quietly celebrate Christmas at home were disciplined. One observer hinted that the Puritans viewed Santa Claus as *the Anti-Christ* and numerous New England colleges and universities did not have a Christmas break in December until the end of the 1870s.

The Puritan hostility to Christmas slowly eroded but it wasn't until the late nineteenth century when authors began praising the holiday for its liberality, family togetherness and joyful observance. In 1887 for example, the *St. Nicholas Magazine*, (a popular American children's publication that circulated from 1873 to 1940) printed a story about a sickly Puritan boy of 1635 being restored to health when his mother brings him a bough of Christmas greenery.

A "CHRISTIAN NATION"

Religious discrimination has been and continues to be glossed over by most American History textbooks, mainly out of fear of offending the religious beliefs of a specific community. Many are surprised to learn that from the earliest arrival of Europeans on the continent of North America, religion was often been used as a justification to victimize, oppress and eventually execute peoples who don't comply with the oppressor's religious beliefs. People were first branded as *heretics, unbelievers* or *foreigners* and sadly, this included indigenous people who were first identified by European settlers as *heathen native savages* who were living in the Americas before the European settlers arrived. It should also be noted that battles between Catholics and Protestants and quite often between different Protestant sects also serve to portray an unavoidable contradiction to the widely held belief that America was founded as a "Christian" nation.

The first settlement established by people fleeing the religious persecution in Europe was located on the St. Johns River in what is the state of Florida, (about 10 km inland from the current coastline, close to what is now the city of Jacksonville). A colony called Fort Caroline was established in 1564 by French Huguenots (a Protestant minority living in predominantly Roman Catholic France). It was a triangular earth and timber fort, built more than fifty years before the Pilgrims arrived at Plymouth Massachusetts. The first wave of settlers at the fort comprised 200 soldiers, craftsmen and several women. These settlers looked forward to building homes and clearing fields, all in preparation for the arrival of several hundred more Huguenots the following year.

Difficulties quickly overcame the colony after an attempt to establish good relations with a local group of native Americans did not end well. The colonists began to suffer from hunger, disease and other hardships and many chose to give up and return to France, but a core of the most committed settlers clung to their North American foothold. The following year, ships from France brought supplies and an additional 600 soldiers and settlers. Predictably, all this activity began to attract the attention of King Philip II of Spain who had laid claim to all of Central America, Mexico, all of what is now Florida and sections of what are now New Mexico and Arizona as Spanish territory.

The king sent Admiral Pedro Menendez de Aviles, (based at St. Augustine, the capital of Spanish Florida) to dispose of the French, a duty that Menendez performed with merciless efficiency. Fort Caroline was quickly captured and about 200 survivors of the battle were taken prisoner. 140 French men were declared heretics and *put to the sword*, while the remaining 60 women and children were loaded on a ship and deported to Havana Cuba, were they were left to find their own way home from there. Several weeks later, survivors of a shipwrecked French fleet washed up on the beaches of Florida after a severe Atlantic storm and Menéndez, using a captured Frenchman as translator, explained how Fort Caroline had been seized and destroyed, he urged the French to surrender. The French, having lost most of their food and weapons in the shipwreck, agreed.

When Menéndez then demanded that they give up their Protestant faith and embrace Catholicism, most refused. In total, 111 Frenchmen were killed and of the sixteen who were spared, several by declaring that they were Catholic, a few who claimed to be impressed sailors from the Breton Isles and four survivors who allowed that they were skilled craftsmen with talents that were needed at St. Augustine, (their religious affiliation apparently notwithstanding). The Spanish forces destroyed Fort Caroline and a short time later, built their own fort on the same site.

Three years later, in April of 1568, Dominique de Gourgues led a French force to re-take the installation. They captured and burned the fort, then slaughtered the Spanish prisoners in retribution for the 1565 massacre. So by most accounts, the first few encounters between European 'Christians' in the new world – *ended in a blood bath*.

Yes, the Pilgrims who arrived in New England in the early 1600s did so to flee the religious persecution they experienced in England, but as ecumenical as this idea may sound, the Puritan fathers of the Massachusetts Bay Colony could not and would not tolerate any opposing religious (or political) views to defile their 'city upon a hill.' From Puritan Boston's earliest days, Catholics (often and openly referred to as 'Papists') were considered an *abomination* (again, that word) and were banned from the colonies, along with other non-Puritans.

Protestant hostility toward Catholics, principally *French and Spanish Catholics*, prompted religious leaders like Cotton Mather to emphasize this schism in his Sunday sermons. Across the region, local laws covering property ownership and voting rights were drafted deliberately to discriminate against Catholics. Anti-Catholic feelings began to fan the flames of revolution in colonial America after England's King George III extended an olive branch to French Catholics living in Canada when England drafted the Quebec Act of 1774, an act which officially recognized their religion.

When he sent Benedict Arnold on a mission to encourage the French Canadians to support the American Revolution in 1775, George Washington cautioned Arnold *not to let their religion get in the way* with this piece of advice, "Prudence, policy and a true Christian Spirit will lead us to look with compassion upon their errors, without *insulting them*." Arnold later stated that America's alliance with Catholic France was *one of his reasons* for his betrayal of the American cause.

Nor would this idea go away after the War of Independence. America, *feeling flushed with independence*, proceeded to create a crazy quilt of state laws regarding religion. In Massachusetts for example, only Christians were allowed to hold public office, while Catholics were allowed to do so only if they renounced papal authority. In 1777, New York State's constitution banned Catholics from public office, and this law would remain in effect until 1806. In Maryland, Catholics had full civil rights *but Jews did not*. Delaware required an oath affirming *belief in the Trinity* and several states, including Massachusetts and South Carolina, all had official, state supported churches. Many colonies drafted oaths and pledges that were required to be administered before anyone could assume public office, but these required oaths of office primarily targeted specific religions, all of this the result of the proliferation of religious beliefs held by groups of immigrants that had spread throughout the colonies in the years leading up to the War of Independence.

Again if I may digress, while it's true that most Puritans were very pious and faithful, those living in the colonies during the time leading up to 1776, lived in a society far removed from the settlers of 1620. While it appears that America's early elected leaders were models of religious tolerance, *entrenched attitudes* were still slow to change. The anti-Catholic sentiment of America's Calvinist past found a fresh new voice in the 19th century. A belief that was widely held and actually preached by some of the most prominent ministers in America at the time, was that Catholics would, *if not stopped*, turn America over to the pope (an idea that has never totally gone away). Even children were not spared, anti-Catholic hostility and rancor was part of every school day, as was selected classroom Bible readings, all of this was carefully orchestrated to keep the sentiment alive and in the forefront of everyone's mind.

Mount Benedict was a Roman Catholic convent, located in Charlestown, Massachusetts, just across the river from Boston. It was being run by a Catholic Order of Ursuline nuns (an order of nuns dedicated to the education of young girls) who also opened and operated a private school for girls. The school was founded in 1820 with an enrollment of approximately 100 female students, principally the daughters of predominantly Protestant, liberal Unitarian members of the upper classes of Boston. By 1834, the school census had dropped to 47 students, *with as few as six of whom were Catholic.*

However, the middle and lower classes of Boston society, who were for the most part *conservative Protestants*, came to see the convent school as the symbol of a union between two classes of people, both of whom they mistrusted. Roman Catholic institutions, especially convents, were often rumored (usually by anti-Catholics) to be dens of *immorality and corruption*. The Charlestown facility specifically was seen by lower class Protestants as a place where Catholics and wealthy Unitarians assembled to plot against them. To compound the problem even further, the Convent stood close to the site where a monument to the battle of Bunker Hill was being constructed. For many local residents, this nearby complex made the school's location a personal affront and worst of all, the school was seen by many as a symbol of a foreign faith that was evil, hateful and was seen as a threat to the nation.

As night fell on August 11, 1834, a few hundred citizens morphed into a mob that assembled at the convent and, as the nuns and their young charges cowered outside, both the convent and school were ransacked and torched by the crowd. As emotions grew, a mausoleum was opened, several coffins were overturned and the remains desecrated. After three nights of arson and unchecked lawlessness, both the convent and the school it operated had been reduced to a smoking ruin.

A committee established by then Mayor Theodore Lyman met every day (except Sunday) from August 13 to August 27. Testimony taken by this committee and by the Charlestown selectmen's committee led to thirteen arrests, where eight suspects were charged with the capital crimes of arson or burglary. Eventually, 12 of the 13 defendants were acquitted and only the thirteenth, *a 16 year old* whose only crime was burning books during the riot, was convicted. The young man was sentenced to *life at hard labor* but was pardoned by the governor a short time later and finally, there was no restitution for the destruction of the school or the convent.

Also during this time, a new religion in America appeared, begun by a man named Joseph Smith. His religion very quickly angered the Protestant majority, and by 1832, a mob tarred and feathered Smith and thus began the start of a long battle between Christian America and Smith's Mormon ideology.

Haun's Mill was a gristmill established by Jacob Hawn in 1835 and was situated on the banks of Shoal Creek in Fairview Township in Caldwell County, Missouri. By October of 1838, there were approximately 75 Mormon families who had fled persecution in the east and were living along the banks of Shoal Creek, about 30 of them in the immediate vicinity of the Mill. In October 1838, following a series of disagreements over land and the growing opposition to Smith's religion, Missouri Governor Lilburn Boggs ordered all Mormons expelled from his state. Local non-Mormon residents of Livingston, Missouri heard (what were later found to be false stories spread by Mormon dissenters) that the Latter-Day Saints living in the vicinity of the mill were planning an attack on settlers in Livingstone County. Missouri Militia Colonel Thomas Jennings, Sheriff of Livingston County, without any authority or orders from his superiors, elected to lead an attack on the settlement about 4:00 that afternoon.

After the initial engagement, several of those who had been wounded or had surrendered were shot dead. A 78 year-old man surrendered his musket to a militiaman who then shot the man and hacked his body apart with a corn knife. Several other bodies were mutilated or had their clothing stolen, many of the women were assaulted, houses were robbed, wagons, tents and clothing were stolen, horses and livestock were driven off and the few surviving women and children were left destitute. Two years later, a mob murdered Joseph Smith and his brother Hyrum while they were jailed in Carthage, Illinois. It should be noted that *no one was ever convicted* for any of these crimes.

Nativism in the 1800s was understood to mean the opposition to immigration and objection to the support of any effort to lower the political or legal classification of certain ethnic or cultural groups. It was felt that, because these immigrant groups were *hostile to a natural culture*, they would not be able to assimilate into society. Ten years after the events in Charlestown Massachusetts, in the city of Philadelphia, (a Greek word for 'brotherly love' chosen by the Quaker, William Penn when he named the city) anti-Catholic sentiment and animosity powered by the nation's growing anti-immigrant sentiment, served to fuel what came to be known as the Philadelphia Nativist Riots (or alternately the Philadelphia Prayer Riots, the Bible Riots or the Native American Riots, (native American Indians notwithstanding).

The Philadelphia began to emerge as a sizable industrial center during the years leading up to the War Between the States, and as the number of immigrant workers in the city increased, tensions resulting from religious, economic and cultural differences began to fester between residents. Due to a number of circumstances, the majority of immigrants migrating to Philadelphia were Catholic and the predominantly indigenous Protestant majority saw this as a challenge to their way of life. As the Catholic population continued to grow, Protestants felt the need to draw a line in the sand and chose to do this *at the front door of the public school.*

In 1838, the Pennsylvania State Legislature passed a law authorizing that The Bible (which everyone at the time understood to be *the King James Version*) should be used as a *public school textbook.* This law was a calculated slap in the face directed at Catholics because it was completely unnecessary, *public schools state wide were already using the King James Bible for daily instruction.* Additionally, many textbooks contained clear cut and thinly veiled anti-Catholic bias, one text even going so far as to openly refer to the pope as *the anti-Christ.* Stories quickly began circulating about how priests and nuns who had engaged in illicit affairs, killed the offspring and were burying them beneath the floor of the convent. As bizarre as these stories may sound today, they were taken as gospel (*sorry*) by many Americans living in the 1840's and predictably, the position of both sides grew more polarized and extreme.

In 1842, over 50 Protestant clergy (some estimates suggest that the number was as high as at 90) formed the American Protestant Association, a group committed to halting the spread of Catholicism in the United States, believing that it was "subversive of civil *and* religious liberty." At the same time, the Catholic Church dogmatically clung to its time honored theological precepts, the net result only serving to widen the gap between the two groups.

The Catholic church's official stance was that the separation of church and state was a *flawed concept*; governments, the church maintained, had an obligation to submit to Rome, in fact as we saw, Augustine taught that human beings cannot be trusted to govern themselves because our nature has become corrupt as the result of Adam's sin. Furthermore, Catholics believed that there could be no salvation for anyone outside the Catholic Church, so none of the other religions had any rights and the Pope should not in any way be compelled to recognize or support non-Catholics.

In 1843, a wave of Protestant fervor swept Philadelphia. Church leaders joined forces to bring the community *back to God,* including the reestablishment of a time for reverence and sanctity on Sunday. Protestant clergy in Philadelphia joined a growing and successful national movement to suspend train travel and stop mail delivery on Sunday, (see the list of legislative efforts to weave religion into everyday life in the appendix). The group of clergy also decided to launch a crusade to end the sale of liquor on Sunday. Against this backdrop, hostility over the divergent religious influence in the city's public school system quickly escalated.

As a sidebar, statutes called 'Blue Laws' were put in effect in the 17th century that prohibited various recreational and commercial activities on Sunday. These laws, which today are more often referred to as Sunday Closing Laws, still prohibit certain types of commercial activity on the Sabbath. For example, in Texas, blue laws prohibited selling housewares such as pots, pans and washing machines on Sunday until 1985. Originally, these laws were written to stop people from engaging in personal activities that officials regarded as 'moral offenses' such as gambling or the consumption of alcohol, however, in the 19th century, state and local governments passed laws that forbade businesses from operating at all on Sunday. Although these laws were clearly based on Christian beliefs, the U.S. Supreme Court has until very recently, consistently ruled that they do not violate the First Amendment's Establishment Clause. Many lower court rulings have repealed these laws since the 1960s but laws banning the sale of alcohol on Sunday still remain in force in many states across the country.

In the mid-1800s, Pennsylvania's public schools were a microcosm of a neighborhood filled with generic Protestantism. The school day began with the recitation of the Lord's Prayer, readings from the King James Bible and group participation when singing Protestant hymns. The Bible was also frequently used as a spelling book in classes. Biblical reading in class were conducted *without comment,* (meaning that the teacher reads a number of verses, usually 10, without any elaboration or interpretation). Most students, (who were Protestant) found this rubric appropriate because it agreed with their own theology, but Catholics, who had been taught to refer all questions to church leaders who would then interpret Scripture, saw the practice as *heretical and alien.*

On May 3rd, 1844, the long simmering dispute between Protestant and Catholic factions over the use of the King James Bible as part of public school instruction spilled violently into the streets and became a brawl that resulted in the death of four nativist protesters. Calling on Philadelphians to defend themselves from *"the bloody hand of the Pope"* and further asserting that Catholics (without disclosing how) had somehow desecrated the American flag, bands of young nativist sympathizers heard the call and marched into Kensington (then a township north of Philadelphia) on May 7th. When gunfire broke out, the nativists rioted, torching the Hibernia firehouse and a market before local militia dispersed the crowd.

On May 8th, the nativists again took to the streets. As one group returned to Kensington, where they burned down St. Michael's Catholic Church, the Seminary of the Sisters of Charity and several homes, a second mob gathered at St. Augustine's Catholic Church and began throwing stones at Mayor John Morin Scott as he pleaded for calm. Ignoring the (badly outnumbered) National Guard troops on duty, the mob burned the church to the ground, cheering when the steeple fell. Before it all ended, over 30 buildings were set ablaze an destroyed, two Catholic churches were severely damaged, at least 20 people were killed, over 100 were wounded and 200 families, both Catholic and Protestant, were left homeless.

In 1849, Charles B. Allen founded a nativist society in New York City that he called the Order of the Star Spangled Banner. This was an oath-bound secret society, created to protest the rise of Irish, Roman Catholic and German immigration into the United States. The group saw Catholics as treacherous, illegal voters who were (of course) under control of a Pope in Rome. In order to become a member of the order, a man had to be at least 21 years old, a Protestant and a believer in God, and he must be willing to obey *without question,* the dictates of the order. Those who joined promised during secret rituals, to vote only for native born Protestants for public office and the organization endorsed and supported carefully selected candidates or designated its own nominees during secret council meetings. Every new member was required to take the following oath;

> "In the presence of Almighty God and these witnesses, you do solemnly promise and swear that you will never betray any of the secrets of this society, nor communicate them even to proper candidates, except within a lawful council of the order; that you never will permit any of the secrets of this society to be written, or in any other manner made legible, except for the purpose of official instruction; that you will not vote, nor give your influence for any man for any office in the gift of the people, unless he be an American-born citizen, in favor of Americans ruling America, nor if he be a Roman Catholic; that you will in all political matters, so far as this order is concerned, comply with the will of the majority, though it may conflict with your personal preference, so long as it does not conflict with the Constitution of the United States of America or that of the State in which you reside; that you will not, under any circumstances whatever, knowingly recommend an unworthy person for initiation, nor suffer it to be done, if in your power to prevent it; that you will not, under any circumstances, expose the name of any member of this order nor reveal the existence of such an association; that you will answer an imperative notice issued by the proper authority; obey the command of the State council, president or his deputy, while assembled by such notice, and respond to the claim of a sign or cry of the order, unless it be physically impossible . . ."

Several members of the order actually got elected to public office and managed to introduce a few bills in Congress, but the order was largely unsuccessful in getting any meaningful legislation passed. The society became known as 'the no-nothing society' because members were instructed to answer "I don't know" to anyone asking questions about the organization.

The Know-Nothing movement spread rapidly, such that by 1852, supporters of the movement had achieved significant results with many of their candidates winning seats in local and state elections. With the passage of the Kansas Nebraska Act of 1854, the order gained more supporters. Although originally allied with the Whigs, the phenomenal success of the Know-Nothings, as well as growing debate over the issue of slavery helped cause the decline and demise of the Whig Party. In the 35th Congress, which assembled in December, 1855, there were 75 Know-Nothing members elected as such. In 1856 Horace Greeley wrote:

> "The majority of the Banks* men, are now members of Know-Nothing councils and some twenty or thirty of them actually believe in that swindle. Half of the Massachusetts delegation, two thirds of that of Ohio and nearly all of that of Pennsylvania are Know-Nothings."

> *(Nathaniel Prentice Banks, candidate for Speaker of the House of Representatives and member of the Know-Nothing Party. He was reelected to Congress in 1854)

The Know-Nothings elected the governor and all but two members of the Massachusetts state legislature as well as 40 members of the legislature in the state of New York. Despite the number that held elective office, the Know-Nothings were for the most part, unsuccessful in passing significant legislation. Several bills were introduced in Congress that called for the prohibition of immigration of foreign born paupers and convicts, while legislation was introduced in several states that called for registration and literacy tests for voters. The Know-Nothings decided to follow the path laid out for them by precedents going all the way back to the Revolutionary War and the Constitution and ignore slavery by adhering to the current set of laws, betting that their anti-Catholic, anti-immigrant, pro-American message would trump the race card. The only problem with this idea was that by the end of the 1850s, the subject of slavery had moved to the front of the national political debate.

The increasing controversy over slavery led to the rapid fragmentation of the Know-Nothing movement. Many antislavery adherents joined remnants of the Whigs in the newly emerging Republican Party, while pro- supporters joined the Democratic Party. By 1859, as the country approached the War Between the States, the Order saw dwindling support in all but a few Northern and border states and was no longer a significant participant on the national political stage.

The effort to eliminate religious disqualifications that remained in state constitutions that affected Roman Catholics and other religious minorities moved very slowly and with a great deal of opposition from a large segment of many of the state's populations. It was not until 1833 that the union between Church and State in the Commonwealth of Massachusetts was dissolved and Catholics no longer had to pay taxes to support of the state (that is, Protestant) Church. New Jersey retained its anti-Catholic provision in its Constitution until 1844, and it wasn't until 1877 that New Hampshire struck the provision from its Constitution that disqualified Catholics from holding state office.

It should be noted that the anti-Catholic feeling isn't limited to early history in our country. With the pervasive threat of what was held as *godless Communism* looming during the Cold War, the country's fear of atheism also reached new heights of paranoia and fear. As late as 1960, presidential candidate John F. Kennedy, in the face of a mounting public objection to the candidate's Roman Catholic religion and a growing political campaign claiming that he would be a proxy and (once again) *America would be governed by a Pope in Rome*, found himself compelled to make a national speech in which he attempted to clarify that his loyalty was to America, not the pope.

America's anti-Semitism was practiced, institutionally as well as socially for decades and as recently as 2008 Presidential candidate Mitt Romney, (a Mormon) in the face of mounting cacophony from the media, felt compelled to address the public's concerns and suspicions about his membership in the Church of Jesus Christ of Latter-day Saints.

"IN GOD WE TRUST"

The motto IN GOD WE TRUST has been viewed by some as a back door attempt to get God into the government. It was actually not placed on United States coinage until just before the Civil War, when the motto was added to several coins because of the increased religious fervor that swept the nation during that War. Treasury Secretary Salmon P. Chase received frequent requests from devout citizens from all across the country, all urging the United States to recognize the Deity on United States coins. From Treasury Department records, it appears that one of the first such appeals came from a letter to the secretary. It was dated November 13, 1861 and written by Reverend M. R. Watkinson, Minister of the Gospel from Ridleyville, Pennsylvania and is presented here;

Dear Sir:

You are about to submit your annual report to the Congress respecting the affairs of the national finances. One fact touching our currency has hitherto been seriously overlooked. I mean the recognition of the Almighty God in some form on our coins.

You are probably a Christian. What if our Republic were not shattered beyond reconstruction? Would not the antiquaries of succeeding centuries rightly reason from our past that we were a heathen nation? What I propose is that instead of the goddess of liberty we shall have next inside the 13 stars a ring inscribed with the words PERPETUAL UNION; within the ring the allseeing eye, crowned with a halo; beneath this eye the American flag, bearing in its field stars equal to the number of the States united; in the folds of the bars the words GOD, LIBERTY, LAW.

This would make a beautiful coin, to which no possible citizen could object. This would relieve us from the ignominy of heathenism. This would place us openly under the Divine protection we have personally claimed. From my hearth I have felt our national shame in disowning God as not the least of our present national disasters.

To you first I address a subject that must be agitated.

As a result, Secretary Chase directed James Pollock who was Director of the Mint at Philadelphia, to prepare a motto in this letter dated November 20, 1861:

Dear Sir:

No nation can be strong except in the strength of God, or safe except in His defense. The trust of our people in God should be declared on our national coins.

You will cause a device to be prepared without unnecessary delay with a motto expressing in the fewest and tersest words possible this national recognition.

Because of an Act of Congress from January 18, 1837, the mint was prohibited from adding mottoes and devices on the coins of the United States and thus, the mint could not make any changes without the Congress enacting separate, specific legislation. In December 1863, the Director of the Mint submitted his designs for new one cent coin, two cent coin and three cent coin to Secretary Chase for approval and in a letter to the Mint Director in that month, Secretary Chase stated:

I approve your mottoes, only suggesting that on that with the Washington obverse the motto should begin with the word OUR, so as to read OUR GOD AND OUR COUNTRY. And on that with the shield, it should be changed so as to read: IN GOD WE TRUST.

The Congress passed the Act of April 22, 1864 and the legislation changed the composition of the one cent coin and authorized the minting of a two cent coin. The Mint Director was directed to develop the designs for these coins for final approval of the Secretary. IN GOD WE TRUST first appeared on the 1864 two cent coin and a second Act of Congress passed on March 3, 1865, allowed the Mint Director, with the Secretary's approval, to place the motto on all gold and silver coins that "shall admit the inscription thereon."

Under this Act, the motto was placed on the gold double eagle, the gold eagle and the gold half eagle coins, and was also placed on the silver dollar, the half and quarter dollar coins and on the nickel three cent piece beginning in 1866. Congress later passed the Coinage Act of 1873 that also said that the Secretary "may cause the motto IN GOD WE TRUST to be inscribed on such coins as shall admit of such motto."

However, the use of IN GOD WE TRUST has not been consistently applied, it disappeared from the five cent coin in 1883 and did not reappear until production of the Jefferson nickel began in 1938, but all United States coins bear the inscription since 1938. Later, the motto was found missing from the new design of the double eagle and the eagle gold coins shortly after they appeared in 1907. In response to broad demand, Congress directed that it restored and an act passed in May of 1908 made it the motto mandatory on all coins upon which it had previously appeared.

IN GOD WE TRUST was not mandatory on the one cent and five cent coins but could be placed on the coins at the request of the Secretary or the Mint Director with the Secretary's approval. The motto has been in continuous use on the one cent coin since 1909 and on the ten cent coin since 1916. It's also appeared on all gold coins and silver dollar coins, half dollar coins, and quarter dollar coins struck since July 1, 1908. (Are you confused yet?)

Over the years, many have argued against the presence of the religious motto on American currency. President Theodore Roosevelt, in a letter published in the New York Times in 1907, wrote that keeping the motto on coins was unwarranted and possibly sacrilegious:

> "My own feelings in the matter is due to my very firm conviction that to put such a motto on coins, or to use it in any kindred manner, not only does no good, but does positive harm, and is in effect irreverence, which comes dangerously close to sacrilege,"

It wasn't until 1956, (again, during the height of the Cold War) that a law was passed by the 84th Congress on July 30, 1956 and approved by the President, that 'IN GOD WE TRUST' was declared the national motto of the United States. The motto first appeared on paper money in 1957 on the one dollar silver certificate and this began circulating on October 1, 1957. Legislation approved July 11, 1955, made the appearance of the motto mandatory on all coins and paper currency of the United States.

In response to the first court case challenging this addition to our currency and coinage, the 9th U.S. Circuit Court of Appeals ruled in 1970 that "...its use is of patriotic or ceremonial character and bears no true resemblance to a governmental sponsorship of a religious exercise." The Supreme Court of the United States declined to review the case.

THE PLEDGE OF ALLEGIANCE

The Pledge of Allegiance was written by a man named Francis Julius Bellamy. Born in Mount Morris, NY in 1855, Bellamy attended the Rome Free Academy in Rome, New York, then entered the University of Rochester in 1872, graduating in 1876. He entered the Rochester Theological Seminary in the fall of 1876 and graduated in 1880. Bellamy was a Christian Socialist and an outspoken advocate for the rights of working people and the equal allocation of economic resources, (ideas that are still kicked around today). Bellamy however, believed that these rights were inherent in *the teachings of Jesus Christ*. He served as a Baptist minister from 1880 to 1891, but was forced out of his Boston pulpit when his sermons took on an increasingly socialist tone, such that at one point, he portrayed Jesus Christ as a socialist. Shortly thereafter, Bellamy stopped attending church.

In 1895, Bellamy took a position as editor and manager at *The Illustrated American*, a magazine that focused on current national political affairs. This presented him with an opportunity to write editorials on his political ideology. In 1896, Bellamy attacked William Jennings Bryan as a demagogue who was the first U.S. Presidential candidate to attempt to stir up class warfare, pitting the multitudes against the upper class. He further claimed that Bryan was urging crowds to raise a red flag of armed rebellion. Bellamy also expressed his personal biases against southern Europeans in his commentaries, again directly attacking the government policy of open immigration and the idea of universal suffrage.

In a May 22, 1897 editorial, Bellamy briefly explained his assessment of the Mexican labor force:

"Cheap peon labor in Mexico is of a shiftless and unreliable kind. The native Mexican works only that he may live. If he can live for a month on the rewards of a week's work, he will work for twelve weeks out of the year and not a week more."

And in an August 28, 1897 editorial, again using the publication *The Illustrated American* as a vehicle, he stated the following positions on race and the demographics that made up America:

"The hard inescapable fact is that men are not born equal. Neither are they born free, but all in bonds to their ancestors and their environments..."

"The success of government by the people will depend upon the stuff that people are made of. The people must realize their responsibility to themselves. They must guard, more jealously even than their liberties, *the quality of their blood.*"

Bellamy went on to state that:

"A democracy like ours cannot afford to throw itself open to the world. Where every man is a lawmaker, every dull-witted or fanatical immigrant admitted to our citizenship is a bane to the commonwealth. Where all classes of society merge insensibly into one another every alien immigrant of inferior race may bring *corruption to the stock.*

There are races, more or less akin to our own, whom we may admit freely, and get nothing but advantage from the infusion of their wholesome blood. But there are other races which we cannot assimilate without a lowering of our racial standard, which should be as sacred to us as the sanctity of our homes." *(All emphasis mine)*

Bellamy was living in Boston Massachusetts when he drafted the Pledge of Allegiance for a campaign sponsored by a popular patriotic circular entitled the *Youth's Companion* (one of the most widely circulated weekly magazines with 475,000 readers). In 1888, the publisher of the *Youth's Companion* introduced a promotion to sell American flags to public schools as a premium to increase the magazine's subscription base. In 1891, Daniel Ford, the owner of the publication, hired Bellamy to work in the magazine's premium department with Ford's nephew James Upham. Under the direction of Upham and Bellamy, the flag promotion became more than a basic marketing ploy. The approach the two dreamed up to promote the American flag effort was to offer to pupils in every school, one hundred cards *at no cost*, that had the following words printed on them:

> This Certificate, representing a 10 cent contribution, entitles the holder to One Share in the patriotic influence of the School Flag.

Each set of 100 cards, worth ten cents each, covered the wholesale cost of a sizable American flag. Soon, under their guidance, *Youth's Companion* became a lively and energetic champion of the schoolhouse flag effort that envisioned an American flag flying above every school in the country. By the close of 1891, the magazine had managed to sell American flags to just under *26,000 schools* across the nation. As the campaign spread, the magazine began to augment the campaign by encouraging citizens to fly the flag on national holidays.

Then, on the 400th anniversary of Columbus' arrival, the President, Benjamin Harrison issued a proclamation calling Columbus a "pioneer of progress and enlightenment," and that people everywhere should "let the national flag float over every schoolhouse in the country and the exercises be such as shall impress upon our youth the patriotic duties of American citizenship." The proclamation went on to say that citizens should "cease from toil and devote themselves to such exercises as may best express honor to the discoverer and their appreciation of the great achievements of the four completed centuries of American life."

Upham decided to use the anniversary of Christopher Columbus' voyages to the New World as a means to enhance the schoolhouse flag movement. The magazine called for a national Public School Celebration to coincide with the World's Columbian Exposition and a national flag salute would be part of the official Columbus Day celebration planned for schools all over America.

On September 8th of that year, Bellamy's pledge was published in the magazine and the campaign was quick to make use of it. Bellamy subsequently spoke at a national convention for school superintendents, where he sold them on the idea that his pledge should be instituted as a part of this "official Columbus Day program." He was ultimately elected chair of the committee that was formed and they structured the entire holiday around an elaborate flag-raising ceremony and his pledge. With the sanctions of the national education leaders in hand, Bellamy's committee spread the word across the country, drafting an official program for schools to follow on the national day of celebration that included using his pledge, all centered around the flag raising ceremony. Bellamy was soon lobbying governors, congressmen and even approached the President.

As a socialist, Bellamy stated that he had originally considered using the words *equality* and *fraternity* but changed his mind after realizing that there were state superintendents of education on the committee who were against equality for women and African Americans. The pledge was originally recited with the *Bellamy salute*. He visualized this as a person holding his or her right arm stretched out towards the flag with the hand lifted and the palm turned downward, but in the years leading up to World War II, it resembled the Nazi salute and was replaced by holding the right hand over the heart and remained that way from then on. In 1954, in response to the widely publicized threat of secular and *godless communism*, President Dwight Eisenhower urged Congress to add the words "under God" which created the 31 word pledge we have today.

When the Pledge was first published, no specific author was credited with its creation. Instead, and out of deference to the magazine that sponsored the flag program, it was simply known as the *"Youth's Companion Flag Pledge"*. As the Pledge gained fame, many tried to claim credit for its authorship and it took Bellamy's son many years before his father was finally given public recognition as author of the Pledge. The original Pledge was supposed to be quick and to the point, such that it could be recited in as little as 15 seconds. Bellamy saw his Pledge "as an *inoculation* (his word) that would protect immigrants and native born but inadequately patriotic Americans from the *virus* (again, his word) of radicalism and subversion."

The Pledge has been modified four times since its composition and the official changes are indicated below in parentheses:

> 1892, as it was first drafted: "I pledge allegiance to my Flag and the republic for which it stands, one nation indivisible, with liberty and justice for all."

> 1892: "I pledge allegiance to my Flag and (to) the republic for which it stands: one nation indivisible, with liberty and justice for all."

> 1923: "I pledge allegiance to (the) Flag (of the United States), and to the republic for which it stands; one Nation indivisible with liberty and justice for all."

> 1924: "I pledge allegiance to the Flag of the United States (of America), and to the republic for which it stands; one Nation indivisible with liberty and justice for all." *(Note: Bellamy objected to the addition of 'of America' as being overly redundant).*

> 1954 to the present: "I pledge allegiance to the Flag of the United States of America, and to the republic for which it stands, one Nation (under God), indivisible, with liberty and justice for all."

In 1940 the Supreme Court, in *Minersville School District v. Gobitis*, ruled that students in public schools, including Jehovah's Witnesses who considered the flag salute to be a form of idolatry, could be compelled to swear the Pledge. A rash of mob violence and intimidation against Jehovah's Witnesses followed the ruling and in 1943 in *West Virginia State_Board of Education v. Barnette*, the Supreme Court reversed its decision. Justice Robert H. Jackson writing for the 6 to 3 majority went beyond ruling that public school students are not required to say the Pledge on narrow grounds, but asserted how such ideological dogma is antithetical to the principles of the country, concluding with;

> "If there is any fixed star in our constitutional constellation, it is that no official, high or petty, can prescribe what shall be orthodox in politics, nationalism, religion, or other matters of opinion or force citizens to confess by word or act their faith therein. If there are any circumstances which permit an exception, *they do not now occur to us." (Emphasis mine)*

RELIGION & POLITICS

As I've tried to show, religion was deeply entrenched in pre-revolutionary colonial America, and it was slow to change. One of the primary attacks on our country's religious neutrality from the Religious Right is the insistence that this country was founded as a Christian Nation...not just that the people were Christians, but the country itself was founded *by* Christians exclusively *for* Christians and this idea remains dominant in many sectors of society to this day. However, people who perpetuate this fantasy tend to be Christian revisionists who are attempting to rewrite history, much the way holocaust deniers do.

The oldest Jewish Synagogue in America is the Turro Synagogue in Newport, Rhode Island. Founded in 1685, a small but growing colony of Newport, Rhode Island received its first Jewish residents, fifteen families who came from Barbados, where a Jewish community had existed since the 1620s. They were of Spanish and Portuguese origin and the community had migrated from Amsterdam and London to Brazil before arriving in the new world. In 1790, George Washington wrote to the members of the synagogue (where his letter is still read aloud to the congregation every August). In his message, Washington stated the following;

> "All possess alike liberty of conscience and immunities of citizenship. It is now no more that toleration is spoken of, as if it was by the indulgence of one class of people that another enjoyed the exercise of their inherent natural rights. For happily the Government of the United States, which gives to bigotry no sanction, to persecution no assistance, requires only that they who

live under its protection, should demean themselves as good citizens."

Washington also included a phrase that applies specifically to Jews as well as Muslims:

"May the children of the Stock of Abraham, who dwell in this land, continue to merit and enjoy the good will of the other inhabitants, while every one shall sit in safety under his own vine and figtree, and there shall be none to make him afraid." *(A copy of the full letter can be found in the appendix).*

The men responsible for laying the groundwork for the United States were not men of deep Christian beliefs, they were Deists, men who did not believe or accept the bible as an inerrant, absolute truth. These men were also free thinkers who relied on their reason more than their faith. If this country was founded on the Christian tradition, the Constitution would clearly say so, but nowhere does the document say: 'These States form a Christian Nation', or anything close to that. In point of fact, the words Jesus Christ, Christianity and God never appear in the Constitution, religion is only mentioned in the Constitution in *exclusionary* terms.

It may upset people to read this, but the Declaration of Independence is *not a governing document,* and while it refers to 'Nature's God' and our firm 'Reliance on the Protection of Divine Providence', this is the language of Deism, not Christianity. In fact, one of the early criticisms of the Founding Fathers was that, because of their position on religion, many of them had to be atheists. However, as Deists, they did believe that the universe had a creator, but that this creator does not concern himself with the day to day lives of humans, nor does it directly communicate with humans through any form of revelation or in sacred writings. The Founding Fathers occasionally spoke of Nature's God or the God of Nature, but again, this was not the God of the Bible, nor do they deny the existence of a person called Jesus. While they praised Christ for his benevolent teachings, almost all of them vigorously dismissed his divinity.

In a letter from Ben Franklin to friend William Strahan, (a fellow printer, publisher and British Parliamentarian) in 1784, Franklin said,

> "....I believe in one God, Creator of the universe. That He governs it by His *Providence*. That He ought to be worshiped." *(Emphasis mine)*

At the Constitutional Convention in 1787, again, Franklin again made this reference to Providence;

> "The frequent instances of a superintending Providence in our favour."

George Washington, in his Thanksgiving Proclamation of 1789, said,

> "That we may then all unite in rendering unto him our sincere and humble thanks--for his kind care and protection of the People of this Country previous to their becoming a Nation–for the signal and manifold mercies, and the favorable interpositions of his Providence which we experienced in the course and conclusion of the late war,"

Many are surprised to learn that Congress removed Thomas Jefferson's words that condemned the practice of slavery in the colonies from the documents and also changed his wording concerning equal rights. Jefferson's original text was that "All men are created equal *and independent. From that equal creation they derive rights inherent and inalienable."* Congress changed that phrase, increasing its religious overtones "All men are created equal. *They are endowed by their creator with certain unalienable rights."*

It is true that there were Christian men among America's Founders, many of whom used theology to justify the institution of slavery. According to the *King James Version of the Bible*, in the 25th chapter of Leviticus, verses 44-46, we find the following;

[44] Both thy bondmen, and thy bondmaids, which thou shalt have, shall be of the heathen that are round about you; of them shall ye buy bondmen and bondmaids.

[45] Moreover of the children of the strangers that do sojourn among you, of them shall ye buy, and of their families that are with you, which they begat in your land: and they shall be your possession.

[46] And ye shall take them as an inheritance for your children after you, to inherit them for a possession; they shall be your bondmen for ever,

The term bondman is an old English word that was first used around 1200 to 1250 and is defined this way;

...a slave or serf, a man bound to service without wages.

A good example of this idea would be Frederick Dalcho, who was born in London, England, baptized on Oct. 15, 1770 and immigrated to Baltimore in May of 1787 at the age of 15 years. He went to live with his father's sister who was married to Dr. Wiesenthal, and under the guidance of Dr. Wiesenthal, young Frederick pursued his education, studying medicine and eventually becoming a surgeon's mate in the United States Army in April of 1792. In 1799 he settled in Charleston, South Carolina, where he practiced medicine and in 1807 he became one of the two editors of the Charleston Courier, a Federalist daily newspaper, and about this time, he also became a 33° Mason. Dalcho began to study theology in 1811 and was ordained in the Episcopal Church as a deacon on Feb. 15, 1814, and became a priest on June 12, 1818. On Feb. 23, 1819, he became assistant minister at St. Michael's Church, Charleston, where he remained until his death in 1836.

In 1823, South Carolina Episcopal Clergyman Frederick Dalcho used an obscure passage in Genesis 9:20-27 to justify slavery in the United States. It is presented here:

[20] And Noah began to be an husbandman, and he planted a vineyard:

21 And he drank of the wine, and was drunken; and he was uncovered within his tent.

22 And Ham, the father of Canaan, saw the nakedness of his father, and told his two brethren without.

23 And Shem and Japheth took a garment, and laid it upon both their shoulders, and went backward, and covered the nakedness of their father; and their faces were backward, and they saw not their father's nakedness.

24 And Noah awoke from his wine, and knew what his younger son had done unto him.

25 And he said, Cursed be Canaan; a servant of servants shall he be unto his brethren.

26 And he said, Blessed be the LORD God of Shem; and Canaan shall be his servant.

27 God shall enlarge Japheth, and he shall dwell in the tents of Shem; and Canaan shall be his servant.

Genesis 9:20-27 KJV

Dalcho's position was that the prophecy in Genesis was not fulfilled in the individuals named, but nationally in their descendants, making it plain that scripture was (in this case) referring to the Africans. His contention was that we are taught by the Bible that human beings lost immortality through disobedience and sin, that slavery was condoned through a divine degree with the curse of Cane, as recounted in scripture by saying,

"The prophecy of Noah was to be fulfilled, not in the individuals named, but nationally in their descendants. Canaan's whole race was under the malediction. Thus the descendants of Canaan, the Africans, were to be the 'servants of servants', the lowest state of servitude, slaves to the descendants of Shem and Japeth, the present day Jews and Christians."

He then went on to reference a pamphlet that outlined the different parts of the world inhabited by Noah's sons to prove that the prophecy had come true. While Dalcho validated the effects of the curse in Genesis at length, he remained silent on the exact character of Ham's transgression. He advanced the idea that these descendants were somehow markedly wicked and offensive to God and characterized slavery as God's punishment of and remedy for this peculiar moral degradation of a part of the race, once again without ever completely explaining the nature of the sin responsible for such degradation. Many Americans are surprised to find out that discussions about whether slavery was right or wrong in our nation's history began 70 years before the Civil War.

As I said above, somehow, history has lost sight of the fact that the Founding Founders were students of the European Enlightenment. The Age of Enlightenment (or alternately, The Age of Reason) was a time in the early 1600s into the late 1700s when powerful cultural and intellectual thinkers in Western Europe emphasized reason, analysis and individualism rather than time honored lines of authority. These ideas were promulgated by philosophical theorists and logical thinkers in coffeehouses, salons and masonic lodges and the ideas challenged the authority of social institutions deeply rooted in society, such as the Catholic Church. Lengthy discussions were held about ways to reform society, using toleration, science and skepticism as tools.

Leading minds of the day included Francis Bacon, René Descartes, John Locke, Pierre Bayle, François-Marie Arouet, (writing under the pseudonym Voltaire, who was a strong proponent of freedom of religion), Francis Hutcheson, David Hume and Isaac Newton, all of whom had a strong influence on society when they presented their ideas, ideas that were widely circulated. As public awareness grew around these modern and radical views, many European rulers tried to introduce reforms based on these ideas, allowing toleration and occasionally going so far as to acknowledge and accept multiple religions in what became known as enlightened absolutism. And as you might expect, there were also more than a few who refused to buy into this idea.

With this in mind, let's look at how these ideas shaped the religion and politics on this new and predominantly unexplored continent...

In 1624, the king of England granted a royal charter to the colony of Virginia. The Church of England (head of the Anglican

Church) became the established church, with tax monies going to support the church and the clergy. Preachers who were members of other religious groups needed a license in order to preach and those who refused to obtain this license ran the risk of imprisonment and fines. By 1779, Virginia's then governor Thomas Jefferson, drafted a bill that guaranteed legal equality for citizens of all religions, including those of no religion who were living in the state. It was during this time that Thomas Jefferson summed up his position with this statement;

> "But it does me no injury for my neighbor to say there are twenty gods or no God. It neither picks my pocket nor breaks my leg."

Jefferson's plan had little acceptance and support until Patrick Henry introduced a bill in the Virginia legislature in 1784 that encouraged state support for 'teachers of the Christian religion.' Henry's basic position was that the inclusion of religion was essential to support and maintain a moral focus for the people. He further insisted that without firm State control and support, religion would gradually decline and fade away, much to the detriment of society. *(A copy of this bill can be found in the appendix).*

While few copies of Patrick Henry's speeches supporting his bill exist, Madison's notes from the legislative sessions suggest that Henry introduced the measure to forestall what in his own words, was "*a decay of civility, morality and piety in the state.*" In the preamble to his bill, Henry expresses his rationale for it;

> "The general diffusion of Christian knowledge hath a natural tendency to correct the morals of men, restrain their vices, and preserve the peace of society; which cannot be effected without a competent provision for learned teachers, who may be thereby enabled to devote their time and attention to the duty of instructing such citizens, as from their circumstances and want of education, cannot otherwise attain such knowledge..."

While many colonials had no problem with this idea, it was Henry's following rationalization that Madison and Jefferson saw as an early example of a 'slippery slope';

> "...and it is judged that such provision may be made by the Legislature, without counteracting the liberal principle heretofore adopted and intended to be preserved by abolishing all distinctions of pre-eminence amongst the different societies or communities of Christians."

Patrick Henry painted a bleak and hopeless future for society if his measure failed. With support for the bill gaining momentum, Madison worked to get the vote postponed and before the Assembly reconvened. He then skillfully worked hard to help Patrick Henry win the gubernatorial election, because as governor, Henry could no longer support a bill he introduced. This bought Madison enough time to draft and circulate one of his most important documents entitled *"A Memorial and Remonstrance Against Religious Assessments."*

In his document, Madison eloquently laid out his reasons why the State had no business making Christian instruction available to its citizens. 2,000 Virginians signed the document and Madison's argument became the foundation of America's powerful endorsement of a secular ideology. Among the documents 15 points was an assertion that,

> "The Religion then of every man *must be left to the conviction and conscience of every man*; and it is the right of every man to exercise it as these may dictate. This right is in its nature, *an inalienable right." (Emphasis mine)*

Madison stressed his key points in a way that any believer of a religion, regardless of their religious affiliation should be able to comprehend; any government sanction of a single religion was a threat to all religions. *(A copy of Madison's full document can be found in the appendix).*

From his education, Madison understood that the spread of Christianity was *in spite of* and often *in the face of* persecution from those with both secular and religious authority. As written in his treatise, Madison maintained that Christianity;

> "...disavows a dependence on the powers of this world; it is a contradiction to fact: for it is known that this Religion existed and flourished, not only without the support of human laws, but in spite of every opposition from them."

Madison also asserted that Henry's proposal would signify, as he expressed it;

> "a departure from that generous policy, which offering an Asylum to the persecuted and oppressed of every Nation and Religion, promised a lustre to our country."

After a long debate, Patrick Henry's bill was defeated by a vote of 12 to 1. The Virginia General Assembly then took up Jefferson's plan for the separation of church and state and in 1786, the Virginia Act for Establishing Religious Freedom, slightly modified from Jefferson's original draft, became law. After the bill was passed, Jefferson proudly wrote that the law was

> "...meant to comprehend, within the mantle of its protection, the Jew, the Gentile, the Christian and the Mahometan, the Hindoo and Infidel of every denomination." *(A copy of this bill is included in the appendix.)*

Jefferson wanted to be remembered for what he saw as his three most important accomplishments, and instructed that they be inscribed on his tombstone. They were; writing the Declaration of Independence, writing the Virginia Statute for Religious Freedom and founding the University of Virginia.

Not everyone realizes that the University of Virginia originally did not have a chapel and offered no study of theology in its curriculum and amazingly, Jefferson *did not list his presidency* on his tombstone. With his exposure to the doctrines of the Period of Enlightenment, Jefferson fully expected that organized religion would die out, thinking that everyone would eventually become Unitarians. He became very disappointed as the ranks of Baptists and Methodists grew and gradually became aware that after the Revolution, religions in the United States began to grow and flourish.

James Madison wanted Jefferson's vision of a separation of church and state to become a cornerstone of the new government in America. As it was framed in Philadelphia later that year, the Constitution clearly stated this in Article VI that federal elected and appointed officials;

> "The Senators and Representatives before mentioned, and the members of the several state legislatures, and all executive and judicial officers, both of the United States and of the several states shall be bound by Oath or Affirmation, to support this Constitution, *but no religious Test shall ever be required* as a Qualification to any Office or public Trust under the United States." (*Emphasis mine*)

This familiar passage, along with the fact that the Constitution does not mention God or a deity, other than the time-honored pro forma "In the year of our Lord..." commonly used to format and date official documents, and the fact that the very first amendment forbids Congress from making laws that would interfere with the free expression and exercise of religion, demonstrates the founders' resolve that America was intended to be a secular republic.

Contrast this with ideas expressed today. Bryan Fischer hosts the talk radio program *Focal Point* on American Family Radio. On a broadcast on Tuesday, December 10th, 2013, (and is posted on YouTube) Mr. Fischer publicly stated his personal position on the subject, maintaining that;

> "...because the words of the 1st amendment have *never been changed*, they mean exactly what the Founding Fathers wrote in 1789."

and he went on to clarify his point;

"By the word *religion* in the First Amendment, *the founders meant Christianity.* They weren't providing any cover or shelter for the free exercise of Islam or even Judaism or even atheism," (*Emphasis mine*)

Mr. Fischer later clarified his position by saying,

"My argument all along has been that the purpose of the First Amendment is to protect the free exercise of *the Christian religion...*"

He continued to speak for the Founding Fathers on a broadcast of Focal Point in September of 2011 (and once again, it can be viewed on YouTube), he proclaimed that:

"Mormonism is not an orthodox Christian faith. It just is not...it's very clear that the Founding Fathers did not intend to *preserve automatically religious liberty for non-Christian faiths.*" (*Emphasis mine*)

I checked Mr. Fischer's Curriculum Vitae, it lists an undergraduate degree in philosophy from Stanford University and a graduate degree in theology from Dallas theological Seminary, but nowhere is there any mention of a degree awarded or even any study of American Political History or Constitutional Law.

Judges and politicians have been trying to wrap religious beliefs around the law almost as long as America has been a country. A fairly recent example took place in June of 1958, two residents of Virginia, Mildred Jeter, an African American woman, and Richard Loving, a Caucasian man, were married in the District of Columbia in accordance with its laws. Shortly after their marriage, the Lovings returned to Virginia and established their home in Caroline County. During the October 1958 Term of the Circuit Court of Caroline County, a grand jury issued an indictment charging the Lovings with violating Virginia's Racial Integrity Act of 1924. On January 6, 1959, the Lovings pleaded guilty to the charge, and were sentenced to one year in jail; however, the trial judge suspended the sentence for a period of 25 years on the condition that the Lovings leave the State and not return to Virginia together *for 25 years*. Judge Leon M. Bazile stated in his opinion that:

> "Almighty God created the races white, black, yellow, malay and red, and He placed them on separate continents. And, but for the interference with His arrangement, there would be no cause for such marriage. The fact that He separated the races shows that *He did not intend for the races to mix*."
>
> (*Emphasis mine*)

January 22, 1965, the ACLU filed a motion on behalf of Richard and Mildred Loving to vacate their 1959 conviction which was denied and the case was appealed to the U.S. Supreme Court, which issued a unanimous ruling in the Loving's favor in 1967.

And then we have a purely religious position, expressed by Pastor Dennis Terry of the Greenwell Springs Louisiana Baptist Church. On Sunday, March 18th, 2012, a rally was held for then Presidential candidate Rick Santorum. Pastor Terry was preaching from the pulpit (and his sermon is also available on rightwingwatch.org) when he said;

> "I don't care what the liberals say, I don't care what the nay-sayers say, this nation was founded as a Christian nation. The God of Abraham, the God of Isaac, and the God of Jacob-there's only one God...*THERE IS ONLY ONE GOD AND HIS NAME IS JESUS!*...I'm tired of people telling me that I can't say those words," he continued, "I'm tired of people telling us as Christians that we can't voice our beliefs or that we can no longer pray in public...*Listen to me*, if you don't love America, if you don't like the way we do things, I've got one thing to say: *GET OUT!* We don't worship Buddha, *I said we DON'T WORSHIP BUDDHA!* We don't worship Mohammad, we don't worship Allah! *We worship GOD*, we worship *GOD'S SON JESUS CHRIST!*...I tell you my friend, I believe that Christians in America are the

key to revival. I believe that Christians in America is the key to the economy turning around. I believe that Christians in America is the key to the jobless rate continuing to go down. *I believe it's a spiritual thing.* If we'll put God *back in America, put God back in our pulpits, put God back in our homes and in our State House and then in Washington D.C.*, then we can have a *revival* in America and the Holy Spirit will show up *and great and mighty things will happen for this country.*" He concluded by saying, "…but if you disagree with my comments, then you are in turn *disagreeing with the Word of God*, and *that* may be part of our nation's problems." *(All emphasis mine)*

Realizing that the sermon was posted online, Pastor Terry tried to walk his statements back and a video of the service was scrubbed from the church website, all while he maintained that he never said any of this and that the media *misreported* his remarks.

Scott Douglas Lively is an American author, attorney and a former independent candidate for Governor of Massachusetts in the 2014 election. He is the president of Abiding Truth Ministries, a conservative Christian organization based in Temecula, California. He was the state director of the California branch of the American Family Association and a spokesman for the Oregon Citizens Alliance. In an interview, (again posted YouTube) Lively insisted that Christians are being denied their First Amendment rights because of gay rights, while simultaneously asserting that the First Amendment's guarantee of religious freedom applies only to Christians, "In fact," Lively clarified, "it is because the United States has grown to accept *religious pluralism* that God is now punishing us with abortion rights and LGBT equality." He went on to state, "Well, I don't actually believe in *religious freedom* the way that the term is used, I know that when you use it and when most people use it, you're talking about Christianity. We're not talking about freedom for Islam and freedom for Buddhism and Hinduism as if they're equal with God."

As I said, all these speeches can be viewed online and I encourage you to watch them and draw your own conclusions…

This is a small sampling of the underlying forces that influenced and shaped religion in the years leading up to the revolution and in the balance of our nation's history to date. To be sure, there were and are incidents in favor of other views, but these are shouted down in most cases and my primary purpose is to examine the religious beliefs that existed when America was just starting out as a nation and how they carried forward. Today's pundits and proponents have drawn from this time in history to create the idea that America was founded a "Christian Nation", and I suggest that this may not be the case, based on all the available evidence.

As we are about to see, many of the men who fought the Revolution believed in a god and many thanked Providence. They may have attended church regularly or they may not as they chose, but a vital fact to keep in mind is that they fought a war against a country *where the head of state* was also the head of the *church*. These men clearly knew the history of religious conflict that led to America's colonization and eventual evolution as a country, many having witnessed it firsthand. They also clearly understood the jeopardy to individual freedom a government based religious system presented, and the inevitable prospect of sectarian conflicts that would follow. It was only the Founding Father's knowledge, recognition and acceptance of the country's divisive history, most notably by Washington, Jefferson, Adams and Madison, that would secure America as a secular republic.

America can still be, as Madison perceived the new nation in 1785 as being, "...an Asylum to the persecuted and oppressed of every Nation and Religion..." but *recognizing* and perhaps more importantly, *accepting* that there is a deep religious discord that has been part of America's history that predates its beginning *is a healthy and necessary first step.* When and if we are able to acknowledge this dark and troubled past and accept the fact that traces of that past history lingers still, perhaps then we as a nation can fulfill Madison's vision.

Let's look at a few of the men who founded this nation and examine their views:

George Washington

Let's begin by looking at George Washington, *the man*, and to begin to understand him, we should first begin with his parents and grandparents. George Washington's great grandfather, John Washington was born in 1633 to Amphilis Twigden and Lawrence Washington in Purleigh, Essex County, England. The Washingtons were Royalists and property owners, which placed them in the upper class of English society. When John was eight years old, King Charles I nominated the boy for a position at Sutton's Hospital (later known as Charterhouse School), a prestigious center of learning in London. While John waiting for a slot to open at the school, his educational opportunity was interrupted by the English Civil War and his schooling at Sutton's Hospital never came to pass.

The English Civil Wars (perhaps more properly called the wars of the three kingdoms) comprise some the most important events in British history, beginning with the Bishop's war with Ireland and Scotland in 1639 and the great rebellion, fought between 1642 and 1651. This became a bitter conflict that pitted two major elements of the government (the King and Parliament) against each other. It tested the prerogative of the king and challenged the theory of a monarch's divine right to rule (Charles believed that kingship was a divine right and members of his court supported this belief and the righteousness of his actions). It also encompassed the first public execution of an English king when Charles I was convicted of treason, causing the one and only *republic* in the history of the British Empire.

King Charles was ardently pro-Catholic and anti-Puritan during his reign and more worrisome for him was the fact that he'd married a French woman named Henrietta Maria, the daughter of King Henry IV of France and mother of England's Kings Charles II and James II (being Catholic made her very unpopular in England and as she was Catholic, she could not be crowned in an Anglican service and never had a coronation). To compound the King's problems even further, Charles also had a powerful antagonist to contend with, that being the Church of England.

The Church of England had managed to maintain a connection with the early Medieval church through its use of the catholic creeds, its pattern of ministry, its architecture and through significant portions of its liturgy. Anglicans traditionally date the origin of their Church to the arrival of the Gregorian mission to the pagan Anglo-Saxons in the Kingdom of Kent, (an early medieval kingdom located in what is now South East England) toward the end of the 6th century. The church continues to embody Protestant insights in its theology and in the overall outline of its liturgical tradition took on a Roman Catholic structure. It broke away from the church in Rome in 1534 but church officials planned to keep the church more or less Catholic but isolated from Rome, describing itself as *both catholic and reformed*, which was deeply troubling to both sides of the discussion after the reformation as it tried to walk a very delicate religious line between the two.

When Charles married Princess Henrietta Maria of France, this decision deeply exacerbated the king's problems because the queen openly celebrated her religion in public. In addition, her influence over the King and the royal children was once again seen as some sort of *international* Papist conspiracy against the Protestant faithful and their church. While Charles was faithful and devout, his religious policies were deeply divisive. In collaboration with Archbishop Laud, (William Laud served as Archbishop of Canterbury, beginning in 1633. He was later arrested, tried for treason in 1640 and executed in 1645) the King insisted upon religious conformity across the aforementioned three kingdoms (England, Ireland and Scotland). This went disastrously wrong when the Scottish church was forced to use the Anglican liturgy and Prayer Book in 1637. The King also attempted to replace the Scottish Presbyterian system of church government with the Episcopalian or High Anglican system, in an effort to standardize the churches of England and Scotland. This resulted in the creation of the Scottish National Covenant against interference in religion, ultimately leading to the Bishops' Wars between the two nations in 1639 and 1640.

In the aftermath of all this, Lawrence Washington was branded a Malignant Royalist and stripped of his post as a clerical 'Don' (a fellow or tutor at a college or university). Most of his land was seized by the Crown and Lawrence was demoted to the position of Anglican Rector, assigned to an impoverished parish in Essex and his sons were subsequently barred from entering Oxford University. John Washington, his mother and his siblings were given shelter by the family of a relative by marriage, Sir Edwin Sandys. Washington found an apprenticeship with a London merchant with the assistance of his relatives, and it was here that he received a basic education in colonial trade.

In 1656, John Washington partnered with Edward Prescott, captain of the ketch *Sea Horse*, to serve as the second master or 'second man' (an experienced sailor capable of taking charge of the ketch). The *Sea Horse* was one of several dozen ships devoted almost exclusively to the growing trade for tobacco, one the one of the most profitable crops available in the New World at the time. The *Sea Horse* sailed to Virginia, probably with a cargo of household goods and supplies to exchange for tobacco, and Washington signed on with the expectation of receiving part of the profits of the voyage. On its return voyage in early 1657, the *Sea Horse* succumbed to a common fate on the Potomac waterway that many other ships succumbed to during this time in history, it ran aground on a poorly marked shoal and sank during a winter storm.

After he helped refloat the ship, Second Officer Washington decided to stay in the area as a guest of Nathaniel Pope, an established land owner in the County of Westmoreland, Virginia. Washington spent April and May in court in a dispute with Prescott how much was owed two each party. Each partner embarked on a tirade of accusations, resulting in a long, drawn out conflict. Prescott sought legal remedy against John Washington for his abandonment of their partnership and the subsequent loss of his capital investment and at one point, John Washington retaliated during a proceeding in a Maryland court by accusing Prescott of a witch hanging aboard his ship.

John's fortunes turned for the better when Pope bailed him out by paying off Prescott with in beaver skins at eight shillings per pound and assisted John to sever his legal ties with Prescott. Conveniently, Nathaniel Pope was one of the magistrates hearing his case and concluded that Washington would be useful to him, while John realized the same thing about Pope. A short time later, Washington met Pope's daughter Anne, and fell in love with her. He and Anne were married in 1658 and they received 700 acres on Mattox Creek as a wedding gift from her father. The couple had five children together, two of whom died in childhood and their names are lost to history. One of the three remaining children was the eldest child, Lawrence, grandfather of George Washington.

Lawrence was born in 1659 at Mattox Creek and after Anne's death in 1668 (or 69, the records are not quite clear on this), John married twice more before his death in 1677. His father saw to it that Lawrence was educated in England to become a lawyer and the young Washington developed an intense interest in politics upon returning to the colonies. Little more is known about the family until we get to George's father, Augustine, born in Westmoreland, Virginia on November 12, 1694. He was a son of Lawrence Washington and Mildred Warner. Augustine was only four years old when his father died and when he became of age, he inherited about 1,000 acres on Bridges Creek in Westmoreland County. His sister Mildred inherited the property called the Little Hunting Creek, which became a plantation and was later to be named Mount Vernon. Augustine Washington was an ambitious man who acquired land and owned slaves, built mills and grew tobacco. In addition to supervising overseers and slave labor as a tobacco planter, Washington was active in the Anglican Church and in local politics. He took the oath as justice of the peace for the county court in July 1716 and served as county sheriff. He married his first wife, Jane Butler and the young couple settled on the Bridges Creek property.

In 1718, Augustine Washington purchased additional land on Popes Creek that adjoined his property on Bridges Creek. Sometime in 1726, he had a new house built there (later called Wakefield) with the help of slave labor and skilled craftsmen. In the same year, he purchased the Little Hunting Creek property from his sister Mildred. His marriage produced three children. Augustine's wife Jane died in 1729 and Washington married Mary Ball in 1731. George was the eldest of Augustine and Mary's six children, all of which survived into adulthood. The family lived on Pope's Creek in Westmoreland County, Virginia and became moderately prosperous members of what was Virginia's "middling class" at the time. Augustine Washington died in April of 1743 at the age of 48 when George was only 11 years old.

While little is known about George Washington's childhood, it is generally known that it was customary for children of the upper class in Virginia to be educated at home by private tutors or sent to local private schools. Boys usually started their education around the age of seven with lessons in reading, writing and basic arithmetic. Later they were schooled in Latin and Greek as well as more down-to-earth, useful subjects such as geometry, bookkeeping and surveying. Wealthy families often sent their sons to England to complete their education and this was done with George's older half-brothers, Lawrence and Augustine but not young George. What is known is that from age seven to 15, George was home schooled and he studied with the local church sexton and later with a schoolmaster, where he learned practical math, geography, Latin and the English classics. But most of the knowledge he acquired during this time, he would use for the rest of his life. Washington went on to work as a backwoodsmen and as a plantation foreman and by his early teens, he had mastered planting and raising tobacco, raising livestock and became a successful surveyor.

When George Washington's father died, George became the ward of his half-brother, Lawrence, who gave him a good upbringing. Under his brother's tutorage, George was schooled in some of the finer aspects of culture that Lawrence learned during his time in the English educational system. When he was 16,

George Washington wrote a copy of a set of 110 rules composed by French Jesuits in 1595, entitled *Rules of Civility & Decent Behavior in Company and Conversation*, most likely as part of a penmanship assignment. They were originally translated into English and published in 1640 by Francis Hawkins, an English Jesuit, child prodigy and translator. English copies circulating at the time underscored respect for others and the idea of treating others in a civilized and cultured way. *(A copy of this can be found in the Appendix).*

It's been suggested that manners and social customs that developed in western civilization during the period that we call the renaissance, originated with the upper classes and aristocracy in society of the time. Today's dictionary definition of courtesy is *polite behavior* or *a polite action*, but during the Middle Ages, courtesy meant *behavior that was appropriate at court*. Again referring to the 1826 copy of Webster's dictionary, courtesy was defined as:

> Elegance or politeness of manners; especially, politeness connected with kindness; civility; complaisance; as the gentleman shows great courtesy to strangers; he treats his friends with great courtesy.

Washington's purpose and intent after the war for independence was to create a government that would free America from the effects and influence of the royalty and aristocracy of European countries, but that didn't change his views on courtesy and respect. The 110 rules and edicts composed by the Jesuits that he copied during his early education, created in Washington a personal sense of courtesy, respect and a belief that everyone should be treated as equals. This would guide and influence his thoughts and actions for the rest of his life.

In 1748, while he was still a young man, George Washington found employment with a group of surveyors who were working to plot the land in Virginia's western territory. Over the following year, Washington was appointed an official surveyor of Culpeper County Virginia and spent the next two years surveying land in Culpeper, Frederick and Augusta counties in Virginia. The experience from this experience made him resourceful and toughened his mind and body. It also stimulated his interest in the vast stretches of open land to the west, an interest that stayed with him throughout his life. As he was able, he engaged in speculative land purchases and held a belief that the future of the country lay in colonizing the territories to the West.

By the end of July of 1752, Washington had lost his half-brother Lawrence to tuberculosis and two months later, Lawrence's only child, Sarah passed away at the age of four, so at the grand old age of 20, George Washington found himself the head of one of Virginia's most prominent estates, *Mount Vernon*. For the rest of his life, he would regard farming as one of the most honorable and noble professions. He was extremely proud of Mount Vernon and as time allowed, he increased his land there to about 8,000 acres.

In the early 1750s, France and Britain were officially at peace but the French military maintained a presence in America, occupying much of the Ohio Valley, their stated purpose being to protect France's land interests, fur trappers and French settlers. The borders in this territory were often in dispute between England and France and Washington, at the age of 23, was appointed a major in the Virginia Militia and headed several campaigns against the French. In August of 1755, he was ordered to patrol and protect nearly 400 miles of the frontier border with some 700 undisciplined colonial troops and a Virginia colonial legislature that was not willing to support him and these early campaigns ended in failure. His health had begun failing him in the closing months of 1757 and he returned home with dysentery.

In 1758, Washington resumed his duties, leading another expedition to capture Fort Duquesne. This time, 14 men were killed and 26 of Washington's men were wounded due to a friendly fire incident but at the end of the day, British forces scored a major victory when they captured Fort Duquesne. This allowed the British to regain control of the Ohio Valley and Washington retired from his Virginia regiment in December 1758. He later applied for a commission with the British Army but was turned down, so he returned home to Mount Vernon, a deeply disillusioned man. Involvement with the war was personally frustrating for him because he felt that decisions took forever, his men received little or no support from the colonial legislature and his new recruits were poorly trained.

During the time between his retirement from the militia until the beginning of the Revolutionary War, Washington dedicated himself to managing his land. He loved horseback riding, fox hunting, fishing and attending cotillions. He regularly worked six days a week and would often stop, take off his coat and work alongside his laborers. While Washington kept over 100 slaves, he made it known that he disliked the institution of slavery, but he acknowledged the economic advantage and the fact that it was allowed under the law.

In January of 1759, Washington married Martha Dandridge Custis, a widow who was only eight months older than he. Martha brought a considerable fortune with her, consisting of an 18,000-acre estate from which George personally acquired 6,000 acres. With this and a tract of land he was granted for his military service, Washington became one of the wealthier landowners in Virginia. Martha also had two young children by her previous marriage, John Parke Custis, (Jacky) age 6 and Martha (Patsy), age 4 and Washington lavished great affection on both children. Patsy was 17 years old when she died from an epileptic seizure and Washington was heartbroken when, about two weeks after the battle at Yorktown, Jacky died of camp fever (typhus) at the age of 27. Jacky was a spoiled and apathetic young man who had not fought in the war but had by its end, traveled to Yorktown to serve as a civilian aide to his stepfather. He was the last of Martha's remaining children and she was devastated by her son's death.

Although opposition to British rule in the colonies had been increasing during the years leading up to the War of Independence, Washington tried to prevent events from drawing him into the conflict. He was vexed by the British Proclamation Act of 1763 that prohibited settlements beyond the Alleghenies and was opposed to the Stamp Act of 1765. This act was a direct tax on the colonies of British America that the Parliament in Great Britain levied, requiring that any printed materials in the colonies, such as legal documents, magazines, playing cards, newspapers and many other types of paper used throughout the colonies, be produced on paper produced in London that carried an embossed revenue stamp. One of the purposes of the tax was to help pay for troops stationed in North America after the British victory over France in the Seven Years' War (often referred to in U.S. history books as The French and Indian War).

Washington didn't take on a significant role in the mounting colonial resistance against the British until the growing protest began over the Townshend Acts in 1767. By this time, Washington saw no opposition to what he saw were basic, fundamental abuses of the rights of Englishmen by Great Britain. In 1769, Washington introduced a resolution to the House of Burgesses calling for Virginia to boycott British goods until the Townshend and Stamp Acts were repealed.

When the Colonials banded together and resisted the Stamp Act, the British Parliament tried to avoid a repeat of the confrontation, while trying to extract revenue from the colonies, and at the same time remind the colonies that Great Britton still had the power to control and tax them. A series of measures were then introduced into Parliament by Charles Townshend, Chancellor of the Exchequer. These actions resulted in duties on glass, lead, paints, paper and tea imported into the colonies. Many colonialists viewed this taxation as an abuse of power and retaliated by passing measures to limit imports from Britain. In 1770, the British Parliament repealed all the Townshend duties except the tax on tea, leading to a temporary truce between the two sides in the years leading up to the American Revolution.

However, the British Parliament then legislated a series of measures known as The Intolerable Acts. These were:

> The Quartering Act: established on March 24, 1765 when the King sent British troops to Boston. The colonists were ordered to house and feed the British troops and if anyone refused, well…they *would be taken out and shot.*

The Administration of Justice Act: this became effective May 20, 1774, and allowed that British Officials could not be tried in colonial courts for crimes. They would have to be taken back to Britain for trial, leaving the British *free to do whatever they wanted to do to the Colonists and whatever they wanted to do in the colonies.*

Massachusetts Government Act: also effective May 20, 1774, this act placed the British Governor in charge of all the town meetings in Boston, putting an *end to self-government in Boston.*

The Quebec Act: again established on May 20, 1774, this act extended the Canadian borders, effectively *cutting off the western colonies of Connecticut, Massachusetts and Virginia.*

The Boston Port Bill: the King of England closed Boston Harbor to *all but British ships. (This became effective on June 1, 1774.)*

With the passage of The Intolerable Acts, Washington felt the need to get involved and he led a meeting where a document with several agreements that are referred to as the Fairfax Resolves was adopted. This was basically a position paper drafted in the early stages of the American Revolution by a committee in Fairfax County in the colony of Virginia on July 18, 1774. Composed principally by George Mason, they rejected the British Parliament's claim of supreme authority over the American colonies. The first one is rather blunt and is presented here:

> 1. *Resolved* that this Colony and Dominion of Virginia can not be considered as a conquered Country; and if it was, that the present Inhabitants are the Descendants not of the *Conquered*, but of the *Conquerors. (Emphasis Mine)*

Over thirty additional counties in Virginia passed similar resolutions in 1774, but the Fairfax Resolves were the most detailed, influential and the most far-reaching documents. The resolutions led to the creation of a Continental Congress that met to decide the fate of the colonies, with the prospect of armed resistance seen as a last resort.

After the battles of Lexington and Concord in April 1775, the political disagreements between Great Britain and the North American colonies quickly intensified and became an armed confrontation. In May, Washington traveled to the Second Continental Congress in Philadelphia, dressed in his military uniform, this to send the message that he was prepared for an armed conflict, should it come to that. On June 15, Washington was appointed Major General and Commander in Chief of the colonial forces against Great Britain. While Washington didn't seek the office of commander, he did not face any serious competition for it. In June 1775, the Congress commissioned George Washington to take command of the Continental Army besieging the British in Boston. He wrote home to Martha that he expected to return safely to her in the fall, but the command actually kept him away from Mount Vernon for *another 8 years.*

Washington's small army had a few small victories and in March of 1776 when his army placed artillery on Dorchester Heights, located above Boston that forced the British to withdraw. He then moved his troops into New York City, but in June, a new British commander named Sir William Howe, arrived in the Colonies with the largest expeditionary force Britain had ever deployed to that point in history. By August 1776, the British army launched a major attack, quickly taking New York City in what was the largest battle of the war. Washington's army was routed and suffered the surrender of 2,800 men and he ordered the remains of his army to retreat across the Delaware River into Pennsylvania. Confident the war would be over in a few months, General Howe made a tactical decision many military historians have questioned since then, when he wintered his troops at Trenton and Princeton, leaving Washington free to attack at a time and place of his choosing.

On Christmas night, 1776, Washington and his men crossed the Delaware River and attacked 1400 unsuspecting Hessian mercenaries at Trenton, taking over 1000 prisoners and forcing their surrender. (Hessian mercenaries were 18th century German soldiers in the employ of the British government. The British Parliament found it more expedient to borrow money and hire foreign troops than it was to recruit and train British soldiers.) A few days later, evading a force that had been sent to destroy his army, Washington attacked the British again, this time at Princeton and the British army suffered a second embarrassing loss. The darkest time for Washington and the Continental Army was during the winter of 1777 at Valley Forge, Pennsylvania. The 11,000-man force went into winter quarters and over the next six months suffered thousands of deaths from cold and disease.

Martha, General Washington's wife, joined her husband in his winter quarters every year of the war, where they entertained his officers and guests. A patriot in her own right, Mrs. Washington made it her war. When she wasn't nursing sick and wounded soldiers, she was helping to raise money for the troops. Needlework helped her to pass the time through the long, cold winters and by war's end, she had spent about half the war in camp with her husband.

It may be well be time to interrupt this narrative and clear up a large myth about Washington's encampment at Valley Forge and take a look at *the George Washington Prayer Journal* controversy. This story begins with an inspiring artistic work by the artist Arnold Friberg. Officially known as 'The Prayer at Valley Forge'. Friberg tried to capture what he called 'The spirit of 1776' when he painted the picture in 1975 for the American bicentennial celebration the following year. Since then, the painting has become one of the top selling pieces of contemporary American art and has inspired countless knock-offs and copies by various artists who sought to capitalize on the painting's popularity. The painting has also become a source of controversy between Christian conservatives and secularists who seem to be locked in a continuing battle over America's founding ideology. Copies can be found hanging in several state governors' offices, principally located in one geographic area of the U.S.

There is also a prayer attributed to George Washington at Valley Forge that is presented here:

> "Help me thoroughly to examine myself concerning my knowledge, faith and repentance. Increase my faith and direct me to the true object Jesus Christ the way, the truth and the life. Bless, O Lord, all the people of this land, from the highest to the lowest, particularly those whom thou has appointed to rule over us in church and state ... for the sake of thy dear son, Jesus Christ our Lord, Amen."

The truth (however unpopular it may be for some) is that Washington did not pray this prayer, it was actually found in a document that the religious right continues to call *the George Washington Prayer Journal,* but the actual title on the manuscript is "The Daily Sacrifice." The religious right has insisted that this work was written by Washington, who began writing entries some time in his youth to his early 20s. The original manuscript is handwritten and has twenty four pages, typical of a pocket memo book of the time. As the story of its discovery is recounted, Washington's descendant who ironically was also named Lawrence Washington, came across the journal in an old trunk in 1890 and had it evaluated for authenticity by document specialists. Their conclusion was that it was not written by George Washington.

The manuscript was later submitted to the Smithsonian in Washington, D.C. where again, the handwriting was analyzed by staff handwriting experts who compared it to other (readily available) documents written by Washington. The document experts at the Smithsonian confirmed that the manuscript was not written by George Washington. A few years later, Dr. W.A. Croffutt, a Washington D.C. newspaper correspondent, attempted to settle the issue once and for all when he traced some of the prayers in the manuscript back to an English prayer book used during the reign of the English King James I, who died 107 years *before George Washington was born.*

The advocates for the document's validity vehemently suggest that Washington's handwriting changed over time as he aged and matured, thus the writing in the journal may not resemble documents on file and dismissed the other arguments against the document as lies and misrepresentations.

Despite the document's questionable authenticity, Philadelphia auctioneer Stan V. Henkels who, as he prepared the catalog of sale for an April 1891 auction of Washington family possessions, summarily dismissed the opinions of all the experts and insisted that the document was absolutely written in Washington's own hand and the prayers were his own composition. From that point on, Christian apologists have embraced the idea that the work must be authentic and it has been published in both facsimile and contemporary print form, however, it is *not* now recognized by the Library of Congress as part of the definitive collection of George Washington's papers.

So what facts do we actually know about the "Prayer at Valley Forge"? Well, there are several different versions of the story by some accounts, and the original story of George Washington kneeling in prayer comes from a source that is troublesome if not suspect, to say the least. A brief recitation of the tale was first published in an 1808 edition of a biography of Washington by Mason L. (Parson) Weems;

Mason Locke Weems, better known as Parson Weems was an American author and book agent and is best known as the originator of some of the most celebrated stories about George Washington, the most famous of which is the tale about Washington as a child, chopping down the cherry tree, i.e.; *"I cannot tell a lie, I did it with my little hatchet."*, a fable that's included in *"A History of the Life and Death, Virtues and Exploits of General George Washington"*. It was written in 1800 and is considered Weems' most famous work. It became a 19th century bestseller and was purported to portray Washington's virtues, eventually becoming an entertaining and perhaps more importantly, the morally enlightening primer for children at the time.

Weems never revealed his source for the Prayer at Valley Forge, but he did identify Washington's observer as "a certain good old FRIEND of the respectable family and name of Potts." The story actually does begin with a young man named Isaac Potts who professed to have witnessed this event. Isaac Potts was a 26 year old Quaker who (because of his religious beliefs) was opposed to the Revolutionary War. His house was used by Washington as his headquarters at Valley Forge during the winter of 1777-78 but Isaac Potts didn't live at Valley Forge during the encampment. Potts actually rented the house in Valley Forge to his aunt, the widow Deborah Hewes, who then sublet it to Washington while Potts actually took up residence in Pottsgrove, Pa. between 1774 and 1782.

Anyway, Potts, so the story goes, was at Washington's encampment and was out riding sometime during the winter of 1777 (the exact date and location was never disclosed), when he encountered General Washington in a secluded area of the woods, deep in prayer. Potts, explained that when he witnessed seeing the general in prayer, Potts withdrew from the scene to allow the general some privacy but it caused him to have a change of heart about the war.

This part of the story poses a curious question; if Washington left the camp to pray in seclusion, why was he praying so that every word could be heard by Potts. From his own account, he was standing several yards away and from here, the story becomes really interesting because the full, detailed episode remained unreported, (other than the brief reference by Weems) until Potts allegedly recounted his experience to his pastor, Reverend Nathaniel Snowden a good *40 years* after the event allegedly happened, with no explanation about why Potts waited until then to recount the story ever offered. The Reverend Snowden came from a prominent family, his father Isaac Snowden helped start the First Presbyterian Church in America. Snowden was a personal friend of the general and a frequent visitor at the encampment and at some point, the reverend allegedly copied Potts' story into his personal journal to 'protect and preserve it for posterity'. This is a short passage from Potts' story, as it is recorded in Reverend Snowden's journal:

> "I tied my horse to a sapling & went quietly into the woods & to my astonishment I saw the great George Washington on his knees alone, with his sword on one

side and his cocked hat on the other. He was at Prayer to the God of the Armies, beseeching to interpose with his Divine aid, as it was ye Crisis, & the cause of the country, of humanity & of the world.

Such a prayer I never heard from the lips of man. I left him alone praying. I went home & told my wife. I saw a sight and heard today what I never saw or heard before, and just related to her what I had seen & heard & observed. We never thought a man c'd be a soldier & a Christian, but if there is one in the world, it is Washington. She also was astonished. We thought it was the cause of God, & America could prevail."

That this story evokes a very moving and deeply emotional image of General George Washington beseeching God to bless and protect his army is to say the least, powerful and symbolic, but there is a problem with it in that there is no proof of its validity. First, there's little if any evidence that Reverend Snowden knew of or associated all that closely with Isaac Potts and there's another annoying little fact; Reverend Snowden's journal account contains the name of Potts's wife as Sarah but her name was actually *Martha*, Isaac's wife in 1777 was named Martha, after she died in 1798, Potts married Sarah in 1803, this more than three years after Washington's death. Also, Snowden's journal states that he got the story from a man named "John" and not Isaac Potts, John was actually the name of Isaac's *brother*.

In addition to his dubious journal entries, it should be noted that Potts never changed his opposition to the war and better yet, several critics of Snowden maintained that the reverend retracted his story when he was presented with these contradictions. It's not difficult to conclude that the story in the good Reverend's journal is not supported by the historical facts as they are known. For example, in 1866, artist John McRae was commissioned by the United States to create an engraving of this event. However, when the Valley Forge Park Commission was given a grant to create a statue of McRae's engraving that would be placed at the entrance to Valley Forge Park, historians on staff at the Park turned down the offer, saying that there was insufficient evidence to support the idea that the event ever happened.

Perhaps the most damning piece of evidence against the Valley Forge painting is the simple fact that George Washington refused to pray on his knees. Historians and biographers of Washington all agree that Washington elected to stand, refusing to kneel when everyone else did during prayer. In this case, Washington made it clear to his military staff and advisers that he rejected anything that reduced a man to his knees.

The historical record also establishes that, during this time, religious leaders from a number of different churches all tried to claim George Washington as their congregant, and who could blame them? Washington was a legend in his own time, and to have his mere presence would be seen as a religious endorsement from America's General and First President that would be inspiring in the eyes of the community. As a result, numerous religious leaders during the 18th century have distorted the true character of Washington's faith, bending it to conform to their own vision of history.

It was definitely public knowledge that Washington attended church with some regularity and while he held religion in high regard, it's important to remember that Washington was far from being an orthodox believer. While Washington attended many religious services over the course of his life, he refused to be confirmed as a member of any one denomination. He also strongly opposed any orthodox allegiance in religious or political affairs. It's also generally known that Washington refused to take communion of any kind when attending church services, in fact, a number of religious leaders expressed distress at the fact that Washington would not participate in communion. When communion was offered, it was quite commonplace for Washington to get up and leave church at that point in the service.

All this being said, the religious right will not let go of the idea that the book is authentic and written by Washington and he actually knelt in the snow and recited it. The first printed copy was published in 1907 by William Herbert Burk in a work entitled *Washington's Prayers*, followed by William J. Johnson's work, *George*

Washington the Christian, an apologetic work published in 1919 that is populated with additional historical errors. The prayers appear in the second chapter of the book and the book is still available from devotional publishers as well as the Internet Archive.

The fact that the manuscript never had any connection with George Washington and that there is not one credible historical scholar who thinks Washington wrote it *doesn't seem to matter,* the manuscript is still celebrated as a prime example of George Washington's strong piety and faithfulness.

But let's get back to the conflict. Amazingly, the army emerged from the winter at Valley Forge still intact and in relatively good order. For the remainder of the war, Washington was content to keep the British bottled up in New York, although he never totally discarded the idea of retaking the city and driving them out. The northern, southern, and naval theaters of the war come together in 1781 at Yorktown, in Virginia. General Charles Cornwallis was settled on the York River in Yorktown, where he was ordered to occupy and hold a fortified position that could be resupplied and, should it become necessary, be evacuated by sea.

Cornwallis knew that the arrival of the French fleet from The West Indies would give the Americans control of the Chesapeake, allowing Washington to move the American and French forces south toward Virginia in August. In early September, French naval forces engaged and defeated a British fleet at the Battle of the Chesapeake, cutting off Cornwallis' escape. When Washington arrived outside Yorktown, the combined Franco-American force of 18,900 men began the final attack against Cornwallis in early October. For several days, the French and Americans bombarded the British defenses, then began capturing the British outer defensive positions before Cornwallis decided his position was becoming untenable.

Facing the combined French and Colonial armies and a French fleet of 29 warships at his back, Cornwallis held out as long as he could before surrendering his army on October 19, 1781. Faced with the surrender at Yorktown, King George III lost control of the British Parliament to the Peace Party and there were no further major military activities in North America, although the war continued elsewhere for two more years, including the siege of Gibraltar and naval operations in the East and West Indies, until a peace treaty was signed on September 3, 1783.

The Continental Congress named a five-member commission to negotiate a treaty; John Adams, Benjamin Franklin, John Jay, Thomas Jefferson, and Henry Laurens. However, Laurens ship was captured by a British warship and held in the Tower of London until the end of the conflict and Jefferson did not leave the United States in time to take part in the negotiations, so they were conducted by Adams, Franklin, and Jay. The last British troops left New York City on November 25, 1783, and the United States Congress of the Confederation ratified the Paris treaty on January 14, 1784.

Okay, I've spent some time trying to show the events in Washington's life that shaped his character and moral convictions, because they have a direct impact on what happens next. Three years later, in 1787, Washington was again called into the service of his country when he was elected president of the Constitutional Convention in Philadelphia. Finally free of Great Britain, the young republic began struggling with the Articles of Confederation, a structure of government that centered power with the states. But the thirteen colonies had fought the Revolution as if they were thirteen independent nations and resisted any attempts at unification. Many were fighting among themselves over boundaries and navigation rights, while others refused to contribute to pay the country's war debt. In some instances, state legislatures arbitrarily imposed oppressive tax policies on their own citizens.

Washington became extremely discouraged at the state of affairs and slowly came to the realization that something had to be done, but it wasn't until Congress approved a convention to be held in Philadelphia to amend the Articles of Confederation. At the convention, James Madison, Alexander Hamilton and Washington all came to the conclusion that it wasn't amendments that were needed, but a completely new constitution, one that would give the national government more authority...they also realized that this would be a formidable task.

In the end, the Convention produced a plan that could not only address the country's current problems, but would hopefully survive the test of time. In the months after the convention adjourned, Washington's reputation and endorsement of the new government became central if the Constitution was to be ratified. Opposition was clamorous but not well organized, with many of America's leading political figures, including Patrick Henry and Sam Adams, all of whom condemned the proposed plan as a government grab for power. Their argument was so convincing that even in Washington's home state of Virginia, the Constitution was ratified by only one vote.

As the first president, Washington was perceptively aware that everything he did in his presidency would set a precedent that everyone coming after him would likely feel bound to follow. He carefully attended to the responsibilities and duties of his office, paying particular attention to avoid the trappings of a European royal court. He selected the title "Mr. President" to of more grandiose forms of address that had been suggested and also declined the $25,000 salary that Congress offered with the office of president, asserting that he was already wealthy and wanted to protect his image as a selfless public servant. Congress finally persuaded him to accept the compensation to avoid giving the impression that only the wealthy could serve as president.

George Washington may have been drawing on his experience in the army when he surrounded himself with the most qualified people in the country, appointing Alexander Hamilton as Secretary of the Treasury and Thomas Jefferson to the post of Secretary of State. Throughout his two terms as president, Washington was becoming dismayed at the growing partisanship between government and the nation. The power granted to the federal government by the Constitution allowed for making key decisions and required people to join together to make those decisions. Washington saw that the formation of political parties were influenced more by personalities than by issues and this made him long to return to Mount Vernon and his farming. He was experiencing a decline in his stamina and endurance with advancing age and refused the idea of serving a third term, although there is no doubt that there would be no strong opposition had he chosen to do so. Because Washington was very aware of the precedent he established with each decision as the "first president," he set out to create a peaceful transition of governmental leadership.

I've recounted these events to again show the character of George Washington, these were experiences that shaped a man who gave so very much of himself to a fledgling country, both as a military leader and as a statesman, but the question that is still looming is, *was Washington a church member*, or perhaps better asked, *was he in any way a Christian*, since the political and religious right insists that these two *must go hand in hand?*

During George Washington's early life, he did hold a formal adherence to the Church of England, serving, for a time as a vestryman in the parish in which he resided. But this position was purely a secular position in the church that did not require his being a communicant, *or even a believer in Christianity*. As an adult, he was actually not affiliated with any church. George Washington as a young Virginia planter might, with some degree of frankness, have been called a Christian but George Washington, the soldier, the statesman and sage was actually not a Christian as most people would define it, he is best a Deist.

Similarly, Washington actually did not say "so help me God" at the presidential oath of office, despite what those who desperately want this to be true are maintaining. The words do not appear in the original text as laid out in laid out in Article 2, Section 1 of the Constitution.

The actual text is presented here;

> "I do solemnly swear (or affirm) that I will faithfully execute the Office of President of the United States, and will to the best of my Ability, preserve, protect and defend the Constitution of the United States."

There is no verifiable evidence to support any claim that any president used the phrase "so help me God" in their inauguration *until Abraham Lincoln* said it at the start of his second term as President, although this is disputed by some critics. A local newspaper account of Lincoln's 1865 inauguration states that Lincoln appended the phrase "so help me God" to the oath. There is also a corroborative account, offered in a newspaper the same year after Lincoln's death (April 15, 1865), that Lincoln included "so help me God" in his oath of office, but conversely, there was a claim made by A.M. Milligan, a Presbyterian minister, (Milligan was part of the movement for an official Christian Government) that several letters were sent to President Abraham Lincoln, insisting that he swear to God during his inaugurations and Lincoln is alleged to have responded by stating that *God's name was not in the Constitution* and he therefore could not depart from the letter of that instrument.

I will expand on this below, but Getting back to George Washington, after the War of Independence, when Washington found himself helping to organize the new government, his Deism almost immediately began to cause problems. A newspaper, The *Massachusetts Centinel* for December 5, 1789 contains correspondence between George Washington and the leaders of the Presbyterian Churches in Northern New England. The Presbyterian Church was alarmed because of the omission of any reference to God or the Christian Religion in the Constitution.

Washington's response to their letter alleviated some of these concerns when he clarified his position in his communiqué; the reason for the absence of any mention of the Christian religion in the constitution was very simple; the path of true piety is *so plain*, it required little if any *political direction*. Washington felt that this direction was best left to the ministers of the various religious sects, given in the course of instruction, encouragement and various religious laws, as his response so eloquently states here:

> To *the* MINISTERS *and* Ruling ELDERS *delegated to represent the Churches in Massachusetts and New-Hampshire, which compose the first* PRESBYTERY *of the* Eastward.
>
> Gentlemen,
>
> The affectionate welcome, which you are pleased to give me to the eastern parts of the Union, would leave me

without excuse, did I fail to acknowledge the sensibility which it awakens; and to express the most sincere return, that a grateful sense of your goodness can suggest.

To be approved by the praise-worthy, is a wish as natural to becoming ambition, as its consequence is flattering to our self-love. I am, indeed, much indebted to the favourable sentiments, which you entertain towards me, and it will be my study to deserve them.

The tribute of thanksgiving, which you offer to the *gracious* FATHER OF LIGHTS, for his inspiration of our publick councils with wisdom and firmness to complete the National Constitution, is worthy of men, who, devoted to the pious purposes of religion, desire their accomplishment by such means as advance the temporal happiness of their fellow men. And, here, I am persuaded, you will permit me to observe, that *the path of true piety is so plain, as to require but little POLITICAL direction.*

To this consideration we ought to ascribe the absence of any regulation respecting religion from the Magna Charta of our country. To the guidance of the Ministers of the Gospel, this important object is, perhaps, more properly committed. It will be your care to instruct the ignorant, and to reclaim the devious: And in the progress of morality and science, to which our Government will give every furtherance, we may confidently expect the advancement of true religion, and the completion of our happiness.

I pray to the munificent Rewarder of virtue, that your agency in this work, may receive its compensation here and hereafter.

G. Washington.   *(Italics mine)*

U.S. Army General Adolphus Washington Greely (veteran, polar explorer and a recipient of the Medal of Honor) did an in-depth analysis of Washington's papers and correspondence. In an article he wrote entitled *Washington's Domestic and Religious* Life, Greely published in the *Ladies' Home Journal* in April of 1896, he offered the following statements:

> "But even if he was ever confirmed in its (the Episcopal) faith there is no reliable evidence that he ever took communion with it or with any other church. Some years ago, I met at Paris, Texas, an old gentlemen, Mr. F.W. Miner, who was born and who lived for a considerable time near Mt. Vernon. He told me that when a boy he was once in company with a party of old men, neighbors in early life of Washington, who were discussing the question of his religious belief. He says that it was admitted by all of them that *he was not a church membe*r, and by the most of them that *he was not a Christian.*
>
> Mr. George Wilson of Lexington, Mo., whose ancestors owned the Custis estate, and founded Alexandria, where Washington attended church, writes as follows: 'My great-grandmother was Mary Alexander, daughter of 'John the younger,' who founded Alexandria. The Alexander pew in Christ church was next to Washington's, and an old lady, a kinswoman of mine, born near Alexandria and named Alexander, told me that the tradition in the Alexander family was that Washington *never* took communion.'
>
> In regard to Washington being a vestryman, Mr. Wilson says: 'At that time the vestry was the county court, and in order to have a hand in managing the affairs of the county, in which his large property lay, regulating the levy of taxes, etc., Washington had to be a vestryman.'"
> *(All emphasis mine)*

In an article conceding that Washington was not a communicant, the 1804 issue of the Western Christian Advocate published this:

"This is evident and convincing from the Life of Bishop White, bishop of the Episcopal church in America from 1787 to 1836. Of this evidence it has been well said: 'There does not appear to be any such undoubtable evidence existing. The more scrutinously the church membership of Washington is examined, the more doubtful it appears. Bishop White seems to have had more intimate relations with Washington than any clergyman of his time. His testimony out-weighs any amount of influential argumentation on the question.'"

Here are some additional quotations from various sources close to General and President George Washington:

"Gen. Washington never received the communion in the churches of which I am the parochial minister." (Bishop White, considered by many to be the father of the Protestant Episcopal church of America.)

"On sacramental Sundays, Gen. Washington, immediately after the desk and pulpit services, went out with the greater part of the Congregation." - Reverend Dr. Abercrombie, (Reverend Dr. Abercrombie was a minister in one of the churches Washington attended).

"The General was accustomed, on communion Sundays, *to leave the church* ...sending the carriage back for Mrs. Washington." Reverend Dr. Beverly Tucker (of the Episcopal church Washington was known to attend). *(Emphasis mine)*

"He never was a communicant in them (Dr. White's churches)." - Reverend Dr. Bird Wilson, (a contemporary of the early statesmen and presidents who meticulously researched the subject of their religious beliefs).

"I find no one who ever communed with him." - Reverend William Jackson, (rector of the Episcopal church of Alexandria, Virginia, the church which Washington had attended).

"The President was not a communicant" - Reverend E.D. Neill, (in the Episcopal Recorder, the organ of the church of which it is claimed Washington was a communicant).

"This (his ceasing to commune) may be admitted and regretted." Reverend Jared Sparks, (American historian, educator, and Unitarian minister, President of Harvard College (now Harvard University) from 1849 to 1853).

"I have never been a communicant." George Washington, quoted by Reverend Dr. Abercrombie, (*see above*).

In October 1831, The Reverend Dr. Bird Wilson devoted an entire sermon on the subject of our Founding Fathers' religious beliefs, giving particular attention to those of George Washington. Wilson noted that:

"Among all our presidents from Washington downward, not one was a professor of religion, at least not of more than Unitarianism."

Reverend Wilson then went on to say;

"...that *the founders of our nation were nearly all Infidels,* and that *of the presidents who had thus far been elected,* namely George Washington, John Adams, Thomas Jefferson, James Madison, James Monroe, John Quincy Adams, and Andrew Jackson, that *not one had professed a belief in Christianity." (Emphasis mine)*

It's important to note that the reverend said "...*not one had professed a belief...*", and not that they said that *they did not believe.* Here's a further excerpt from his sermon:

"When the war was over and the victory over our enemies won, and the blessings and happiness of liberty and peace were secured, the Constitution was framed and God was neglected. He was not merely forgotten. He was absolutely voted out of the Constitution. The proceedings, as published by Thompson, the secretary, and the history of the day, show that the question was gravely debated whether God should be in the Constitution or not, and, after a solemn debate He was deliberately voted out of it...There is not only in the theory of our government no recognition of God's laws and sovereignty, but its practical operation, its administration, has been conformable to its theory. Those who have been called to administer the government have not been men making any public profession of Christianity...Washington was a man of valor and wisdom. He was esteemed by the whole world as a great and good man; but he was not a professing Christian."

Dr. Wilson's sermon was published in the Albany NY Daily Advertiser a short time later, where it drew the attention of a young man named Robert Dale Owen. Owen contacted the author about the statement concerning Washington's belief. The result of their conversation was summarized in a letter to Amos Gilbert, dated Albany, November 13, 1831 and was published in New York two weeks later, as recounted in Thomas Jefferson's papers:

"I called last evening on Dr. Wilson, as I told you I should, and I have seldom derived more pleasure from a short interview with anyone. Unless my discernment of character has been grievously at fault, I met an honest man and sincere Christian. But you shall have the particulars. A gentleman of this city accompanied me to the Doctor's residence. We were very courteously received. I found him a tall, commanding figure, with a countenance of much benevolence, and a brow indicative of deep thought, apparently approaching fifty years of age. I opened the interview by stating that though personally a stranger to him, I had taken the liberty of calling in consequence of having perused an interesting sermon of his, which had been reported in the Daily Advertiser of this city, and regarding which, as he probably knew, a variety of opinions prevailed. In a discussion, in which I had taken a part, some of the facts as there reported had been questioned; and I wished to know from him whether the reporter had fairly given his words or not...I then read to him from a copy of the Daily Advertiser the paragraph which regards Washington, beginning, 'Washington was a man,' etc., and ending, 'absented himself altogether from the church.' 'I endorse,' said Dr. Wilson, with emphasis, 'every word of that. Nay, I do not wish to conceal from you any part of the truth, even what I have not given to the public. Dr. Abercrombie said more than I have repeated. At the close of our conversation on the subject his emphatic expression was -- for I well remember the very words -- 'Sir, *Washington was a Deist.*'"

Dr. Wilson concluded the interview by saying,

"I have diligently perused every line that Washington ever gave to the public, and I do not find one expression in which he (Washington) pledges himself as a believer in Christianity. I think anyone who will candidly do as I have done, will come to the conclusion that *he was a Deist and nothing more." (Emphasis mine)*

It's clear that George Washington did not at any time, take any special interest in church affairs. Again, General Greely is quoted as saying, "He was not regular in church attendance save possibly at home." At home he was the least regular in his attendance, in fact, his diary shows that he attended church about twelve times a year. During the week he supervised the affairs of his farm and on Sunday he usually attended to his correspondence. Sunday visitors at his house were numerous, and if he ever objected to them and this wasn't because they kept him from his devotions, but because they kept him from his work around the plantation.

Washington wrote in his diary:

"It hath so happened, that on the last Sundays -- call them the first or seventh (days) as you please, I have been unable

to perform the latter duty on account of visits from strangers, with whom I could not use the freedom to leave alone, or recommend to the care of each other, for their amusement."

When he visited his tenants to collect the rent, *their* piety, not his, prevented him from doing the business on Sunday, as the following entry in his diary shows:

> "Being Sunday, and the people living on my land very religious, it was thought best to postpone going among them till to-morrow."

His diary also shows that he "closed land purchases, sold wheat, and while a Virginia planter, went fox hunting on Sunday." He didn't believe that Christian servants are better than others, in fact, on one occasion when he needed servants, he wrote:

> "If they are good workmen, they may be from Asia, Africa, or Europe; they may be Mahomedans, Jews, or Christians of any sect, or they may be Atheists."

In August of 1789, Washington received a letter from the Committee of the United Baptist Churches in Virginia, expressing their concern about the lack of religious inclusion guiding the country's fledgling government. Washington wrote this in a letter to the United Baptist Churches in Virginia, expressing his views on religious freedom:

> "If I could have entertained the slightest apprehension that the Constitution framed in the Convention, where I had the honor to preside, might possibly endanger the religious rights of any ecclesiastical society, certainly I should never have placed my signature to it; and, if I could now conceive that the General Government might ever be so administered as to render the liberty of conscience insecure, I beg you will be persuaded that no one would be more zealous than myself to establish effectual barriers against the horrors of spiritual tyranny and every species of religious persecution. For you,

doubtless, remember that I have often expressed my sentiments that every man, conducting himself as a good citizen, and being accountable to God alone for his religious opinions, ought to be protected in worshiping the Deity according to the dictates *of his own conscience.*" *(Emphasis mine) (A copy of both the letter to Washington and this reply can be found in the appendix)*

New York Times Correspondent L. D. Burdick, in a letter to the Times on December 10th 1897, wrote, quoting (The Rev.) Dr. Abercrombie, about "...those in elevated stations who uniformly turned their backs."

"As long as there are people who think Washington ought to have been a member of the Episcopal Church, it will be periodically announced that he was one. It matters little whether he was or not except in the interest of historical truth. It must not be forgotten that when Parson Weems and the Reverend Lee Massey wrote, invention of incident and exaggeration of fact were accounted legitimate biography. It is undisputed that Washington was a vestryman in both Truro and Fairfax Parishes. It was the Rector of Truro Parish who had never known another 'so constant an attendant at church as Washington,' and it was he who had been 'so often at Mount Vernon on Sabbath morning, when his breakfast table was filled with guests; but to him they furnished no pretext for neglecting his God and losing the satisfaction of setting a good example.' But Paul Leicester Ford has shown from Washington's own diary that in one of the years he was 'so constant an attendant' at his church he actually went to church but fourteen times... *(Emphasis mine)*

At the beginning, I made the statement that we need to be careful about how we define 'Christian'. The issue isn't that George Washington wasn't a *Christian*, he was, inasmuch as he held a basic *belief in God*, and from that belief, he developed a basic sense of morality and a basic sense of right and wrong. He wouldn't tolerate profanity by the men under his command, in fact, in August of 1776 he issued the following general order to his troops;

> The General is sorry to be informed that the foolish, and wicked practice, of profane cursing and swearing - a Vice heretofore little known in an American Army - is growing into fashion; he hopes the officers will, by example, as well as influence, endeavour to check it, and that both they, and the men will reflect, that we can have little hopes of the blessing of Heaven on our Arms, if we insult it by our impiety, and folly; added to this, it is a vice so mean and low, without any temptation, that every man of sense, and character, detests and despises it.

As I've shown, Washington preferred to identify God by referring to him as Providence or at times, a Supreme Being. These are terms associated with *Freemasonry*, because Washington was a member of the Masonic Order. In a letter Washington wrote to Benjamin Harrison, Washington said;

> "Providence has heretofore taken us up when all other means and hope seemed to be departing from us; in this I will confide."

In his general orders to his troops in Cambridge in November of 1775, Washington stated;

> "The General hopes such frequent Favors from Divine Providence will animate every American to continue, to exert his utmost, in the defence of the Liberties of his Country, as it would now be the basest ingratitude to the Almighty, and to their Country, to shew any the least backwardness in the public cause."

During the war, when a ship bearing a cargo of flour for the British army fell into the hands of hungry Continental troops, Washington concluded;

"I cannot consider this as anything but a most Providential Event."

His own position notwithstanding, Washington recognized the need for his men to have access to their individual religious beliefs as they fought. In June of 1776, he sent an additional plea to the Continental Congress. In part it reads;

I would also beg leave to mention to Congress, the necessity there is of some new regulations being entered into respecting the Chaplains of the Army.

Few people are aware that George Washington did not want a priest in attendance at his deathbed. There were no prayers uttered and no Christian rituals or rites offering the comfort and reassurance of everlasting life performed. Washington's funeral was actually a simple affair, organized by the local Masonic lodge and held on December 18, 1799. In his will, Washington stated, "It is my express desire that my Corpse may be Interred in a private manner, without parade, or funeral Oration." Reverend Thomas Davis, rector of Christ Church, Alexandria, read the Episcopal Order of Burial, then the Reverend James Muir, minister of the Alexandria Presbyterian Church and Dr. Elisha Dick conducted the traditional Masonic funeral rite.

If I may repeat myself one more time, the Founding Fathers, especially George Washington, had to have studied and understood the religious struggles and conflicts that occurred in Europe and England, these led to his personal struggle with organized religions in general. Consider the environment he grew up in, a colonial outpost of Great Britain, a country with a state church who's head was also the head of the government, then factor in his Great-Great Grandfather Laurence's family history under such rule. Washington's knowledge of world history left him with some serious concerns about how church and political systems had evolved over time. This led Washington to the inescapable conclusion that would be a disastrous error if he or by extension the government forced others to accept his or anybody else's religious views.

As for John Adams and Thomas Jefferson, while they would disagree vehemently over matters of political policy, they were united on the question of religious freedom. Adams and Jefferson would certainly look back and feel satisfied with what they may have considered one of their greatest achievements; the part they played to establish a secular government whose elected members would never have to rule on the legality of theological views in government.

JOHN ADAMS

John Adams was born and raised in Braintree, Massachusetts in the township now known as Quincy Massachusetts. He was a descendant of Henry Adams, who (also) fled to America in 1632, in the face of the persecution in England during the reign of the first King Charles. As such, the young Adams learned about the risks of a state sponsored religion, such as persecution of minorities and became aware of a government's temptation to wage holy wars that an established religion presents. Adams was a statesman, a diplomat and was a strong advocate of independence from Great Britain for America. He was a well-educated, Period of Enlightenment political theorist who worked to promote republicanism and a strong central government.

Adams rose to prominence in the early stages of the American Revolution. A cousin of revolutionary leader Samuel Adams, John was a lawyer and public figure in Boston and became a delegate from Massachusetts to the Continental Congress, where he played a leading role in persuading Congress to declare independence from Great Britain. Adams' revolutionary efforts secured him two terms as vice president under George Washington and was elected in 1796 and served one term as the second president of the United States. Like most New Englanders, Adams opposed slavery all his life and never bought or owned a slave.

So, was John Adams a Christian? Well, like some of the other Founding Fathers, President John Adams was a raised a Congregationalist but, like many of our country's early leaders, he ultimately grew to reject many of the fundamental doctrines of conventional Christianity, such as the Trinity and the divinity of Jesus. As a young man, Adams was urged by his father to become a minister but Adams refused, he viewed the practice of law to be a more noble calling. Along with many Congregationalists of his time, Adams became a Unitarian when he reached adulthood and both he and his wife Abigail attended the First Parish Church in their hometown, where they were active members throughout their lives. As a Unitarian, Adams held a personal religious position that was based *on the moral teachings* of Jesus Christ, but not on *the miraculous events* associated with Christ. In fact, Adams wrote the following after the signing of the Declaration of Independence:

> "We have this day restored the Sovereign to whom alone men ought to be obedient. He reigns in Heaven, and with a propitious eye beholds his subjects assuming that freedom of thought and dignity of self-direction which He bestowed on them. From the rising to the setting sun, may His kingdom come!"

Historians have debated whether or not John Adams' religious views were influenced by the growing movement of Deism. Several popular ideas circulating during this time that were structured around the idea of an Intelligent Creator but not in miracles or divine intervention in the affairs of human beings. Although he referred to himself as a "church going animal," Adams' overall view of religion was generally ambivalent. Because he recognized the abuses, *both large and small*, that religion and religious belief lends itself to, Adams also recognized that religion could be a force for good in individual lives as well as in society. He read extensively, delving into many of the classics that led him to believe that his view applied equally to Christianity as well as other religions. This also suggested to Adams that religion, *provided it united and morally guided people*, could have a positive role in public life.

The Massachusetts Bay Colony that the Adams family helped establish had a significant influence on the laws, culture and tradition of the area during this time and Adams accepted that he had a responsibility to live up to his family's heritage. By the time of John Adams' birth in 1735, many of the Puritan tenets, such as predestination were no longer widely accepted and many of the Puritan's harsher practices had been relaxed. Adams did however, consider the Puritan founders to be supporting freedom with a cause that still had a *holy urgency*. He considered this a personal value system that he worked hard to live up to.

There are many famous quotes of John Adams on religion, especially in response to what was perceived as the Atheism of Thomas Paine (his profile is presented below). Adams was one who felt that Atheist beliefs were a threat to a decent and moral society, and he rebuked Thomas Paine's criticism of Christianity by declaring that no other religion had more "wisdom, virtue, equity and humanity."

But like many of his contemporaries in colonial America during this time, Adams position on Christianity was viewed from the standpoint of a student of history, which was that the basic theology had been twisted by church authorities who used superstition and fear to control the populace, abuse minorities and frequently initiate and sponsor large scale wars. When writing on the subject of religion, Adams would single out the Roman Catholic Church by name for its lengthy history of corrupt exercise of power and deceit.

Despite his assertion that religion could have a role in public life, Adams was committed to his position about separating Church and State and his overall public view of religion was seen by those around him to be apathetic. Adams could also not see where religious interpretations should be called upon to help a politician in matters of law and politics and accepting the idea that these could be accomplished with sound reason and common sense, and that allowing for a free conscience would cause men of all religious beliefs to succeed in uniting together *for the common good of society and the state.* Even with his high level of contempt for Catholics and the flood of Jesuit priests who came to America, he also acknowledged that the nation must accept them on the principle of religious freedom. Adams believed that if freedom of religion was granted by the state, it would be the final blow to all forms of corrupt religious authority.

Adams received his post-secondary education at Harvard at the age of 16 in 1751. After he graduated in 1755 with an Bachelor of Arts degree, Adams had strong misgivings about becoming a minister and these led him to teach school for a few years in Worcester, Massachusetts. This allowed him some time to consider his choice of a career. After much reflection, Adams wrote to his father and explained his decision to become a lawyer by saying that he found lawyers capable of more "noble and gallant achievements" but considered the clergy to afflicted with the "pretended sanctity of some absolute dunces."

As a member of the Unitarian Fellowship, Adams eventually no longer believed in predestination, eternal damnation, the divinity of Christ and most other Calvinist beliefs of his Puritan ancestors. In a letter written on 15 April, 1814 to John Taylor, (a friend, politician and writer and U.S. Senator living in Caroline, Virginia) Adams expressed the following sentiment:

> "The priesthood have, in all ancient nations, nearly monopolized learning. And ever since the Reformation, when or where has existed a Protestant or dissenting sect who would tolerate A FREE INQUIRY? The blackest billingsgate, the most ungentlemanly insolence, the most yahooish brutality, is patiently endured, countenanced, propagated, and applauded. But touch a solemn truth in collision with a dogma of a sect, though capable of the clearest proof, and you will find you have disturbed a nest, and the hornets will swarm about your eyes and hand, and fly into your face and eyes."

It was during this time as a Unitarian that Adams flatly denied the doctrine of eternal damnation. In a letter to Thomas Jefferson that Adams wrote on 3 September, 1816, he made the following point;

> "I almost shudder at the thought of alluding to the most fatal example of the abuses of grief which the history of mankind has preserved - the Cross. Consider what calamities that engine of grief has produced!"

As a child, Adams often wrote about events that had a strong effect on him and he continued to do this in his legal career, where he would take notes during legal cases he would sit in on so that he could later study and learn from them. After Adams earned a Post Graduate Masters of Arts from Harvard in 1758, he was admitted to the bar. His report of the 1761 legal argument of James Otis in the Massachusetts Superior Court as to the legality of Writs of Assistance is a prime example. James Otis, Jr. was a lawyer and member of the Massachusetts provincial assembly whose early advocacy of the patriot views against British policy led to the American Revolution, and his catchphrase *"Taxation without representation is tyranny"* became the basic patriot position and rallying cry. Otis' arguments caused Adams to be swept up in the cause of the American colonies, yet he still believed in the basic rule of law. In 1770 Adams conducted an unpopular but successful legal defense of several British soldiers who were involved in the Boston Massacre, because he believed in every person's right to legal counsel.

Abigail Smith (Adams) was born on November 22, 1744 in the parsonage of the North Parish Congregational Church of Weymouth, to Reverend William Smith and Elizabeth Quincy. She was raised simply and without pretension, though her relatives, especially on her mother's side, were among the leading families in their community. Her father, Reverend Smith was a liberal Congregationalist who had Arminian leanings and did not preach the doctrines of predestination, original sin, or the full divinity of Christ. Rather, he emphasized the importance of reason and morality in religious life.

Reverend Smith's simple faith was the faith his daughter Abigail confessed when she was received into membership in the Weymouth church on June 24, 1759. In that same year, Abigail met John Adams and by 1762, they were exchanging openly affectionate love letters full of mischievous humor. On October 25, 1764, five days before his 29th birthday, the Reverend Smith officiated the marriage of John Adams to his daughter Abigail Smith (who was, as it turned out, Adams' third cousin) in Weymouth, Massachusetts.

Their wedding, on October 25, 1764, began one of history's great partnerships and the marriage produced six children, (their last child was stillborn) including the future president, John Quincy Adams. John and Abigail Adams became active members of the First Parish Church in Quincy, which was already Unitarian in doctrine by 1753. Although she did not sign the membership book (her husband did), Abigail regularly attended the church, supported it, and showed active concern and care for its ministry. Abigail's theology is clearly stated in her correspondence, writing to her son, John Quincy on May 5, 1816, where she said;

> "I acknowledge myself a Unitarian - Believing that the Father alone, is the supreme God, and that Jesus Christ derived his Being, and all his powers and honors from the Father. There is not any reasoning which can convince me, contrary to my senses, that three is one, and one three."

On January 3, 1818, in a letter to her daughter-in-law, Louisa, Abigail wondered

> "...when will Mankind be convinced that true Religion is from the Heart, between Man and his creator, and not the imposition of Man or creeds and tests?"

Like many early Unitarians Abigail discounted sectarian claims and expressed her feeling that she was;

> "...assured that those who fear God and work righteousness shall be accepted of him, and that I presume of what ever sect or persuasion."

Adams' mother was a pious woman but wondered if her son might be unsuited for religious life. There was a strong Puritan strain to Adams' morality, even when he strayed from Puritans' religious precepts: At age 21, Adams wrote this;

> "...this World was not designed for a lasting and a happy State, but rather for a State of moral Discipline, that we might have a fair Opportunity and continual Excitement to labour after a cheerful Resignation to all the Events

of Providence, after Habits of Virtue, Self Government, and Piety. And this Temper of mind is in our Power to acquire, and this alone can secure us against all the Adversities of Fortune, against all the Malice of men, against all the Operations of Nature."

As argumentative as John Adams was about theology, he found members of the clergy equally argumentative. He recalled the conditions under which he decided to switch his intended profession from the ministry to the law:

"Between the years 1751, when I entered, and 1754, when I left college, a controversy was carried on between Mr. Bryant, the minister of our parish, and some of his people, partly on account of his principles, which were called Arminian, and partly on account of his conduct, which was too gay and light, if not immoral. Ecclesiastical councils were called, and sat at my father's house. Parties and their acrimonies arose in the church and congregation, and controversies from the press between Mr. Bryant, Mr. Niles, Mr. Porter, Mr. Bass, concerning the five points."

The term Arminian was widely used in religious debates by this time but was co-opted to match later High Church views of Anglicanism. The five points Adams is referring to here are the basic beliefs or ideas of Arminianism. Scholarly debate has not settled the exact content or historical role of English Arminianism. The beliefs are listed here;

Human Free Will—This states that though man is fallen, he is not incapacitated by the sinful nature and can freely choose God. His will is not restricted and enslaved by his sinful nature.

Conditional Election—God chose people for salvation based on His foreknowledge where God looks into the future to see who would respond to the Gospel message.

Universal Atonement—The position that Jesus bore the sin of everyone who ever lived.

Resistible Grace--a type of grace that offsets the effects of the Fall, restores man's free will and enables every person to choose to come to Christ or not.

Fall from Grace--The teaching that a person can fall from grace and lose his salvation.

Adams continues in his diary:

"I read all these pamphlets and many other writings on the same subjects, and found myself involved in difficulties beyond my powers of decision. At the same time, I saw such a spirit of dogmatism and bigotry in clergy and laity, that, if I should be a priest, I must take my side, and pronounce as positively as any of them, or never get a parish, or getting it must soon leave it. Very strong doubts arose in my mind, whether I was made for the pulpit in such times, and I began to think of other professions. I perceived very clearly, as I thought, that the study of theology, and the pursuit of it as a profession, would involve me in endless altercations, and make my life miserable, without any prospect of doing any good to my fellow men."

John Adams was serving in London as a diplomat for his country in 1787 when he wrote and published a three volume work entitled *"A Defence of the Constitutions of Government of the United States of America"*. In it, Adams offered the following;

"The United States of America have exhibited, perhaps, the first example of governments erected on the simple principles of nature; and if men are now sufficiently enlightened to disabuse themselves of artifice, imposture, hypocrisy, and superstition, they will consider this event as an era in their history. Although the detail of the formation of the American governments is at present little known or regarded either in Europe or in America, it may hereafter become an object of curiosity. It will never be pretended that any persons employed in that service had interviews with the gods, or were in any degree under the influence of Heaven, more than those at work upon ships or houses, or laboring in merchandise or agriculture; it will forever be acknowledged that these governments were contrived merely by the use of reason and the senses...Thirteen governments [of the original states] thus founded on the natural authority *of the people alone*, without a pretence of miracle or mystery, and which are destined to spread over the northern part of that whole quarter of the globe, are a great point gained in favor of the rights of mankind." *(Emphasis Mine)*

In his later life, John Adams seriously questioned theology and its impact on everyday life, like this letter to Thomas Jefferson on June 20, 1815, where he asked,

"The question before the human race is, whether the God of Nature shall govern the world by his own laws, or whether priests and kings shall rule it by fictitious miracles?" *(A copy of the letter can be found in the appendix)*

In a letter written to Judge Francis Adrian Vanderkemp (one of the Dutch radical leaders of the Patriots, a minister and publicist. Vanderkemp persuaded Thomas Jefferson to anonymously publish the his religious work entitled a "Syllabus of an estimate of the doctrines of Jesus compared with those of others") that Adams wrote in Quincy on December 27, 1816, Adams said in part;

"Christianity, you will say, was a fresh revelation. I will not deny this. As I understand the Christian religion, it was, and is, a revelation. But how has it happened that millions of fables, tales, legends, have been blended with both Jewish and Christian revelation that have made them the most bloody religion that ever existed? How has it happened that all the fine arts, architecture, painting, sculpture, statuary, music, poetry, and oratory, have been prostituted, from the creation of the world, to the sordid and detestable purposes of superstition and fraud?" (what Adams is referring to here is that in the time leading up to the reformation. The Roman Catholic Church had stranglehold on art in any form, if you were a painter, a sculptor or a musician, every work you undertook *must* have its content or subject matter approved by senior church officials.)

As the future president, Adams brought to religion a lively interest in science that he developed at Harvard where gratitude as well as reason became part of Adams's religious system. Like Jefferson, Adams did not find the divinity of Jesus important. Over time, Adams became adamant as he expressed his Unitarian model in a letter to Thomas Jefferson, 14 September 1813:

> "The human Understanding is a revelation from its Maker which can never be disputed or doubted. There can be no Scepticism, Pyrrhonism or Incredulity or Infidelity here. No Prophecies, no Miracles are necessary to prove this celestial communication. This revelation has made it certain that two and one make three; and that one is not three; nor can three be one. We can never be so certain of any Prophecy, or the fullfillment of any Prophecy; or of any miracle, or the design of any miracle as We are, from the revelation of nature, i.e. natures God that two and two are four. Miracles or Prophecies might frighten Us to lie; to say that We believe that 2 and 2 make 5. But we should not believe it. We should know the contrary."

And in a letter Adams wrote to Jefferson in 1812, he stated in part:

> "I could express my Faith in shorter terms. He who loves the Workman and his Work, and does what he can to preserve and improve it, shall be accepted of Him."

For Adams, worship must accompany work. In a letter from John Adams written on January 21, 1810 to Benjamin Rush, (a signatory of the Declaration of Independence, a civic leader in Philadelphia, a physician, politician, social reformer, educator, humanitarian and founder of Dickinson College in Carlisle, Pennsylvania) Adams said that;

> "The Christian religion, as I understand it, is the brightness of the glory and the express portrait of the character of the eternal, self-existent, independent, benevolent, all powerful and all merciful creator, preserver, and father of the universe, the first good, first perfect, and first fair. It will last as long as the world. Neither savage nor civilized man, without a revelation, could ever have discovered or invented it. Ask me not, then, whether I am a Catholic or Protestant, Calvinist or Arminian. As far as they are Christians, I wish to be a fellow-disciple with them all," and he went on to say, "It is the duty of all men in society, publicly, and at stated seasons, to worship the SUPREME BEING, the great Creator and Preserver of the universe. And no subject shall be hurt, molested, or retrained, in his person, liberty, or estate, for worshipping GOD in the manner most agreeable to the dictates of his own conscience; or for his religious profession or sentiments; provided he doth not   disturb the public peace, or obstruct others in their religious   worship."

In 1812, Adams again wrote Jefferson:

> "I had forgotten the custom of putting Prophets in the Stocks....It may be thought impiety by many, but I could not help wishing that the ancient practice had been continued down to more modern times and that all the Prophets at least from Peter the Hermit, to Nimrod Hews inclusively, had been confined in the Stocks and prevented from spreading so many delusions and shedding so much blood."

In a follow up letter to John Taylor, Adams made some additional points:

"What havoc has been made of books through every century of the Christian era? Where are fifty gospels, condemned as spurious by the bull of Pope Gelasius? Where are the forty wagon-loads of Hebrew manuscripts burned in France, by order of another pope, because suspected of heresy? Remember the 'index expurgatorius', the inquisition, the stake, the axe, the halter and the guillotine."

But Adams presented a less confrontational image in public, as befit his Unitarianism beliefs. In his inaugural address, he expressed "a veneration for the religion of a people who profess and call themselves Christians," and a belief that Christianity was among the best recommendations for the public service. In a thanksgiving proclamation, issued March 23, 1798, Adams asked for His infinite grace, through the Redeemer of the World, freely to remit all our offenses, and to incline us by His Holy Spirit to that sincere repentance and reformation.

Adams attained a level of distinction during the early stages of the American Revolution as lawyer and public figure in Boston. As a delegate from Massachusetts to the Continental Congress, he played a leading role in persuading Congress to declare independence, assisted Thomas Jefferson in the drafting the Declaration of Independence in 1776 and was a principle advocate in the Congress. Later, serving as a diplomat in Europe, he helped negotiate the eventual peace treaty with Great Britain and was successful in obtaining critical monetary loans for the new governmental from several bankers in Amsterdam.

As a political historian and theorist, Adams played a large part in drafting the Massachusetts Constitution in 1780. This effort, together with his earlier publication, Thoughts on Government (the full title is *Thoughts on Government, Applicable to the Present State of the American Colonies)*, had a strong influence on American political thought. *(A copy of this complete document can be found in the appendix)*.

He found himself gravitating toward the Federalist Party, a political party that was formed sometime in 1788 during the ratification debates over the Constitution. This was the group that supported ratification and had a deep-seated preference for a strong, more consolidated central government rather than the loose confederation of semi-autonomous states. After the Constitution was ratified, the term 'federalist' came to be applied to any supporter of the Constitution and was particularly directed at members of the Washington administration.

One of his greatest functions at the convention was nominating George Washington to be commander in chief, and 25 years later as president, he nominated John Marshall to be Chief Justice of the United States. Adams' revolutionary credentials helped him become elected to two terms as vice president under George Washington and then win his election as President in 1796. During his single term as president, he fended off savage attacks from the Jeffersonian Republicans as well as a powerful faction within his own Federalist Party, principally led by his bitter enemy Alexander Hamilton.

As President, Adams signed the controversial Alien and Sedition Acts. These were laws authored by the Federalists and were supposed to strengthen the national security, but critics argued that this was primarily an effort to suppress voters who disagreed with the ideology of the Federalist party, (*tell me again how history doesn't repeat itself*) Adams also built up the army and navy especially in the face of an undeclared naval war with France from 1798 to1800. The major accomplishment of Adams' presidency was the peaceful resolution of this conflict despite Hamilton's opposition.

The Jeffersonians drove the Federalists out of office in 1800 and Adams retired to Quincy, Massachusetts where some time later, he and Jefferson patched up their differences. He and his wife established an consummate family line of politicians, diplomats, and historians now referred to as the Adams political family. His achievements have garnered significantly greater recognition today than when he was alive, as his contributions were not as celebrated as those of other Founders. Adams was the first U.S. president to reside in the executive mansion that eventually became known as the White House. He was as popular a leader as his second cousin, Sam Adams, his efforts had an impact that made itself felt through his work as a constitutional lawyer and his focused analysis of historical examples, his deep knowledge of the law and his commitment to the doctrines of republicanism.

One of the principle reasons the Founding Fathers, namely Washington, Jefferson, Adams, Hamilton and Franklin were deeply suspicious of a European pattern of governmental involvement in religion was because they saw government *corrupting* religion. Ministers who were paid by the state or paid by the government, felt that they didn't need to pay much attention to their parishes. In many cases, the clergy showed little concern for their parishioners, in fact, many sold their church positions and hired in a stand-in to handle the day-to-day obligations. This allowed them to wander off and often live somewhere else while continuing to draw a salary. They didn't need to pay attention to their parishioners because the parishioners weren't the ones paying them, the *state* was.

As we saw, Adams was aware of the both large and small abuses that religious beliefs give rise to, but he also accepted that religion could serve as a force for good in and individual's life, as well as in society at large. His extensive reading especially the classics allowed him to expand this belief, leading him to realize that his view could apply not only to Christianity but to all religions. From his study of history, Adams also knew of the risks an established religion poses, such as persecution of minorities and the temptation to wage holy wars, but he saw that religion, if it united and morally guided the people, could have a role in public life.

As he advanced in years, Adams retained a measure of piety but began to embrace skepticism, although he did believe in God and in God's governance of the world. Adams seldom penned the words 'Christ' or 'Christian' and more often than not, he, like his fellow Founding Fathers, referred to God as 'Providence', a divine power not specifically recognized with New Testament theology. John and Abigail were lovers, friends, counselors and mentors to one another into old age. Early in October, 1818, Abigail fell ill with typhus and died several weeks later. She was buried in the cemetery of First Church in Quincy. John Adams died at the age of 90 just a few hours after Thomas Jefferson, on July 4, 1826, on the 50th anniversary of the adoption of the Declaration of Independence. Except for Charles Carroll, who lived until 1832, Adams and Jefferson were the last two surviving signers.

THOMAS JEFFERSON

I think most would agree that no Founding Father had more effect on the formation of the government in America than Thomas Jefferson, and the best way to understand Jefferson's personal religious beliefs is to examine them through his own words. Many of his letters have survived and they are the best way to understand his ideas and opinions. Following a brief overview of his political accomplishments, I have placed several examples below that illustrate Jefferson's very complex understanding of religion.

Thomas Jefferson was born on April 13, 1743, at Shadwell, a Virginia plantation on a large tract of land near what is now Charlottesville. His father, Peter Jefferson, was a successful planter and surveyor and his mother, Jane Randolph Jefferson, came from a prominent Virginia family. Thomas was their third child and eldest son; he had six sisters and one surviving brother. He was raised in the Church of England and like Washington, Jefferson served as a vestryman in the church. The Church of England was the established church in Virginia at this time and the only denomination funded by state taxes.

In the years before the Revolution, church parishes were considered part of the local government and elected officials from the local level right up to the Virginia House of Burgesses, (which Jefferson was elected to in 1769) were required show an affiliation with the church and agree that the office holder would not express any dissent or do anything that didn't conform to church doctrine. Jefferson had members of the clergy as his friends and he contributed financially to the Anglican Church that he attended.

In 1760, at the age of 16, Jefferson entered the College of William & Mary in Williamsburg, and for two years he studied mathematics, metaphysics and philosophy under Professor William Small. Professor Small introduced the enthusiastic Jefferson to the writings of the British Empiricists, including John Locke, Francis Bacon, and Isaac Newton. By most estimates, Jefferson was influenced by Deist philosophy while at William & Mary, particularly the concepts of Bolingbroke. (Bolingbroke was a philosopher whose writings were not widely distributed until after the philosophers death in December of 1751, when David Mallet published a five-volume compendium of his works.

The philosophical influence in this collection showed Mallet's reliance on Locke, who Bolingbroke allowed was also his greatest influence. Bolingbroke combined his own ideas with those of Locke's in an attempt to justify how one could attain knowledge and what its limits were. Bolingbroke also emphasized his own beliefs about God and religion, while he attacked the position of earlier philosophers such as Plato, Malebranche and Berkley.

Jefferson also studied Roman and Greek classics, especially Cicero, Epictetus, Euripides and Homer for the rest of his life. (*Marcus Tullius Cicero* (107 – 43 BCE) was a Roman philosopher, politician, lawyer, orator, political theorist, consul and constitutionalist who lived in Rome and unsuccessfully tried to maintain and defend the republican principles during the civil war that brought down the Roman Republic, *Epictetus* (CE 55) was a Greek speaking Stoic philosopher, born a slave at Hierapolis, Phrygia, and later lived in Rome, *Epicurus* (341 BCE) was an ancient Greek philosopher and founder of the school of philosophy called Epicureanism, *Euripides* (480 BCE) was a Greek writer who wrote extensively about the human condition, *Homer* (850 BCE) is said to have been the first and greatest of the epic poets, author of the first known literature of Europe and credited with writing what is called the 'Western canon', a body of books, music and art that are accepted by Western scholars as the most significant and influential works that shaped Western culture.)

In 1762, Jefferson graduated from the College of William and Mary in Williamsburg, Virginia where, as a student, he reportedly enjoyed studying for 12 hours then would practice the violin for several more hours on a daily basis. Since there were no established law schools in America at the time, he went on to study law under the tutelage of a respected Virginia attorney and began working as a lawyer in 1767. Elected to colonial Virginia's House of Burgesses from 1769 to 1775, Jefferson, known for his reserved manner, gained recognition for drafting a pamphlet entitled, "A Summary View of the Rights of British America" in 1774. Jefferson intended it to be a set of instructions for the Virginia delegates attending the first Continental Congress, In it, he made the argument that the British Parliament had no right to govern the colonies, which he asserted were independent since their founding. Jefferson went on to describe how King George III and Parliament deprived the colonies' of their power of self-government and ignored the law. The pamphlet was widely circulated in London, New York and Philadelphia where it helped to confirm Jefferson's reputation as a skillful and articulate political writer.

By 1775, with the American Revolutionary War under way, Jefferson was chosen as a delegate to the Second Continental Congress. Although he was not known as a skillful public speaker, Jefferson was asked to be part of 'the committee of five', charged with drafting the Declaration of Independence. It's a little known fact that Jefferson was at first reluctant to writing the document but was talked into writing the draft by John Adams. Adams continued to press Jefferson and eventually he agreed.

Before he began writing, Jefferson had lengthy discussions with the other four members serving on the committee to decide what should be included the document. The other members were John Adams and Benjamin Franklin, Robert Livingston of New York, an American lawyer, politician and diplomat and Roger Sherman of Connecticut. Sherman was a lawyer, a judge and served in Connecticut's general assembly and the Continental Congress. It was Sherman who proposed the Great Compromise which called for a two-part federal legislature, with one part having representation based on the population of each state and district.

The five began work on June 11, 1776 and presented the document to Congress on June 28, 1776. The intent and purpose of the Declaration of Independence was to explain why the 13 colonies wanted to be free of British rule and also detailed the importance of individual rights and freedoms. One principle line of reasoning for these men was the separation of church and state. They saw it as a necessary reform for what they saw as religious tyranny that occurred when a religion received state endorsement, while those who were not of that religion were denied rights and often punished. After lengthy and sometimes difficult deliberation, (the mid-Atlantic colonies weren't in favor of any declaration of independence, such that in the first vote, only nine colonies voted in favor of declaring independence) the document was finally adopted on July 4, 1776.

From 1779 to 1781, Jefferson served as the governor of Virginia and from 1783 to 1784, he served a second term in what became officially known as the Congress of the Confederation. In 1785, Jefferson succeeded Benjamin Franklin as America's Minister to France, but his duties in Europe meant he could not attend the Constitutional Convention in Philadelphia during the summer of 1787. He was however, kept up to date with the effort to draft a new national constitution and later supported the inclusion of a bill of rights and presidential term limits. After his return to America in the fall of 1789, Jefferson was appointed by George Washington to become the nation's first secretary of state. It was here that Jefferson began arguing with Secretary of the Treasury Alexander Hamilton over foreign policy and differing understandings and interpretation of the Constitution.

In the early 1790s, Jefferson, who by now favored strong state and local government, cofounded the Democratic-Republican Party in an effort to oppose Hamilton's Federalist Party which advocated for a strong national government that had widespread control over the economy. In the presidential election of 1796, Jefferson ran against John Adams, receiving the second highest number of votes. According to the law at the time, this made Adams vice president. Jefferson again ran against Adams in the presidential election of 1800, which became a nasty battle between the Federalists and Democratic-Republicans.

Momentum for political campaigns during this time were fueled by newspaper op-eds, letters and perhaps more importantly, by privately published 'pamphlets'. A fairly lengthy pamphlet was published by Reverend William Linn, the first Presbyterian Chaplain of the United States House of Representatives in Washington, D.C. In what today would be considered a violation of the separation of church and state, Reverend Linn held worship services in the chamber for Congressional members and their families, alternating with the Senate chaplain every other week.

Sometime early in the year 1800, (the actual publication date was not recorded) Reverend Lynn published a pamphlet entitled "Serious considerations on the election of a President addressed to the Citizens of the United States" in which he stated the following:

> "I shall only mention what passed in conversation between Mr. Jefferson and a gentleman of distinguished talents and services, on the necessity of religion to government. The gentleman insisted that some religious faith and institutions of worship, claiming a divine origin, were necessary to the order and peace of society. Mr. Jefferson said that he differed widely from him, and that 'he wished to see a government in which no religious opinions were held', and 'where the security for property and social order rested entirely upon the force of the law.' Would not this be a nation of Atheists? Is it not natural, after the free declaration of such a sentiment, to suspect the man himself of Atheism? Could one who is impressed with the existence of a God, the Creator, Preserver, and Governor of all things, to whom we are under a law and accountable...?"

With reference to Jefferson's statement in a bill guaranteeing legal equality for citizens of all religions, including those of no religion who were living in Virginia, "But it does me no injury for my neighbor to say there are twenty gods or no God. It neither picks my pocket nor breaks my leg." Reverend Linn had this to say:

> "PUTTING the most favorable construction upon the words in the Notes, (referring to Jefferson's Notes on Virginia from 1782) they are extremely reprehensible. It is true that a mere opinion of my neighbour will do me no injury. Government cannot regulate or punish it.

The right of private opinion is inalienable. But let my neighbour once persuade himself that there is no God, and he will soon pick my pocket, and break not only my leg but my neck. If there is no God, there is no law; no future account; government then is the ordinance of man only, and we cannot be subject for conscience sake. No colours can paint the horrid effects of such a principle, and the deluge of miseries with which it would overwhelm the human race.

SOME of the friends of Mr. Jefferson, being ashamed the he should be reputed an Infidel and wishing that he had a little religion, *were it ever so little*, whisper that he is a sort of a Christian. Rather than give him up, they hint that he is as good a Christian as Dr. Priestley*, or thereabouts. I shall not dispute a moment whether he is as good as Dr. Priestly, or Dr. Priestly is as bad as him; but ask for the proofs of his professing Christianity in any shape.

How does he spend the Lord's day? Is he known to worship with any denomination of Christians? Where? When? How often? Though going to church is no certain sign of a man not being an infidel, any more than his pretending a regard for the Christian religion in his writings, yet a total or habitual neglect of public worship, must be admitted a strong proof against him. That wretch Voltaire partook of the sacrament of the supper, while he blasphemed Christ, and endeavoured, with the malice of a devil, to extirpate his religion from the earth. Hume, Kames, Gibbons, and many infidels pretended a regard for divine revelation, while they fought directly and secretly to destroy its credibility. I have exhibited proofs of Mr. Jefferson's infidelity. I wait for the proofs that he is as good as even Dr. Priestly*, which will be still bad enough; *and I shall exceedingly rejoice if any man should be able to prove him better.*"

*(The Dr. Joseph Priestley that Reverend Linn was comparing Jefferson to was an 18th-century English theologian, a dissident

clergyman, natural philosopher, chemist, educator and liberal political theorist. His work, *History of Early Opinions concerning Jesus Christ*, which he wrote in 1786, reignited a period of controversy because it defended Unitarianism and attacked established religious doctrines such as the inspiration of scripture, the virgin birth, the Trinity and the atonement).

Following the Revolutionary War with Great Britain, the Church of England in America was reorganized as the Episcopal Church in America. Margaret Bayard Smith, whose husband was a close friend of Jefferson, acknowledged that during the beginning of Jefferson's first term as president, he regularly attended a service on Sunday in a small humble Episcopalian church, out of respect for public worship. This was the only church in the new city of Washington D.C., other than a small Catholic chapel. Throughout his administration Jefferson permitted church services in executive branch buildings. Jefferson had no problem with this because the services *didn't discriminate and were voluntary*.

Jefferson's views on religion:

As the principal author of the United States Declaration of Independence, Jefferson included a statement about human rights that most of us hold sacrosanct. While Jefferson was not necessarily opposed to supporting people "acknowledging and adoring an overruling providence" as he expressed in his First Inaugural Address, or articulating the need for "the favor of that Being in whose hands we are, who led our fathers, as Israel of old" as he said during his second inauguration, both he and James Madison campaigned against any state sponsored support of churches in Virginia. This religious belief held by Thomas Jefferson differed significantly from orthodox religious views of this time. This being said, Jefferson was extremely interested in theology, religious studies and how they influenced and affected morality. Jefferson identified with Unitarianism and the religious philosophy of Christian Deismand like most Deists, he denied Christianity's closely held concepts of miracles and the Trinity.

Phrases such as 'Nature's God', which Jefferson used in the Declaration of Independence, are typical of Deism, although they were also used at the time by non-Deist thinkers, such as the Scottish-Irish Presbyterian philosopher Francis Hutcheson (who's moral criterion was whether or not an act tends to support the general welfare of mankind). Jefferson was influenced in part by Roman ideas about natural law after reading Cicero's views on this topic. Although Jefferson had a lifelong esteem for Jesus' moral teachings, he like others, did not believe in miracles or the divinity and the miracles of Christ. So, Jefferson was sympathetic and in agreement with many of the *moral teachings* of Christianity, his position was that the Christian religion contained, as he expressed it, "the most sublime and benevolent code of morals which has ever been offered to man."

On August 10, 1787, Jefferson wrote a lengthy letter of advice about religion and the study of religion to his nephew Peter Carr :

> "Man was destined for society. His morality therefore was to be formed to this object. He was endowed with a

sense of right & wrong merely relative to this. This sense is as much a part of his nature as the sense of hearing, seeing, feeling; it is the true foundation of morality. The moral sense, or conscience, is as much a part of man as his leg or arm. It is given to all human beings in a stronger or weaker degree, as force of members is given them in a greater or less degree. It may be strengthened by exercise, as may any particular limb of the body. This sense is submitted indeed in some degree to the guidance of reason; but it is a small stock which is required for this: even a less one than what we call common sense. State a moral case to a ploughman & a professor. The former will decide it as well, & often better than the latter, because he has not been led astray by artificial rules." *(A complete copy of the letter can be found in the appendix.)*

It annoys religious conservatives to no end when they find out that one of the most famous quotes by Thomas Jefferson might have a slightly different meaning, because the statement they're all so fond of was taken *totally out of context*. The quote I'm referring to is displayed in the Jefferson Memorial in Washington D.C. and was carved into the stone around the cornice of the rotunda and is finished in large gold painted letters. Here is the quote:

"I HAVE SWORN UPON THE ALTAR OF GOD, ETERNAL HOSTILITY AGAINST EVERY FORM OF TYRANNY OVER THE MIND OF MAN."

Those memorable words were taken from a letter written by Jefferson to Dr. Benjamin Rush in 1800, in response to the doctor's warning about the clergy in Philadelphia who were attacking Jefferson during his election for President. In his letter to Dr. Rush, Jefferson spoke about the Christian clergy who were working against his being elected President by labeling Jefferson an infidel. The quote above, *reinserted in the original text below*, clearly shows Jefferson's intended meaning was not necessarily the pious sentiment that has often been portrayed:

"I promised you a letter on Christianity, which I have not forgotten...The delusion...on the clause of the Constitution, which, while it secured the freedom of the press, covered also the freedom of religion, had given to the clergy a very favourite hope of an establishment of a particular form of Christianity through the United States; and as *every sect believes its own form the true one*, every one perhaps hoped for his own...the returning good sense of our country threatens abortion to their (the Christian clergy) hopes, and they believe that any portion of power confided to me, *will be exerted in opposition to their schemes*. And they believe *rightly;* for I have sworn upon the altar of god, eternal hostility against every form of tyranny over the mind of man. But this is all they have to fear from me: & enough too in their opinion, & this is the cause of their printing lying pamphlets against me . . ." *(Emphasis mine) (A complete copy of the letter can be found in the appendix.)*

In his letter, Jefferson explains that the "tyranny over the mind of man" that he is opposed to are *the schemes of the Christian clergy.* Although Jefferson believed in a Creator, his concept of it was that of the God of deism, or 'Nature's God' as it was used by Deists of the time. With his deep scientific interest, Jefferson organized his thoughts on religion, rejecting the superstitions and mysticism of Christianity, and going so far as to edit the gospels in the Bible, removing the miracles and mysticism of Jesus and leaving only what he saw as the correct moral philosophy of Christ, (more on this below).

Misrepresentations of history take root in the minds of many Christians whenever they see the word 'God' engraved on statues or cast in memorial concrete. Many who visit the Jefferson Memorial in Washington will read the words that are engraved in stone and, seeing the word 'God', many Christians will point to this as 'proof' of Jefferson's Christianity, without seeing that the word 'God' can have many definitions, ranging from nature to the supernatural. Many of these visitors are unwilling or unable to realize that this passage was intended to attack the tyranny of the

Christian clergy of Philadelphia, *or that Jefferson's God might not be the personal God of Christianity.*

Jefferson was also opposed to Calvinism, Trinitarianism and what he identified as Platonic elements he found in Christianity. In his private letters, Jefferson at various times in his life, referred to himself as 'Christian' (1803), 'a sect by myself' (1819), an 'Epicurean' (1819), a 'materialist' (1820), and a 'Unitarian by myself' (1825). In his later years, Jefferson refused to serve as a godparent for infants being baptized because he couldn't believe in the dogma of the Trinity. Despite the many reports of Jefferson attending church regularly, there is no record that he was ever confirmed or like Washington, that he was a communicant.

Most Founders were students of religion as well as students of the enlightenment and they studied religion *even if they doubted it.* Jefferson studied classic works by Locke and Milton and he knew the New Testament quite well and was able to read it in Greek. However, this familiarity with them did not bring whole-hearted acceptance and respect. Jefferson was suspicious of the King James Bible, especially with anything he thought was added to the theological mystery of the teachings of Jesus. While he admired Jesus the man, he did not admire how the Bible presented him. Jefferson was accused of being an atheist by Christian ministers of his day in an attempt to block his presidency. In a Letter to James Monroe, May 26, 1800, Jefferson wrote the following;

> "As to the calumny (*defamation*) of Atheism, I am so broken to calumnies of every kind, from every department of government, Executive, Legislative, and Judiciary, and from every minion of theirs holding office or seeking it, that I entirely disregard it, and from Chace it will have less effect than from any other man in the United States. It has been so impossible to contradict all their lies, that I have determined to contradict none; for while I should be engaged with one, they would publish twenty new ones." *(A complete copy of the letter can be found in the appendix.)*

During Jefferson's second presidential campaign in 1804, the New England Palladium (a semiweekly newspaper that covered the greater Boston area. It was published by Young & Minns from 1803 to 1814) wrote,

> "Should the infidel Jefferson be elected to the Presidency, the seal of death is that moment set on our holy religion, our churches will be prostrated, and some infamous 'prostitute', under the title of goddess of reason, will preside in the sanctuaries now devoted to the worship of the most High."

Federalists began attacking Jefferson as a "howling atheist" and an "infidel", maintaining that his attraction to the religious and political extremism of the French Revolution should disqualify him from holding *any* public office. It was an accusation frequently hurled at Deists, and calling someone an infidel was used to describe anyone judged to malign the Christian faith, usually the denomination the accuser belonged to. Despite public opinion, while Jefferson opposed the institutions of organized religion, he consistently expressed his belief in *a god*.

Jefferson was however, not much of a conformist about *theological doctrine* but he was a believer in Divine Providence, in the efficacy of prayer, in a future state of rewards and punishments and in the meeting of friends in another world. Jefferson had long held a deep suspicion of organized religion and a negative impression of Christian clergy, believing that many had corrupted Christian beliefs from the start. In a letter to Dr. Benjamin Rush, Jefferson wrote;

> "To the corruptions of Christianity, I am indeed opposed," adding that, "I am a Christian, in the only sense in which he (the clergy) wished any one to be; sincerely attached to his doctrines, in preference to all others; ascribing to himself every human excellence, and believing he never claimed any other."

In 1814, he wrote a letter to his friend Horatio Spafford, (a business and political leader in New York), in which he said,

> "In every country and in every age, the priest has been hostile to liberty. He is always in alliance with the despot, abetting his abuses in return for protection to his own..."

Jefferson's animosity toward organized religion and religious leaders was grounded in his lifelong conviction that 'revealed' religion, such as the fundamentalist insistence that the Bible is "the first, last and Word of God" was a superstition, and by definition, was therefore incompatible with democracy. The battle between mystery and rationality was really no contest for Jefferson. He felt that his reasoned version of religious truth would eventually win out. Still, Jefferson understood the civil uses of religion and understood the function of religion primarily to be *a moral force*.

Jefferson wrote to William Short (Jefferson's private secretary when he was ambassador in Paris, from 1786 to 1789) in October of 1819 that;

> "...the greatest of all the reformers of the depraved religion of his own country, was Jesus of Nazareth. Abstracting what is really his from the rubbish in which it is buried, easily distinguished by its lustre from the dross of his biographers, and as separable from that as the diamond from the dunghill, we have the outlines of a system of the most sublime morality which has ever fallen from the lips of man....Epictetus and Epicurus give laws for governing ourselves, Jesus a supplement of the duties and charities we owe others."

In a letter written in 1816 to his friend Wilson Cary Nicholas (who served in the U.S. Senate from 1799 to 1804 and was the 19th Governor of Virginia from 1814 to 1816), Jefferson made the following point;

> "On the dogmas of religion, as distinguished from moral principles, all mankind, from the beginning of the world

to this day, have been quarreling, fighting, burning and torturing one another, for abstractions unintelligible to themselves and to all others, and absolutely beyond the comprehension of the human mind."

In Jefferson's Letter to Timothy Pickering, (the third U. S. Secretary of State) written on February 27, 1821, he made the following observation;

> "The religion-builders have so distorted and deformed the doctrines of Jesus, so muffled them in mysticisms, fancies and falsehoods, have caricatured them into forms so monstrous and inconceivable, as to shock reasonable thinkers, to revolt them against the whole, and drive them rashly to pronounce its Founder an imposter. Had there never been a commentator, *there never would have been an infidel." (Emphasis Mine) (A full copy of this letter can be found in the appendix.)*

Jefferson also railed against what he saw as society's carefree liberalism in the name of individual freedom. He felt that any government control, not just of religion but of individual methods of commerce, constituted tyranny. Jefferson believed that civil rights should not depend on our religious opinions any more than they should depend on our opinions about geometry or physics.

In a letter to John Adams, written on May 5, 1817 Jefferson and Adams exchanged ideas;

> "If by religion we are to understand sectarian dogmas, in which no two of them agree, then your exclamation on that hypothesis is just, 'that this would be the best of all possible worlds, if there were no religion in it'. But if the moral precepts, innate in man, and made a part of his physical constitution, as necessary for a social being, if the sublime doctrines of philanthropism and Deismtaught us by Jesus of Nazareth, in which all agree, constitute true religion, then, without it, this would be, as you again say, 'something not fit to be named even, indeed, a hell.'"

In a letter Jefferson wrote to William Canby, (a Quaker who opposed war, slavery and the slave trade. During Jefferson's presidency, Canby implored him on several occasions to earn salvation by deepening his Christian faith) written on September 18, 1813, Jefferson explained;

> "Of all the systems of morality, ancient or modern, which have come under my observation, none appear to me so pure as that of Jesus. He who follows this steadily need not, I think, be uneasy, although he cannot comprehend the subtleties and mysteries erected on his doctrines by those who, calling themselves his special followers and favorites, would make him come into the world to lay snares for all understanding but theirs."

In April of 1820, Jefferson shared some thoughts about Jesus to William Short (Jefferson's secretary who later worked as a career diplomat);

> "It is the innocence of his character, the purity and sublimity of his moral precepts, the eloquence of his inculcation, the beauty of his apologues in which he conveys them, that I so much admire....Among the sayings and discourses imputed to him by his biographers, I find many passages of fine imagination, correct morality, and of the most lovely benevolence."

Jefferson wrote to his friend Samuel Kercheval, (Virginia lawyer and author) on January 19, 1810:

> "Nothing can be more exactly and seriously true, that but a short time elapsed after the death of the great Reformer of the Jewish religion, before his principles were departed from by those who professed to be his special servants, and perverted into an engine for enslaving mankind, aggrandizing their oppressors in Church and State; that the purest system of morals ever before preached to man has been adulterated and sophisticated, by artificial constructions, into a mere contrivance to filch wealth and power to themselves; that

rational men not being able to swallow their impious heresies, in order to force them down their throats they raise the hue and cry of infidelity, while themselves are the greatest obstacles to the advancement of the real doctrines of Jesus, and do in fact constitute the real Anti-Christ."

Thomas Jefferson clearly did not believe that Jesus was God, and he said so in a letter to William Short, dated August 4, 1820;

"The office of reformer of the superstitions of a nation is ever dangerous. Jesus had to walk on the perilous confines of reason and religion; and a step to right or left might place Him within the grasp of the priests of the superstition, a bloodthirsty race, as cruel and remorseless as the Being whom they represented as the family God of Abraham, of Isaac and of Jacob, and the local God of Israel. They were constantly laying snares, too, to entangle Him in the web of the law. He was justifiable, therefore, in avoiding these by evasions, by sophisms, by misconstructions and misapplications of scraps of the prophets, and in defending Himself with these their own weapons, as sufficient, ad homines, at least. That Jesus did not mean to impose Himself on mankind as the Son of God, physically speaking, I have been convinced by the writings of men more learned than myself in the lore."

However, in 1823 Jefferson wrote to John Adams, Jefferson saw himself as a defender of Jesus, the man;

"...that the greatest enemies to the doctrines of Jesus are those calling themselves the expositors of them, who have perverted them for the structure of a system of fancy absolutely incomprehensible, and without any foundation in his genuine words. And the day will come when the mystical generation of Jesus, by the supreme being as his father in the womb of a virgin will be classed with the fable of the generation of Minerva in the brain of Jupiter. But we may hope that the dawn of reason and freedom of thought in these United States will do away with all this artificial scaffolding, and restore to us the primitive and genuine doctrines of this the most venerated reformer of human errors."

Jefferson concluded with a reference to meeting Adams in heaven:

"May we meet there again, in Congress, with our ancient Colleagues, and receive with them the seal of approbation 'Well done, good and faithful servants.'"

Jefferson also had no tolerance for Priests. In a letter written in 1813 to Baron Alexander von Humboldt, (an explorer and fellow amateur scientist), Jefferson said;

"History, I believe, furnishes no example of a priest-ridden people maintaining a free civil government. This marks the lowest grade of ignorance, of which their political as well as religious leaders will always avail themselves for their own purpose."

Also in the letter of March 17, 1814, written to his friend Horatio Spafford, Jefferson wrote;

"… they have perverted the purest religion ever preached to man into mystery and jargon, unintelligible to all mankind, and therefore the safer engine for their purpose." *(A copy of this letter can be found in the appendix)*

During this time, Jefferson fell under another attack by religious conservatives in New England. Spafford asked Jefferson about his views on the priesthood so he could defend his friend. He wrote a response to Horatio Spafford, outlining his reaction to the attack. Jefferson omitted the following paragraph, recognizing that it bordered on inappropriate, but couldn't let it go. He sent a transcript of it to Thomas Ritchie, editor of the Richmond Enquirer with a note of explanation. (A copy of the statement that prefaces a full copy of the text can be found in the appendix.) In the letter written in 1816 to Spafford and then deleted, Jefferson wrote in part;

> "... I am not afraid of priests. They have tried upon me all their various batteries of pious whining, hypocritical canting, lying and slandering. I have contemplated their order from the Magi of the East to the Saints of the West and I have found no difference of character, but of more or less caution, in proportion to their information or ignorance on whom their interested duperies were to be played off. Their sway in New England is indeed formidable. *No mind beyond mediocrity dares there to develop itself.*" *(Emphasis Mine)*

THE JEFFERSON BIBLE

In the midst of the public scandal over his relationship with Sally Hemings, President Jefferson got the idea for and produced a document he named "A Syllabus of an Estimate of the Doctrines of Jesus, Compared with Those of Others". While he was writing the Syllabus, Jefferson conceived the idea of making his own personal, expurgated New Testament by stripping out, (as he referred to them) 'corruptions' and eliminating all references to the supernatural (the virgin birth, miracles, the resurrection and the crucifixion), leaving only as he described it, "the matter which is evidently his, and which is as easily distinguishable as diamonds in a dunghill."

In a letter to his daughter Martha, written in 1803, Mr. Jefferson wrote:

> "A promise made to a friend some years ago, but executed only lately, has placed my religious creed on paper. I have thought it just that my family, by possessing this, should be enabled to estimate the libels published against me on this, as on every other possible subject."

Jefferson completed this project in the winter of 1804 - 05 and in a letter to Benjamin Rush, he stated his intention to do this, was;

> "The result of a life of enquiry and reflection, and very different from that anti-Christian system, imputed to me by those who know nothing of my opinions."

Further correspondence indicates that Jefferson assembled 46 pages of New Testament passages in *The Philosophy of Jesus of*

Nazareth but unfortunately, that first volume has been lost to us. The work focused on the moral teachings of Christ as Jefferson saw them, organized by topic. The 1820 volume contains what Jefferson saw as the relevant teachings of Jesus and key events from the life of Jesus. His effort was literally a cut and paste job in every sense of the word; he used a jar of paste, a blank journal and what is believed to be his straight razor. The small amount of actual writing he did took the form of margin notes and editorial commentary. His effort covered the span of one month between February and March of 1804 as Jefferson reduced the Gospels to just 46 pages that he combined from copies of two King James Bibles. He himself said of his abridged gospels: "It was the work of two or three nights only in Washington after getting through the evening task of reading the letters and papers of the day."

Jefferson kept his efforts a secret and although it was not published until after his death as 'The Jefferson Bible', Jefferson himself named it *"The Philosophy of Jesus of Nazareth, extracted from the account of his life and teachings as given by Matthew, Mark, Luke and John, being an abridgment of the New Testament for the use of the Indians, unembarrassed with matters of fact or faith beyond their comprehension."*

The controversial nature of his work convinced Jefferson to conceal his effort and this was characteristic of the secrecy with which he tried to downplay his beliefs. Jefferson defended his effort in a letter to Charles Thomson (secretary of the Continental Congress through its entirety) on January 9, 1816 in which he describes his effort;

> "I, too, have made a wee-little book from the same materials, the Philosophy of Jesus; it is a paradigma of his doctrines, made by cutting the texts out of the book, and arranging them on the pages of a blank book, in a certain order of time or subject. A more beautiful or precious morsel of ethics I have never seen; it is a document in proof that I am a real Christian, that is to say, a disciple of the doctrines of Jesus, very different from the Platonists, who call me infidel and themselves Christians and preachers of the gospel, while they draw

all their characteristic dogmas from what its author never said nor saw." *(A full copy of this letter can be found in the appendix).*

Historians suspect that Thompson did not quite grasp the confidentiality of Jefferson's letter or his work and the contents of his correspondence soon became public knowledge. In an attempt to limit the damage to Jefferson, Thomson made things worse by suggesting that Jefferson had become an orthodox Christian and was writing a book on the subject. Rumors began circulating and Jefferson, who did what he could to suppress them, was angry and disgusted with the reaction to the news of his efforts.

Around 1820, with the urgings of his former secretary William Smalls, Jefferson produced a new, expanded edition of *"The Life and Morals of Jesus"* bound in red leather. Jefferson produced the 84-page volume six years before his death at the age of 83. Jefferson pored over six copies of the New Testament, in Greek, Latin, French and King James English. With his classic education from the College of William & Mary, Jefferson was able to compare the different translations. He again cut out and, using blank paper, glued passages from each of the Gospels in a four column format, French and English on one side of the pages and Greek and Latin on the opposite side, creating what may well have been the first Parallel Bible that was also an interlinear edition.

Thomas Jefferson saw himself as a religious reformer rather than a heretic because for him, reason was vital to the support of religion. Jefferson's rationality was clearly expressed in a letter he wrote John Adams in 1823:

> "The movements of the heavenly bodies, so exactly held in their course by the balance of centrifugal and centripetal forces, the structure of the earth itself, with it's distribution of lands, waters, and atmosphere, animal and vegetable bodies, examined in all their minutest particles, insects mere atoms of life, yet as perfectly organised as man or mammoth, the mineral substances, their generation and uses, it is impossible, I say for the human mind not to believe that there is, in all this,

design, cause, and effect, up to an ultimate cause, a fabricator of all things from matter and motion, their preserver and regulator while permitted to exist in their present forms, ad their regenerator into new and other forms."

In 1816, Jefferson wrote Dr. George Logan, (a medical doctor and great friend);

"The sum of all religion as expressed by it's best preacher, 'fear god and love thy neighbor' contains no mystery, needs no explanation. But this wont do. It gives no scope to makes dupes; priests could not live by it."

Thomas Jefferson died of a variety of ailments on July 4, 1826 in Charlottesville Virginia.

JAMES MADDISON

Like Thomas Jefferson, we need to look at the writing of James Madison to understand his life and religious philosophy. As I said above, he and Jefferson shared much the same views on religion and they worked together to keep the fledgling government free from religious abuses. He felt this way all his life, by way of example, late in his life, James Madison wrote a letter to Edward Livingston (appointed the 11ᵗʰ Secretary of State by President Andrew Jackson) on July 10, 1822. In that letter, he summarized his views:

> "And I have no doubt that every new example, will succeed, as every past one has done, in shewing that religion & Govt. will both exist in greater purity, *the less they are mixed together." (Emphasis mine) (A copy of this letter is included in the appendix.)*

"Little Jemmy" as he was known, grew up in the Anglican church. His father was a vestryman and every Sunday, the Madison family went to church. When he was eleven years old, James's parents sent him to a school in King and Queen County, Virginia, about seventy miles from the Madison estate. By the mid 1750s, most Christian teachers believed that the understandings of the Age of Enlightenment were compatible with Christian faith. The school's headmaster was Reverend Donald Robertson, a Scottish minister educated at Aberdeen and the University of Edinburgh, (in the heart of Scottish Calvinism) and was a well-respected scholar and teacher in the colony. At the school, Madison studied literature, French, Greek, Latin, algebra and geometry. Robertson was Madison's first and perhaps most influential teacher and Madison later said of his teacher, "all that I have been in life I owe largely to that man."

Madison decided to go to Princeton and this decision was momentous for the time, as it was an evangelical Christian school. Madison was apparently influenced by a Presbyterian revival while at Princeton and attended Episcopal churches with some regularity, but he left few expressions of his religious convictions. During his time at Princeton, Madison's attention to religion did increase, intellectually at least, and perhaps even spiritually as he had been effected by the pervasive religious awakenings at the school in 1770 and 1772.

Madison spent part of his extra year at Princeton studying Hebrew. His positive attitude toward theology really surfaced in November 1772, after William Bradford (a lawyer and judge from Philadelphia, Pennsylvania and the second United States Attorney General in 1794–1795) asked for advice on a puzzling choice between Law and Divinity. Bradford confessed that he preferred the latter but felt better qualified for the law and Madison replied that;

> "You forbid any recommendation of Divinity by suggesting that you have insuperable objections therefore I can only condole with the Church on the loss of a fine Genius and persuasive Orator."

Madison's post-graduate study of Hebrew and theology, along with some scholarly notes he took on scriptural commentaries toward the end of 1772 have survived as well as a prayer book he used when conducting family devotions. These plus the nature of his letters to Bradford, all suggest a deep religious interest, but when Madison left Princeton, the future president spent little time with theology and was even more reluctant than Jefferson to offer any theological opinions at all. When an Episcopal clergyman wrote him 1825 to solicit his views on the being and attributes of God, Madison replied that he had not thought about those matters in any depth for 50 years."

The political ideology of James Madison was rooted in his early religious training, especially under Presbyterian minister and teacher John Witherspoon at Princeton, but he avoided extremes in politics and religion, preferring to find a balance. When Madison returned to Virginia, he studied both theology and law on his own, but felt that his weak voice would prohibit his participation in both the legal profession and the ministry. In a letter from James Madison to Frederick Beasley, (fifth Provost of the University of Pennsylvania) written in 1825, Madison wrote that religious belief "is so essential to the moral order of the World and to the happiness of man, that arguments which enforce it cannot be drawn from too many sources."

While Madison didn't display much of his theological enthusiasm in his political writings, he did contribute to the selection of books for the religion section of the library at the University of Virginia. The selections were based in Augustinian and reformed theology, this based on the strict rationality that was characteristic of 18th century Calvinist schooling and Madison's writings resonate with the meticulously constructed arguments that were so familiar to the Presbyterian clerics that founded Princeton University. This can be illustrated by his statement in his work, *Memorial and Remonstrance Against Religious Assessments*, where he writes,

> "It is the duty of every man to render to the Creator such homage, and such only, *as he believes to be acceptable to him*. This duty is precedent both in order of time and degree of obligation, to the claims of Civil Society. Before any man can be considered as a member of Civil Society, he must be considered as a subject of the Governor of the Universe." *(Emphasis mine)*

It's been said that James Madison was a man of complicated religious views, and was intensely private about his theology. He stated that he had long held belief that a belief in a God who was All Powerful, wise and good is absolutely essential to the moral stability of the world, as well as the happiness of man. Madison may have been the nation's foremost advocate for separation of church and state, but his thoughts about religion during the period of his greatest political leadership is less known. During his time in governmental service, Madison never openly shared his personal beliefs, but it was known that he had an intellectual belief structure that combined faith with reason, in Madison's mind, they complemented each other for the glory of God. He had a strong interest in religion for most of his life and like so many of the co-founders of the government, Madison saw a strong benefit for the country in the idea of religious liberty.

In 1785, a political struggle began in the Virginia State Assembly over the separation of church and state and its impact on the idea of religious liberty. On one side stood Patrick Henry, an impassioned proponent of individual liberty who ironically thought it permissible for the state to establish (the word used then was 'sponsor') a religious ideology. On the other side of this issue stood James Madison, a proponent of Federalism, an idea many felt eroded some personal liberties, who nonetheless thought religious liberty a natural right.

James Madison wrote his document entitled, '*To the Honorable the General Assembly of the Commonwealth of Virginia, A Memorial and Remonstrance*', in response to Patrick Henry's Assessment Bill, a bill that would authorize taxes to be collected and used for the hiring of religious teachers and state support for churches (*touched on above*).

While Henry's original draft singled out a specific religious sect for preferential treatment, subsequent drafts expanded the wording of the bill to include all Christian sects. In its final form, the bill would allow each taxpayer to designate which church should receive his tax payment. In the absence of any indication, the legislature would apply it to the somewhat nebulously defined "pious uses." Henry was convinced that his measure was desperately necessary to forestall what he saw as the looming deterioration of civility, morality and piety in Virginia. His feelings were so strong about this that during the debate on the bill, he delivered a very eloquent speech describing the bleak future for the country if the measure failed. As mentioned above, there are no copies of this address, but notes taken by others in the Virginia

Assembly state that Henry delivered an impassioned speech in favor of the bill. *(A copy of Patrick Henry's bill can be found in the appendix).*

Here is a rather scathing segment from Memorial and Remonstrance that Madison used to rebut the rationale for Patrick Henry's bill;

> "What influence, in fact, have ecclesiastical establishments had on society? In some instances they have been seen to erect a spiritual tyranny on the ruins of the civil authority; on many instances they have been seen upholding the thrones of political tyranny; in no instance have they been the guardians of the liberties of the people. Rulers who wish to subvert the public liberty may have found an established clergy convenient auxiliaries. A just government, instituted to secure and perpetuate it, *needs them not."(Emphasis mine)*

Madison continues in Paragraph seven;

> "Because experience witnesseth that ecclesiastical establishments, instead of maintaining the purity and efficacy of religion, have had a contrary operation. During almost fifteen centuries has the legal establishment of Christianity been on trial. What has been its fruits? More or less, in all places, pride and indolence in the clergy; ignorance and servility in the laity; in both, superstition, bigotry and persecution."

Yes, James Madison was a 'religious' man, but he worked tirelessly to keep separate, the melding of religion and government. Much of Madison's influence has been displayed in his interactions with other founders, and Madison's Memorial and Remonstrance is still seen as a cornerstone of the idea of separation of church and state.

James Madison died at Montpelier on June 28, and was the last of the Founding Fathers. He was buried in the Madison Family Cemetery at Montpelier, Virginia.

ALEXANDER HAMILTON

Alexander Hamilton was born on January 11, 1755 but he later claimed to have been born in 1757 on the island of Nevis in the Dutch West Indies. His mother, a Frenchwoman named Rachel Fawcett, was married to a French physician named John Michael Lavine. When the marriage failed, Rachel began an adulterous affair with a Scottish trader named James Hamilton and when Rachel's husband learned of his wife's infidelity, he publicly denounced her. The shame and disgrace from his out of wedlock birth was a stigma would follow Hamilton all his life, even with all his tremendous accomplishments. Whether in the West Indies or in New York, family heritage and bloodlines drew a great deal of attention during the 18th century.

Rachel Fawcett moved in with Hamilton's father in 1751, and after living together for about two years, James and Rachel had a son James Jr. and three years after that, she gave birth to Alexander. James was named after his father and Alexander was named after his paternal grandfather. Although James and Rachel were together for 15 years, this living arrangement didn't last and James Hamilton Sr. stated that he abandoned Rachel and their sons to spare Rachel a charge of bigamy after finding out that her first husband intended to divorce her under Danish law on grounds of adultery and desertion. Rachel and her children were left destitute when Hamilton was still a child.

Three years later, Hamilton's mother died at the age of 38. In probate court, John Lavine exerted his legal right at the time and seized Rachel's estate. He was awarded what few valuables Rachel had possessed, including a small amount of household silver. Most of the items were auctioned off and disposed of, but a friend secretly purchased the family's books and returned them to Hamilton. His lifelong disaffection with established religion may have been further solidified when the church decided that a Christian burial was inappropriate for a 'stained woman' such as Rachel but despite all this, Hamilton considered himself religious.

As the illegitimate son of Rachel Fawcett Lavine and James Hamilton, Alexander and his brother were not welcomed by the established church of colonial British West Indies and because Hamilton's parents were not legally married, the Church of England denied Alexander membership and education in the church school. Hamilton received individual tutoring and classes in a private school led by a Jewish headmistress and it's believed that this is where the stories that Hamilton was somehow Jewish got their start. Hamilton supplemented his education with a family library of 34 books.

Among the male adults who befriended the now orphaned boy was Reverend Dr. Hugh Knox, a Presbyterian minister. Reverend Knox encouraged Hamilton's budding literary skills, which often included religious poems and hymns. As an orphan, young Hamilton found himself subject to the charity of the island gentry, and as it happened, he was placed in the trading house of Nicholas Cruger, (one of the most prosperous merchants on the island of St. Croix) as an apprentice clerk in 1769. Cruger's store was in Christianstadt and was the centre of the Islands trade. It was during this time that Hamilton developed his skill at record-keeping, buying and selling, all activities known to successful merchants of the time, although some feel that it may have been Hamilton's Calvinist influence on his mother's side the prepared him for economic life as a model apprentice clerk in his early years, as well as the founder of American capitalism in the years after the Revolution.

Just as Dr. Hugh Knox had been so helpful to his mother, the reverend provided Hamilton with an education in Latin, French and mathematics and by 1772, Knox had made arrangements for Hamilton to take up his studies on the mainland. His first choice was Princeton, perhaps because this is the institution Dr. Knox had graduated from. However, the admissions committee would not accept Hamilton's proposal for an accelerated program of study, so the West Indian, having misrepresented his age, entered Kings College (now Columbia University) in New York City. Hamilton quickly demonstrated that he was serious about his education and was impatient to make his way in the world.

Hamilton confided to a close friend in a letter written to his boyhood friend Edward Stevens at the age of fourteen on Nov. 11, 1769, where he stated;

> "...my ambition is prevalent, so that I condemn the groveling condition of a clerk or the like...and would willingly risk my life, though not my character, to exalt my station."

Hamilton felt that all that was needed to accomplish this was an overpowering cause, one that was noble and would allow him to exploit it to the fullest. He would often dream about experiencing the glory he'd read about in the works of Julius Caesar and Plutarch (Plutarch was a first century biographer and author whose works strongly influenced the evolution of the essay, the biography and historical writing in Europe from the 16th to the 19th century), during his studies as an orphan boy in St. Croix and as history would have it, there was for Hamilton, a perfect storm brewing in the mainland colonies. In May of 1773 Parliament enacted the Tea Act, threatening to give the British East India Company a monopoly on the colonial market. This was one of several laws passed since 1763 that many colonial spokesmen held to be illegal and Hamilton quickly agreed with this position.

Dr. Knox and other opponents of Parliaments had already explained to Hamilton how all Englishmen were being deprived of their historic rights by the Lord Norths and their arrogant schemes, but while he was a student at Kings College, the Boston Tea Party of December 1773 led Hamilton to become personally involved in the crisis when he wrote his Defence of the Destruction of the Tea and published it in Holts Journal. His work attracted the attention of many New York patriots over the next few months. Hamilton contributed other articles and pamphlets and this lead him to give public speeches on Parliamentary oppression. He became determined to take an even more active role in the controversy with the mother country.

Emotions in the mainland colonies festered with just such a cause when in May of 1773, the British Parliament enacted the Tea Act, threatening to give the British East India Company a monopoly on the colonial market. As we saw above, this was only one of a long list of laws, passed since 1763, all of which colonial spokesmen held to be unlawful and it was these resolutions that caused Hamilton to defend the Continental Congress that was meeting in Philadelphia. While in Philadelphia, he wrote another pamphlet, this to attack the liberal Quebec Bill of 1774, which recognized the Roman Catholic Church in Canada, labelling it a ministerial conspiracy out to destroy the Protestantism of the colonist by establishing popery among their neighbours to the north.

His Remarks on the Quebec Bill reflected the thinking of the Continental Congress itself as the 18 year old Hamilton exposed not only the Whig sentiments of his West Indian tutor, Dr. Knox, but included his own personal prejudices as well. The irony was that, the man making this line of argument with such an emotional outburst, the self-same personage who would eventually become the new nation's most vocal spokesman for a centralized, Federal power, had managed to bring about the opposite outcome when the French Canadians, who were offended at this kind of treatment. They would have nothing to do with what they perceived as *anti-papist bigotry* and chose to remain loyal to Britain

While Hamilton had found his noble cause, namely *the cause of liberty*, and his pamphlets and speeches were serving it well by successfully keeping the Parliamentary tyranny before the public eye, he still felt that intense, burning desire for military glory, the need to find the Caesar-like battlefield successes that would rescue him from his obscure and humble beginnings. In his youth, Hamilton had also confided to his friend Edward Stevens in St. Croix that he "...wanted to prepare the way for futurity... *I wish there was a war.*"

In March of 1776, after the blood-letting at Lexington and Concord, he got his wish. Hamilton used his connections among the New York Sons of Liberty to obtain the rank of captain of artillery in the local militia. This turned out to be the perfect political appointment because he'd studied artillery and ballistics on his own, much like his childhood mentor, Henry Knox. This allowed Hamilton to serve the Revolutionary cause with distinction when the opportunity to prove his skills as a military leader quickly presented itself. When the army retreated across to New Jersey later that year, Captain Hamilton was assigned to Washington's rear-guard on the banks of the Raritan River. He handled his battery with great skill and gallantry, allowing the main body to withdraw safely to Princeton. General Washington was impressed, although in the end it was Hamilton's other talents, namely his gift for writing and sharp intellect which led the commander-in-chief on March 1, 1777 to make the young captain his aide-de-camp and promote him to lieutenant-colonel. So, at age 20, Hamilton's meteoric rise to power had begun, and these events fuelled the temptation of some writers and historians to suggest that Hamilton was actually the general's natural son, even though he was born while Washington was in the Barbados, and we know that Washington was unable to father children. But with all this, these rumours still surface from time to time.

As secretary and aide to Washington, Hamilton became the secretary of war as well as commanding general of the army and soon became privy to the inner workings of the Articles of Confederation and the military system. He set about eliminating their shortcomings with a series of constructive reforms and even at this early date, Hamilton made one of the first calls for a constitutional convention to centralize power in Congress. He further urged the creation and establishment of a national bank in a letter to Robert Morris, the new nation's superintendent of finance.

It was of course, Colonel Hamilton who was acting openly as Washington's trusted adviser, rather than just his aide-de-camp that allowed him to write to the older leaders of the Revolutionary cause and propagate his precious theories. There has been speculation that Hamilton began to manipulate Washington who was more than twice Hamilton's age and who may have developed a somewhat fatherly attachment to the brilliant young officer. His manipulative skill and his willingness to use people as a means to reach what he regarded as a higher cause, describes Hamilton best in these politically active middle years and prompted John Adams to one day comment on Hamilton's rise from humble beginnings by describing the him as "the bastard brat of a Scottish peddler."

The following quote is from The Federalist Papers, drafted in 1787 by Alexander Hamilton, James Madison, and John Jay who were all writing under the pseudonym, "Publius."

> "After full experience of the insufficiency of the existing federal government, you are invited to deliberate upon a New Constitution for the United States of America....It has been frequently remarked, that it seems to have been reserved to the people of this country to decide, by their conduct and example, the important question, whether societies of men are really capable or not, of establishing good government from reflection and choice, or whether they are forever destine to depend, for heir political constitutions, on accident and force.

> This idea, by adding the inducements of philanthropy to those of patriotism, will heighten the solicitude which all considerate and good men must feel for the even. Happy will it be if our choice should be directed by a judicious estimate of our true interests, uninfluenced by considerations foreign to the public good. But this is more ardently to be wished for, than seriously to be expected. The plan offered to our deliberations, affects too many particular interests, innovated upon too many local institutions, not to involve in its discussion a variety of objects extraneous to its merits, and of views, passions and prejudices little favorable to the discovery of truth. For, in politics as in religion, it is equally absurd to aim at making proselytes by fire and sword. Heresies in either can rarely be cured by persecution."

Alexander Hamilton, collaborator in the drafting of The Federalists Papers with fellow New Yorker John Jay, still vacillated on his religious devotion. Hamilton's West Indian mother Rachel was by all accounts buried at St. John's Anglican Church, and this may help explain a curious, persistent ambivalence that Hamilton always felt about regular church attendance, despite a stated religious leaning. Hamilton himself had been relatively religious as a youth, Robert Troup, Hamilton's college roommate, testified to his youthful piety, saying at one point, "In addition to church attendance, Alexander prayed on his knees morning and night, apparently aloud, for Troup said that he was affected by the young man's 'fervour and eloquence.'"

During the Revolutionary era, Hamilton had shed his youthful religious inclinations and became a conventional liberal with Deistic inclinations and was an irregular churchgoer at best. Some even told stories about his joking references to religion. After the Constitutional Convention in 1787, Hamilton was asked why God had not been mentioned in the Constitution, he quipped, "*We forgot.*" In 1788, Hamilton convinced New Yorkers to agree to ratify the U.S Constitution and he went on to serve as the nation's first secretary of the treasury from 1789 to 1795.

Hamilton's religious observation decreased markedly as he approached middle age. Like most of his generation, Hamilton believed that he was fully competent to interpret the intentions of the Almighty. Conceiving the universe to be essentially mechanistic, governed by laws which the human intelligence could discover and comprehend, it seemed to Hamilton that human affairs were likewise controlled by laws that could be reduced to a few simple principles. Hamilton wrote out the prerequisites for his ideal wife in 1779, saying, "As to religion, a moderate streak will satisfy me. She must believe in God and hate a saint."

Hamilton's wife, Elizabeth Schuyler Hamilton, sometimes called Betsey or Eliza, believed in God and was considerably more dedicated to religious observance than her less-than-saintly husband. It's been written that Betsey was troubled by her husband's lack of religious faith. He had been more than agreeable when his wife Betsey insisted on having their first three children christened at Trinity Church in New York. But Hamilton rarely accompanied his wife and children to services on Sunday and when he did go, he, like Washington, never partook of communion.

If there was a dark side to his career in public office, it may be that Hamilton had a three-year affair with Maria Reynolds while he was Secretary of the Treasury and wound up paying her husband James blackmail money to maintain secrecy, and this may have prompted some soul-searching on Hamilton's part. The fallout from this affair would follow him for the rest of his political life, prompting occasional comments such as; 'like father, like son.'

It was during the 1790s Hamilton began recovering his earlier interest in religion, partially in reaction to what he perceived to be the atheism of the French revolutionaries and their supporters in America. As he approached the end of his life, Hamilton's religious faith strengthened. Hamilton, who earlier had seemed to abandon his piety for a more casual attitude to religion, had become intensely reverent. He had never found the opportunity to implement his plans for a national organization of Christians that would elect like-minded men to political office, establish schools or to circulate Christian-oriented publications commented on current events. Even before Hamilton left Washington's cabinet, where he had been so influential, his life was on a downward course and he was almost smothered by depression.

Political frustration was not the only cause, financial problems and his wife's lingering illness were strong contributing factors and through all these struggles, religion did little to relieve or comfort him. Hamilton's piety seemed further to increase on his death bed in July 1804. In a letter to his wife shortly before his duel with Vice President Aaron Burr, Hamilton concluded, "The consolations of religion, my beloved, can alone support you; and those you have a right to enjoy. Fly to the bosom of your God and be comforted. With my last idea I shall cherish the sweet hope of meeting you in a better world."

Hamilton himself was denied any consolation with the church's sacraments. New York Bishop Benjamin Moore refused to give Hamilton communion because the former Treasury secretary had never become member of the Episcopal church. A Presbyterian minister came to see Hamilton but refused to offer communion on the grounds that it was a public rather than a private sacrament. Hamilton apparently wished to take communion in order to assure his wife of his state of grace. He repeatedly told his distraught wife, "Remember, my Eliza, you are a Christian." Hamilton died in New York City of a gunshot wound that he sustained during a duel with Aaron Burr on July 12, 1804.

ANDREW JACKSON

Andrew Jackson was born on March 15, 1767. His parents, Andrew and Elizabeth, along with his two older brothers, Hugh and Robert, emigrated from Ireland two years earlier. Jackson was named after his father, but his father died shortly before he was born and young Jackson was brought up by his widowed mother in the Waxhaws settlement located near the border of North Carolina and South Carolina in what is now Pineville in North Carolina. Jackson grew up with a large extended family of Scots-Irish immigrant farmers and while his mother had hopes of him becoming a Presbyterian minister, Jackson quickly dashed those hopes with his propensity for pranks, constant fighting and cursing.

Jackson was raised a strict Presbyterian. Historians who have studied him emphasize that he was not very religious as a young man, but became more so in his later years. As a southerner, Jackson found no conflict between his religious views and his firm support for the institution of slavery, nor did he perceive any conflict with his religion and his support for the forcible relocation of Native Americans. But he also strongly supported the idea of a Constitutional requirement of a strict separation of church and state like so many of his peers. This support was again based on the observed conditions in England and European countries at the time.

In a letter to Ellen Hanson that he wrote on the 25th of March, 1835, Jackson said,

> "The alliance between church and state and the vast power they have again acquired (in England), with the national debt and pauperism which they have

produced, shows that corrupt influence is as potent in suppressing the rights of human nature and rendering the great majority of the people as miserable as the most unlimited sovereignty concerted in a single individual."

He did occasionally speak of his religious upbringing, as is shown in his letter to Ellen Hanson;

> "I was brought up a rigid Presbeterian, to which I have always adhered. Our excellent constitution guarantees to every one freedom of religion, and charity tells us, and you know Charity is the reall basis of all true religion, and charity says judge the tree by its fruit. All who profess christianity, believe in a Saviour and that by and through him we must be saved. We ought therefor to consider all good christians, whose walk corresponds with their professions, be him Presbeterian, Episcopalian, Baptist, methodist or Roman catholic. let it be remembered by your Grandmother that no established religion can exist under our glorious constitution."

Despite his stated faithfulness, Jackson was a staunch defender of the separation of church and state and had no problem lambasting his fellow politicians whose religion shaped their political direction. In short, Jackson preached religious tolerance to them as long as they embraced some form of Christianity.

The Revolutionary War began when Jackson was 13 years old and the fighting was very fierce and bloody in the rural, poor country where they lived, so at 13 years of age, young Jackson joined a regiment. Captured by the British, he was slashed on the side of his head by a British Officer when he refused to polish an officer's boots. Both he and his brother were imprisoned, and during their confinement, they contracted smallpox. Jackson's mother managed to get the boys released but Jackson's brother died on the long trip home.

Shortly after the Revolutionary War, Jackson received a modest inheritance from a grandfather who lived in Ireland. When this money ran out, Jackson finished school and, although he disliked studying, he took a position as a schoolteacher for a short period. Tall and lanky with red hair and piercing blue eyes, Jackson was known for his fiery temper, bold out-going personality and his spirit. When he turned seventeen in 1784, Jackson made the decision to become an attorney. He moved to Salisbury, North Carolina, where he took a position as a clerk for a lawyer in return for access to his books (the usual 'course of study' during this time. In his first independent days, living in a tavern with other students, he had quite a reputation for frequent wild behavior and hooliganism.

After three years, Jackson received his license to practice law in several counties scattered throughout rural North Carolina. To supplement his income he also worked in small-town general stores. While living in North Carolina, Jackson continued his reputation for being charismatic, wild and ambitious. He loved to dance, entertain, gamble and since he lived in a boarding room above one, he spent his free time in the tavern with friends.

Jackson practiced law with extraordinary energy for the next seven years and during this time, he married Rachel Donelson Robards, the estranged wife of an abusive husband. Jackson at one point, threatened the husband's life for implying he (Jackson) was dishonoring his wife. Later, Robards went to Kentucky, still believing that she had divorced her first husband. She and Jackson were married for two years before learning that their marriage was in fact, invalid. They discovered the truth when Rachel's divorce was finally granted and they were quickly married a second time. One would hope that a shrewd lawyer like Jackson should not have believed in a divorce on the grounds of hearsay, so we can only speculate that Jackson perhaps did not want to know the truth. Despite all this, Jackson married into a very prominent family and he and his wife appeared to be very much in love during their life together.

Like so many of our country's early presidents, Andrew Jackson became a Mason, and is listed in the rolls of the St. Tammany Lodge No. 1, Nashville, Tennessee in 1800. This was the first Lodge in Tennessee, organized in 1789, under a Dispensation from the Grand Lodge of North Carolina. His association with the organization would haunt him in later years, especially during the election of 1832, with the establishment of a third party, the Anti-Masons. (The Anti-Masonic Party was a single issue party, formed in upstate New York in 1828 by opponents of Freemasonry, believing that it was a corrupt and elitist secret society that was attempting to rule much of the country in defiance of republican principles.)

It should be noted here that Freemasonry is not a religion, nor is it a substitute for religion. It requires of its members to believe in God as part of the obligation of every responsible adult, but advocates no sectarian faith or practice. Masonic ceremonies include both traditional and spontaneous prayer to reaffirm each individual's dependence on God and to seek divine guidance. Freemasonry is open to men of any faith, and religion is not discussed at Masonic meetings. Masons hold that there is one God and that people employ many different ways to seek, and to express what they know of God. Masonry uses the designation, 'Grand Architect of the Universe,' and other non-sectarian titles to address the Deity. By doing so, followers of different faiths join together in prayer, concentrating on God, rather than differences among themselves. Masonry holds the idea of religious freedom and the relationship between the individual and God is personal, private, and sacred. An open volume of the Sacred Law, 'the rule and guide of life,' is an essential part of every Masonic meeting. The Volume of the Sacred Law in the Judeo/Christian tradition is the Bible; to Freemasons of other faiths, it is the book held holy by them (*Freemasonry played a large part in many of the lives of the Founding Fathers and for those who wish to more, information on the Freemasons can be found at http://www.freemasons-freemasonry.com.*)

Today, while most Christian denominations take no stance on Freemasonry, there are a few that outwardly oppose it and either discourage or outright prohibit their members from joining the fraternity. The largest of these are the Roman Catholic Church and the Eastern Orthodox Church. The Southern Baptist Convention is understood to prohibit Freemasonry, but actually leaves it up to the person's individual conscience. Some of the persistent Roman

Catholic criticisms of Freemasonry is that it advocates a Deist or naturalist view of creation, and that it fails to promote one faith superior to any others, (a belief strongly held by Roman Catholics) while at the same time it also uses rituals that have a religious form and substance that appear to encourage an indifference to religion.

Jackson was elected the General of the Tennessee Militia in 1802. When the war of 1812 began, troops were needed on the southern and western frontiers and the War Department sent Jackson and the Tennessee Militia. During the War, General Jackson led his troops through enemy territory to victory in several tide-turning battles. In doing so, he greatly aided the nation's victory in the war. This led to the addition of millions of acres in the present-day southern United States, including Florida. Just as significant, his victories kindled a spirit of patriotism and pride across the nation at a time when it was desperately needed.

As a general, Jackson made quick, decisive steps, taking personal control of the War of 1812, even when his troops were the underdogs. Jackson and his small army defended New Orleans against a full frontal attack by the British and forced them to withdraw from Louisiana. His unanticipated victory created an enormous sense of pride in America as a nation, as the country began to understand its true potential. This also served to make Andrew Jackson a true American hero, who was seen as a 'common man'.

In 1834, several disparate political elements representing various interests blended to form the Whig Party (the Whigs supported the supremacy of Congress over the Presidency and favored a program of modernization, banking and economic protectionism to stimulate manufacturing). Whatever divided them was not nearly as important as that which united them, specifically their opposition to Andrew Jackson as President. They depicted him as "King Andrew", a dangerous man on horseback with an insatiable appetite for power. While much of the hostility between Jackson and the Whigs centered on key political issues, other factors played a part. For example, as we saw above, the Protestant religious revival movement had injected a moralizing component in the Whig ranks. Many Whigs were seeking to promote social change through activist government and often blended evangelical religion with politics. The Whig Party (which by now included parts of the former anti-freemasons party) proved especially amiable to social and religious reformers who sought to use the power of government to reshape society.

The Democratic Party, on the other hand, denounced the infringement of religious and moral crusades such as temperance into politics, believing these belonged in the private sphere. This tension is shown in a letter by Andrew Jackson to the Secretary of the Navy, Mahlon Dickerson, concerning the travails of one John O. Bradford. In this January 1838 letter, the former President makes his case for Mr. Bradford;

> Hermitage, Ten, 10th January, 1838

> My Dr Sir

> This will be handed you by my friend Mr. J. O. Bradford who is a young Gentleman of good Education and of high moral worth. He was pursuing a course of studies to fit himself for the Ministry of the Episcopalian order, and to enable him to proceed he became Editor of the Nashville Union for a short space of time. This so displeased a few of the Whig Elders, and Deacons (of the church) that they, for his becoming Editor, dropped him as a candidate for orders in their Church--some of whom are believed now never to have had three grains of religion.

> Mr. Bradford is therefore again turned upon the broad World to seek a support with nothing but his moral and private worth of character. He formerly, for a few years, followed a seafaring life in the merchant service, and would be pleased to get employment in our Navy, such as a Purser. Mr. B. has capacity enough to fill any subordinate office in any of the Departments. Col. Polk is well acquainted with his character to whom I refer you, and hope it may be in the power of the government to

give him employment. He has been shamefully treated by his brethren of the Church.

I am very respectfully yours

Andrew Jackson

John Bradford served as the newspaper editor for the *Nashville Union* for five months in 1836 as the newspaper was launched the previous year to essentially serve as a mouthpiece for Andrew Jackson and the Democratic Party. James Polk, a close ally of Jackson, was instrumental in launching the newspaper and had hired Bradford. By taking a job with the pro-Jackson publication, Bradford apparently committed an unpardonable offense in the eyes of the Whig Elders of the Episcopalian Church, who felt that his actions disqualified him from any further religious endeavors.

Jackson suggests Dickerson take Bradford's plight up with "*Col. Polk*", Speaker of the House of Representatives. Curiously, Jackson always referred to Polk's military rank in letters, even though Polk never saw one minute of action. Jackson still considered it a mark of status that he served in the military. In the letter, Jackson suggests that Bradford might be suited for a position as purser in the Navy and evidently, he still possessed the political clout to influence events. The recommendation was a provident one. Bradford received this appointment and went on to become Commodore John O. Bradford, Paymaster-General of the United States Navy.

As further evidence that religion was a large part of Jackson's personal life, as can be seen here in a letter to his wife, Rachel, on 21 December 1823. The tone is typical of his letters to his wife;

"I trust that the god of Isaac and of Jacob will protect you, and give you health in my abscence, in him alone we ought to trust, he alone can preserve, and guide us through this troublesome world, and I am sure he will hear your prayers. We are told that the prayers of the righteous prevaileth much, and I add mine for your health and preservation until we meet again."

And then there is this section from Andrew Jackson's letter to the Synod of the Reformed Church of North America, 12 June 1832, where he explains his refusal of their request that he proclaim a day of fasting, humiliation, and prayer;

> "While I concur with the Synod in the efficacy of prayer, and in the hope that our country may be preserved from the attacks of pestilence 'and that the judgments now abroad in the earth may be sanctified to the nations,' I am constrained to decline the designation of any period or mode as proper for the public manifestation of this reliance. I could not do otherwise without transcending the limits prescribed by the Constitution for the President and without feeling that I might in some degree disturb the security which religion nowadays enjoys in this country *in its complete separation from the political concerns of the General Government." (Emphasis mine)*

Andrew Jackson made this statement during his final illness on June 1, 1845

> "When I have Suffered sufficiently, the Lord will then take me to himself-but what are all my sufferings compared to those of the blessed Saviour, who died upon that cursed tree for me, mine are nothing."

And his final words, uttered on his deathbed were:

> "What is the matter with my dear children, have I alarmed you? Oh, do not cry — be good children and we will all meet in heaven."

Andrew Jackson died on June 8, 1845 in Nashville, Tennessee.

BENJAMIN FRANKLIN

Benjamin Franklin was born in Boston and was raised in a devout Puritan home. His father, Josiah, was a member of Boston's Old South Church and he raised his son on the teachings of traditional New England Calvinism, beginning with the idea that *God was sovereign*. If we are to understand Franklin's view of life, we should look at these Puritan religious influences surrounding him during his childhood, because as we've seen, this was a very strong influence during this time in the history of our country.

As a child, Franklin was taught that human beings were separated from God because of their sin. However, God, through his divine mercy, offered salvation to humankind through the death and resurrection of his only son, Jesus Christ. Furthermore, men and women were required to perform good works in the world, and any attempt in doing them without the aid of the Holy Spirit would be useless in the eyes of God.

Franklin's curiosity about the world as a whole frequently led him back to its Creator and the people He placed in it, along with whatever physical rules might have been prescribed, such as the behavior of water and air and the motion of the planets. As a young man, Franklin contemplated many subjects and changed his mind several times and finally arrived at the conclusion that he didn't want to waste any further time about it. His deductions gave direction to everything he did and what he thought he ought to do. Franklin was first and foremost, a practical man.

At the age of fifteen, Franklin read a series of lectures, published by the estate of British chemist Robert Boyle. The lectures were intended to counter the influence of Deism in English religious life. Boyle considered his scientific experiments, like all his other endeavors, part of his Christian service, believing that the orderliness of the universe reflected God's purposeful design. As Franklin understood it, Deism was the belief that God created the world and allowed it to operate according to natural laws. Deists believed God did not intervene in the lives of his human creation. He did not perform miracles, answer prayer, or sustain the world by his providence. Religious belief was based on reason rather than divine revelation, an idea with roots in ideas from the Period of Enlightenment.

In his Autobiography, Franklin later wrote about this experience;

> "My parents had early given me religious impressions, and brought me through my childhood piously in the Dissenting way. But I was scarce fifteen, when, after doubting by turns of several points, as I found them disputed in the different books I read, I began to doubt of Revelation itself. Some books against Deism fell into my hands; they were said to be the substance of sermons preached at Boyle's Lectures. It happened that they wrought an effect on me quite contrary to what was intended by them; for the arguments of the Deists, which were quoted to be refuted, appeared to me much stronger than the refutations; in short, I soon became a thorough Deist. My arguments perverted some others, particularly Collins and Ralph; but, each of them having afterwards wrong'd me greatly without the least compunction, and recollecting Keith's conduct towards me (who was another freethinker), and my own towards Vernon and Miss Read, which at times gave me great trouble, I began to suspect that this doctrine, tho' it might be true, was not very useful."

Although he claimed that he had become a 'thorough Deist,' Franklin's early commitments to the idea were short lived, and his flirtation with this world view could be thought of as little more than youthful rebellion against the Calvinism of his Puritan upbringing. While he never returned to the Calvinism of his youth, the religion of his parents shaped much of his adult thinking.

Franklin believed in a Creator-God who not only possessed great wisdom, goodness and power and who created the world, but also sustained it.

For example, Franklin was amazed at how God created the stars and the planets, then continued:

> "...to govern them in their greatest Velocity as they shall not flie off out of their appointed Bounds, nor dash one against another to their mutual Destruction."

In short, Franklin had little tolerance for theological squabbles often associated with organized Christianity, realizing that debates over the meaning of Christian orthodoxy usually prevented members of the clergy from preaching the true spirit of Christianity (as he saw it), namely, loving one's neighbor.

Franklin put his faith in an active God who watched over His natural creation and was ready, when it was deemed it necessary, to intervene in the lives of His human creation as well. 36 years after he claimed to embrace Deism, Franklin's tone had begun to sound nothing like an adherent to this religious system;

> "Without the Belief of a Providence that takes Cognizance of, guards and guides, and may favour particular Persons, there is no Motive to Worship a Deity, to fear its Displeasure, or to pray for its Protection."

But he also believed that this God was also one who answered prayer. Franklin wrote prayers for his own personal use and took time to rewrite the Lord's Prayer (see below) so that it was more suitable to contemporary readers. Somewhat surprisingly, in July 1787, during the meeting of the Constitutional Convention in Philadelphia, Franklin called for prayer to bring reconciliation to the political differences of the body.

Franklin's main difficulty with established religion had to do with its incapacity to help individuals serve each other, rather than a tendency to pit people against each other, which led to the detriment of the community. While he often stayed away from churches, he did make donations that they might help some people love their neighbors. Franklin's life was full of ironies, for example, when defending a Presbyterian preacher against accusations of heresy, Franklin wrote:

> "Morality or Virtue is the End, Faith only a Means to obtain that End: And if the End be obtained, it is no matter by what Means."

It is often said that Franklin admired Cotton Mather's emphasis on personal virtue, but that didn't stop Franklin from rebelling against Puritan clergy, loudly and often. The one part of Puritan doctrine Franklin did embrace was the idea that human beings were lazy, malicious, egotistical, and prone to a life of ease. Thus, despite his complaints about the status quo of Christianity, he determined that religion was really quite useful for others. Like many of the Founding Fathers, Franklin saw the public utility of religion, so rather than rejecting religion out of hand, Franklin tailored it, and while he didn't often attend church, he continued to draft prayers for himself.

In November 1728, Franklin created a private practice of devotion, consisting of a very personal creed and a corresponding method of worship. This was inscribed in a small notebook, about the size of the prayer book that Franklin used as a substitute. Some of his dogmata (that is; something clarified and elaborated upon, but not contradicted in novel teachings. Rejection of dogma may lead to expulsion from a religious group) clearly originated with several Deistical authors Franklin read as a teenager, others are highly original and would have come from a mind that combined the imagination of a genius with that of a gifted intellectual.

Franklin understood the importance of religious discipline even as he rejected religious doctrine. As a boy, he wrote;

> "I grew convinc'd that truth, sincerity and integrity in dealings between man and man were of the utmost importance to the felicity of life; and I form'd written resolutions, which still remain in my journal book, to practice them ever while I lived. Revelation had indeed no weight with me, as such; but I entertain'd an

opinion that, though certain actions might not be bad because they were forbidden by it, or good because it commanded them, yet probably these actions might be forbidden because they were bad for us, or commanded because they were beneficial to us, in their own natures, all the circumstances of things considered. And this persuasion, with the kind hand of Providence, or some guardian angel, or accidental favorable circumstances and situations, or all together, preserved me, thro' this dangerous time of youth, and the hazardous situations I was sometimes in among strangers, remote from the eye and advice of my father, without any willful gross immorality or injustice, that might have been expected from my want of religion."

As an adult, Franklin wrote the following in his biography;

"Tho' I seldom attended any public worship, I had still an opinion of its propriety, and of its utility when rightly conducted, and I regularly paid my annual subscription for the support of the only Presbyterian minister or meeting we had in Philadelphia. He us'd to visit me sometimes as a friend, and admonish me to attend his administration, and I was now and then prevail'd on to do so, once for five Sundays successively. Had he been in my opinion a good preacher, perhaps I might have continued, notwithstanding the occasion I had for the Sunday's leisure in my course of study; but his discourses were chiefly either polemic arguments, or explications of the peculiar doctrines of our sect, and were all to me very dry, uninteresting, and unedifying, since not a single moral principle was inculcated or enforc'd, their aim seeming to be rather to make us Presbyterians than good citizens."

Again in his biography, Franklin wrote that his understanding that religion should have an impact on social conduct;

"At length he took for his text that verse of the fourth chapter of Philippians, 'Finally, brethren, whatsoever things are true, honest, just, pure, lovely, or of good report, if there be any virtue, or any praise, think on these things.' And I imagin'd, in a sermon on such a text, we could not miss of having some morality. But he confin'd himself to five points only, as meant by the apostle, viz.: 1. Keeping holy the Sabbath day. 2. Being diligent in reading the holy Scriptures. 3. Attending duly the publick worship. 4. Partaking of the Sacrament. 5. Paying a due respect to God's ministers. These might be all good things; but, as they were not the kind of good things that I expected from that text, I despaired of ever meeting with them from any other, was disgusted, and attended his preaching no more. I had some years before compos'd a little Liturgy, or form of prayer, for my own private use (viz., in 1728), entitled, Articles of Belief and Acts of Religion. I return'd to the use of this, and went no more to the public assemblies. My conduct might be blameable, but I leave it, without attempting further to excuse it; my present purpose being to relate facts, and not to make apologies for them."

Throughout his life, Franklin continued to believe that religion was important, yet he attended services infrequently. Those times when Franklin did attended church, his inclinations varied. In 1774, he was present at the founding of the Essex Street Chapel, London's first Unitarian congregation. While in Britain, Franklin often attended the services led by his friend and fellow scientist, the Reverend Joseph Priestley (also a friend of Thomas Jefferson);

Franklin in 1764 wrote from England to his daughter back in Philadelphia:

"Go constantly to Church whoever preaches. The Acts of Devotion in the common Prayer Book, are your principal Business there; and if properly attended to, will do more towards mending the Heart than Sermons generally can do. For they were composed by Men of much greater Piety and Wisdom, than our common Composers of Sermons can pretend to be. And therefore I wish you wou'd never miss the Prayer Days. Yet I do not mean

that you shou'd despise Sermons even of the Preachers
you dislike, for the Discourse is often much better than
the Man, as sweet and clear Waters come to us thro' very
dirty Earth. I am the more particular on this Head, as
you seem'd to express a little before I came away some
Inclination to leave our Church, which I wou'd not have
you do."

As was his colleagues, Franklin was a product of the
Enlightenment Age and his intuitions were intellectual. He
sought to make his Book of Common Prayer reasonable. As
Franklin grew older, he revisited the characteristic Puritan habit
of self-examination, but with his rational punitive scrutiny there
was no sign of the deep guilt brought about by sin that darkened
Puritan soul searching. Franklin did have a realistic assessment
of human nature that he, *in his skepticism*, came to understand as
well as anyone. While Franklin devoted a great deal of attention to
religion throughout his life, he had no mysticism or deeply spiritual
nature but there was an emotional element to Franklin's thinking.
When he returned in to Philadelphia from France in 1785,
Franklin wrote: "God be praised and thanked for all His mercies!"

While Franklin is usually labeled as a Deist, his theology, like
that of many of his colleagues, actually changed over time and he
apparently ditched his pantheistic (belief that God is everything)
notions in a letter written on March 9, 1790 to Yale President
Ezra Stiles when the 85 year old Franklin wrote and reflected his
experiences as a scientist;

> "I believe in one God, creator of the universe. That
> he governs it by his Providence. That he ought to be
> worshiped. That the most acceptable service we can
> render to him is doing good to his other children. That
> the soul of man is immortal, and will be treated with
> justice in another life respecting its conduct in this.
> These I take to be the fundamental principles of all
> sound religion, and I regard them as you do, in whatever
> sect I meet with them." *(A copy of this letter is included in
> the appendix.)*

Franklin provided a summary of his beliefs in a letter to George Whatley, (a contemporary, friend and correspondent of Benjamin Franklin. Whatley also served as Vice-President and treasurer of the Foundling Hospital in London) written on 23 May, 1785;

> "When I observe that there is great frugality, as well as wisdom, in his works, since he has been evidently sparing both of labor and materials; for by the various wonderful inventions of propagation, he has provided for the continual peopling [of] his world with plants and animals, without being at the trouble of repeated new creations; and by the natural reduction of compound substances to their original elements, capable of being employed in new compositions, he has prevented the necessity of creating new matter; so that the earth, water, air, and perhaps, fire, which being compounded from wood, do, when the wood is dissolved, return, and again become air, earth, fire, and water; I saw, that, when I see nothing annihilated; and not even a drop of water wasted, I cannot suspect the annihilation of souls, or believe, that he will suffer the daily waste of millions of minds ready made that now exist, and put himself to the continual trouble of making new ones. Thus finding myself to exist in the World, I believe I shall, in some shape or other, always exist."

As an adult, Franklin's opinion of Jesus was similar to Thomas Jefferson's;

> "As to Jesus of Nazareth, my Opinion of whom you particularly desire, I think his system of morals and his religion, as he left them to us, the best the world ever saw or is like to see; but I apprehend it has received various corrupting changes, and I have, with most of the present Dissenters in England, some doubts as to his Divinity; though it is a question I do not dogmatize upon, having never studied it, and I think it needless to busy myself with it now, when I expect soon an opportunity of knowing the truth with less trouble. I

see no harm, however, in its being believed, if that belief has the good consequence, as probably it has, of making his doctrines more respected and more observed; especially as I do not perceive, that the Supreme takes it amiss, by distinguishing the unbelievers in his government of the world with any peculiar marks of his displeasure."

And as a young man, Franklin wrote his parents on 13 April, 1738, in part saying;

"Honour'd Father and Mother, I have your Favour of the 21st of March in which you both seem concern'd least I have imbib'd some erroneous Opinions. Doubtless I have my share, and when the natural Weakness and Imperfection of Human Understanding is considered, with the unavoidable Influences of Education, Custom, Books and Company, upon our Ways of Thinking, I imagine a man must have a good deal of vanity who believes, and a good deal of boldness who affirms, that all the doctrines he holds are true, and all he rejects are false. And perhaps the same may be justly said of every sect, church, and society of men, when they assume to themselves that infallibility which they deny to the Pope and councils. I think opinions should be judged of by their influences and effects; and, if a man holds none that tend to make him less virtuous or more vicious; it may be concluded he holds none that are dangerous; which I hope is the case with me."

Like Thomas Jefferson, Franklin tried to modify Christianity to fit his own view. For example, late in 1768, he revised the Lord's Prayer to read;

"Heavenly Father, may all revere thee, and become thy dutiful children and faithful subjects. May thy laws be obeyed on earth as perfectly as they are in Heaven. Provide for us this day as Thou has daily done. Forgive us our trespasses and enable us likewise to forgive those that offend us. Keep us out of temptation and deliver us from evil."

Franklin donated time an effort in the church's business affairs, subscribing to the building fund and serving from 1752 to 1753 as one of the managers of a lottery to raise money for a steeple and a chime of bells. As Franklin explained in his autobiography:

"I had been religiously educated as a Presbyterian; and tho' some of the dogmas of that persuasion, such as the eternal decrees of God, election, reprobation, etc., appeared to me unintelligible, others doubtful, and I early absented myself from the public assemblies of the sect, Sunday being my studying day, I never was without religious principles. I never doubted, for instance, the existence of the Deity; that he made the world, and govern'd it by his Providence; that the most acceptable service of God was the doing good to man; that our souls are immortal; and that all crime will be punished, and virtue rewarded, either here or hereafter. These I esteem'd the essentials of every religion; and being to be found in all the religions we had in our country, I respected them all, tho' with different degrees of respect, as I found them more or less mix'd with other articles, which, without any tendency to inspire, promote, or confirm morality, serv'd principally to divide us, and made us unfriendly to one another. This respect to all, with an opinion that the worst had some good effects, induc'd me to avoid all discourse that might tend to lessen the good opinion another might have of his own religion; and as our province increas'd in people, and new places of worship were continually wanted, and generally erected by voluntary contribution, my mite for such purpose, whatever might be the sect was never refused."

Joseph Galloway was an American politician who became a Loyalist during the War of Independence after serving as delegate to the First Continental Congress from Pennsylvania. For much of his career in Pennsylvania politics, he was a strong ally of Benjamin

Franklin and became a leading figure in the colony. What's interesting about Galloway is that he, like most Tories, believed that the American Revolution had been brought about by *a religious quarrel between Presbyterians and Congregationalists*, whose principles of religion and community were equally averse to those of the established Church and Government.

As a delegate to the Continental Congress and the Constitutional Convention, Franklin said:

> As to Jesus of Nazareth, my Opinion of whom you particularly desire, I think the System of Morals and his Religion...has received various corrupting Changes, and I have, with most of the present dissenters in England, some doubts as to his   Divinity; tho' it is a question I do not dogmatize upon, having never studied it, and think it needless to busy myself with it now, when I expect soon an opportunity of knowing the Truth with less trouble."

As people reach the end of their lives, they tend to look to their religion, in many cases this occurs after a lifetime of neglect or indifference. In a letter to William Strahan, London printer, bookseller, and associate of Franklin's, the statesman said,

> "It is with great sincerity I join you in acknowledging and admiring the dispensations of Providence in our favor. America has only to be thankful and to persevere. God will finish his work and establish their freedom.... If it had not been for the justice of our cause, and the consequent interposition of Providence, in which we had faith, we must have been ruined. If had ever before been an atheist, I should now have been convinced of the being and government of a Deity! It is He who abases the proud and favors the humble. May we never forget His goodnes to us, and may our future conduct manifest our gratitude....I believe in one God, Creator of the universe. That He governs it by his providence. That He ought to be worshiped."

Franklin died a month later on April 17, 1790 and historians consider him, like many other great Americans of his time, to be a Deist, not a Christian. Like Hamilton, Benjamin Franklin seemed to become more religious as he neared death. Franklin had been brought up in the church but as a teenager he rejected many of its beliefs. After moving to Philadelphia at the age of 17 in 1721, Franklin embraced the trappings of religious respectability even as he continued his religious search. Indeed, the Franklin family had a pew in the Episcopalian Christ Church, where the two younger children were baptized and they and both parents were buried.

THOMAS PAINE

No discussion about religion in colonial America during the fight for independence would be complete without a brief profile of one of the most outspoken and controversial figures of the time, Thomas Paine, a man who described himself as "a corset maker by trade, a journalist by profession and a propagandist by inclination." He was also a strong supporter of the concept of separation of church and state.

Thomas Paine's life was difficult even by the standards of the time, this included being thrown into a French prison and sentenced to death by Jacobins, (Jacobin was the name of the most famous and influential political club in France, initially founded by anti-Royalist deputies from Brittany, the club grew into a nationwide republican movement) in the aftermath of the French revolution because he had taken sides against the execution of the dethroned French King, Louis XVI. With all that, his writings were an inspiration that provided momentum to the Revolutionary War effort when it was deeply needed. Paine saw no good reason for the Colonies to remain dependent on Great Britain.

Thomas Paine was born on January 29, 1737 into a family of moderate means in Norfolk, England. His mother was Anglican and his father was a Quaker and it's likely Paine was baptized into the Anglican church. It's also quite likely that his exposure to these two very different religious traditions had a significant impact on Paine's personal religious development. He attended Thetford Grammar School from 1744 to 1749 during a time when there was no mandatory education. His father was a corsetiere by trade and had grand visions for his son, but the boy failed out of school and his Protestant father forbade him studying Latin as part of his education because of its association with the Roman Catholic church, so at the age of 12 he was apprenticed to his father to learn the craft of stay making.

By the time Paine was in his mid-teens, he become drawn to the allure of stories about naval life he'd been told by one of his teachers, so at age 16, Paine twice ran away from home to sea. The first time he was caught and returned home, but the second time he managed to sign on as a member of the crew on a privateer named the *King of Prussia*.

The exact sequence of events over his next ten to fifteen years is unclear. Paine is thought to have lived on and off in London, but also spent time in Sandwich and in Margate, where he continued periodically to ply his skills as a stay maker and may have done some preaching in the Methodist persuasion. In 1759, he married a Mary Lambert who was an 'Orphan of Sandwich', meaning she had no money or relatives to provide for her. Her father had been an excise officer, (typical responsibilities of the job included advising businesses about statutory requirements and ensuring that these are complied with and also handling any enquiries.) She became pregnant but both she and the child died the following year, Mary in childbirth and the child that was premature shortly afterward.

From 1767 to 1768, he served as a school teacher in London and gradually became involved in civic issues in and around the city, and we know that in March of 1771, at the age of 34, he married Elizabeth Ollive, his landlord's daughter. The previous year, he had set up a tobacco business with Elizabeth and her mother after Elizabeth's father passed away. From 1772 to 1773, Paine worked as an excise officer, his principle duties were to hunt for smugglers and collect the excise taxes owed on liquor and tobacco, but his income was insufficient to cover his living costs. He joined a group of excise officers asking Parliament for better pay and working conditions and published *The Case of the Officers of Excise* in the summer of 1772. This was a 21page article that was to become his first political work. He spent the winter in London, distributing 4,000 printed copies to members of Parliament and other officials. At the urging of other excise officers, Paine drew up a memorial urging Parliament to raise their wages, presenting it in 1773 but Parliament was not persuaded by his arguments. Paine wound up having to sell the tobacco shop to escape imprisonment for debt. In spring of 1774, he was discharged from the excise service for being absent from his post without permission and in April of that year, to again avoid debtors' prison, he sold his household possessions to pay off his debts.

A year after that, Paine went to London to press the claims of the excise men for higher pay but was not successful. In the final settlement between Paine and his wife he was awarded £400, whereupon he journeyed to London, managing to secure letters of introduction from Benjamin Franklin, whom he had met during an earlier visit to the capital, then embarked in April 1774 for the New World. The voyage was physically very difficult and ended with Paine being carried ashore on a stretcher in Philadelphia in November 1774, suffering from a severe fever because the ship's water supplies were so bad, (typhoid fever killed five other passengers on the voyage but Paine survived).

Paine settled in Philadelphia where he met up with Franklin and soon began a new career as a journalist and contributed articles to the *Pennsylvania Magazine,* covering a wide range of topics. Although he had been in America less than a year, Paine found himself committed to the cause of American independence. He attacked monarchical government and the alleged virtues of the British constitution, opposing any reconciliation with Great Britain. Paine also urged an immediate declaration of independence and the establishment of a republican constitution.

Common Sense was published in Philadelphia on January 10, 1776 and Paine signed anonymously with the moniker, "by an Englishman." Paine wrote for everyone, as he explained,

> "As it is my design to make those that can scarcely read understand, I shall therefore avoid every literary ornament and put it in language as plain as the alphabet."

The pamphlet became an immediate success and soon about 100,000 copies began circulating over the next three months to the two million residents of the 13 colonies. In all about 500,000 copies total including unauthorized editions were produced and sold during the course of the Revolution. Paine's original title for the pamphlet was *Plain Truth* but Paine's friend and pro-independence advocate Benjamin Rush suggested that *Common Sense* would have a greater impact. Loyalists ferociously attacked the publication; in one written attack by James Chalmers from Maryland, Chalmers said Paine was a political quack and warned that without a monarchy, the government would 'degenerate into democracy'.

Suddenly, Thomas Paine became very important. He traveled with the Continental Army but wasn't successful as a soldier. He did however, produce *The American Crisis*, a series of 16 pamphlets in total. 13 numbered pamphlets were published between 1776 and 1777, with three additional titles released between 1777 and 1783. Paine signed the pamphlets, using the pseudonym, "Common Sense." The Pamphlets set a tone that resonated with the American Revolutionaries and helped inspire the Army during a time when they needed to be uplifted. Written in a language that the common man could understand, they represented Paine's freethinking philosophy. His writings boosted the morale of the American colonists, clarified the issues that were at stake in the war and condemned advocates of a negotiated peace. The first volume begins with these oft quoted words "These are the times that try men's souls."

Virtually every supporter of independence read or it they were unable to read, listened to a reading of his powerful pamphlet *Common Sense*. It stoked the rebellious fervor for independence from Great Britain. Paine's work, *The American Crisis* was part of a pro-revolutionary pamphlet series, and *Common Sense* was so influential that John Adams said, "Without the pen of the author of *Common Sense*, the sword of Washington would have been raised in vain."

Instead of staying in America to help the Revolutionary cause, Paine returned to Europe and pursued other ventures, including working on a smokeless candle and designing a free standing iron bridge. In 1791 and 2, he wrote *The Rights of Man* in response to criticism of the French Revolution. This work caused Paine to be labeled an outlaw in England for his anti-monarchist views. He would have been arrested there, but he fled to France to join the French National Convention, (a single-chamber assembly created during the French Revolution that succeeded the pre-revolution Legislative Assembly.)

As I noted above, Paine was active in the French Revolution but was imprisoned for refusing to support the execution of the French King Louis XVI. As Jacques Mallet du Pan is believed to have said at his trial; *"The revolution devours its own children."* Danton was a leading figure in the early stages of the French Revolution and the first President of the Committee of Public Safety. Ironically, after accusations of leniency toward the enemies of the Revolution were brought against him, Danton was tried, convicted and guillotined.

During his imprisonment, Paine wrote and arranged for the distribution of the first part of what was to become his most famous work at the time, the anti-church text, *The Age of Reason*. He was freed from prison in 1794 after narrowly escaping execution, thanks to the efforts of James Monroe, U.S. Minister to France at the time. Paine remained in France until 1802, then returned to America on an invitation from Thomas Jefferson, where he discovered that his contributions to the American Revolution had been all but obliterated due to his religious views. Derided by the public and abandoned by his friends, he died on June 8, 1809 at the age of 72 in Greenwich Village, New York.

Although he is often thought of as an atheist, Paine was actually a Deist. He wrote extensively on the subject of religion, both promoting Deism and criticizing Christianity and other religions, essentially dismissing any belief in miracles other non-natural occurrences. For a man so frequently labeled an atheist, Paine shows a remarkable confidence in the divine order of the creation. The major work that destroyed his reputation in America and also divided his supporters in Britain was his *Age of Reason*, followed by an additional section written a year later, with all his miscellaneous writings compiled by later editors into a third part in 1804.

But his critics were wrong, the *Age of Reason* was not an atheist treatise, it was written during a period of significant, wide ranging church excess and abuse, all combined with ideas formed during the Age of Enlightenment. These ideas were combined to shape a scathing criticism of any claim of authority for the Bible by religious authorities, yet it had an expression of confidence in a divinely ordered world, a world revealed in nature through the exercise of reason that drew heavily on the lectures given by James Ferguson and Benjamin Martin (both eighteenth-century lecturers on experimental philosophy). Paine had attended their lectures in London, prior to leaving for America and by most accounts, he seemed to have committed their accounts to memory. He skillfully lays out the order of the universe, speculates on the possibility of a plurality of worlds and dismisses all claims for mystery, miracles and prophecy.

Paine takes the view that God is an unmoved first cause who designs and sets the universe in motion for the benefit of man. Here, he summarizes the beginning of part one of *The Age of Reason*:

> "Having now extended the subject to a greater length than I first intended, I shall bring it to a close by abstracting a summary from the whole. 'That the moral duty of man consists in imitating the moral goodness and beneficence of God, manifested in the creation toward all his creatures. That seeing, as we daily do, the goodness of God to all men, it is an example calling upon all men to practise the same toward each other; and, consequently, that every thing of persecution and revenge between man and man, and everything off cruelty to animals, is a violation of moral duty.'"

While many of Paine's critics feel that the later sections of *Age of Reason* descend into extensive detail, interpretation and controversy, the beginning is a powerful testament of rationalist faith in a Divine Creator. whose design can be appreciated by man in the Bible of Creation. It describes a Creator whose principles are eternal, who rejects as meaningless the claims to authority and the theology of the Christian Churches. As Paine put it,

> "The study of theology, as it stands in the Christian churches, is the study of nothing; it is founded on nothing; it rests on no principles; it produces no authorities; it has no data; it can demonstrate nothing; and it admits of no conclusion. The only religion that has not been invented, and that has in it every evidence of divine originality, is pure and simple Deism. And as simple government avoids us becoming the dupes of fraud, so simple belief protects us from the fraud of priest craft, which so often runs hand in hand with despotism."

In his work *Common Sense*, Paine had this to say;

> "As to religion, I hold it to be the indispensable duty of every government, to protect all conscientious professors thereof, and I know of no other business which government hath to do therewith. Let a man throw aside that narrow ness of soul, that selfishness of principle, which the niggards of all professions are so unwilling to part with; and he will be at once delivered of his fears on that head. Suspicion is the companion of mean souls, and the bane of all good society. For myself, I fully and conscientiously believe, that it is the will of the Almighty, that there should be a diversity of religious opinions among us: it affords a larger field for our Christian kindness. Were we all of one way of thinking, our religious dispositions would want matter for probation; and on this liberal principle, I look on the various denominations among us, to be like children of the same family, differing only, in what is called, their Christian names."

In *The Age of Reason*, Paine had this to say about his work, *Common Sense*;

"Soon after I published the pamphlet COMMON SENSE, in America, I saw the exceeding probability that a revolution in the system of government would be followed by a revolution in the system of religion. The adulterous connection of church and state, wherever it had taken place, whether Jewish, Christian, or Turkish, had so effectually prohibited, by pains and penalties, every discussion upon established creeds, and upon first principles of religion, that until the system of government should be changed, those subjects could not be brought fairly and openly before the world; but that whenever this should be done, a revolution in the system of religion would follow."

While Paine never described himself as a Deist, he did write the following in *The Age of Reason, Part II*, after recently been freed from French captivity where he wrote the second part of his treatise:

"The quotations I then made were from memory only, but they are correct; and the opinions I have advanced in that work are the effect of the most clear and long-established conviction that the Bible and the Testament are impositions upon the world, that the fall of man, the account of Jesus Christ being the Son of God, and of his dying to appease the wrath of God, and of salvation, by that strange means, are all fabulous inventions, dishonorable to the wisdom and power of the Almighty; that the only true religion is Deism, by which I then meant, and mean now, the belief of one God, and an imitation of his moral character, or the practice of what are called moral virtues-and that it was upon this only (so far as religion is concerned) that I rested all my hopes of happiness hereafter. So say I now-and so help me God"

While, as an ordained minister, I personally don't agree with much of his theology, I must admit that I have a favorite quote from Thomas Paine and with your indulgence, I present it here...

> "Persecution is not an original feature of any religion; but it is always the strongly marked feature of all religions established by law."
>
> *The Rights of Man*, 1791

As I've tried to show, founding a new country isn't as easy as it sounds, and one of the biggest obstacles for America was the various opinions and positions of a society comprised of multiple backgrounds and cultures, something that still exists today. Our Founding Fathers struggled with many cultural differences and beliefs, but were united on one subject, they recognized that religious principles were deeply personal and should remain that way. Many religious leaders today insist that there is only one way to worship and lay down only one set of rules that everyone has to live by. Principally, one religion is right, all the others are wrong and these leaders will fight to force others to accept their position. Sadly, this is not what was intended when it started a little over 2000 years ago.

In the appendix, there are letters and documents written by these men and I encourage you the reader, to read through them and listen to the tone and the feelings that are expressed by the author. These men had first-hand experience and based on that, they were trying desperately to prevent this fledgling new democracy from becoming one more victim of a failed governmental system. The Founding Fathers felt so strongly about this that, when they drafted the Bill of Rights, the very first right listed was *freedom of religion*, "Congress shall make no law respecting an establishment of religion, or prohibiting the free exercise thereof..."

Their intent was to guarantee that all of us can live freely, under the guidelines of our chosen religious belief for all of us who have a personal relationship with that entity that we identify and call God. Any law that is centered around one religious tenet or standard that prevents an individual who follows a different religion from following the dictates of that religion violates this right.

Our country has struggled in the past and continues to struggle with this idea. There are many in America today who insist that our country is a "Christian Country" and are trying to force everyone to believe and accept this. When I read through the list of religious measures introduced in congress since 1888, I was amazed at how many attempts there were to circumvent the first amendment and there is no evidence to suggest that this effort will not continue. For each of us, religious beliefs boil down to a personal relationship with a supreme being, regardless of what name we choose to give him (or her). This is the message that religion is passing along to each of us, but we have to be willing to listen...

APPENDIX

Rules of Civility & Decent Behaviour in Company and Conversation: a Book of Etiquette

1 Every Action done in Company, ought to be with Some Sign of Respect, to those that are Present.

2 When in Company, put not your Hands to any Part of the Body, not usualy Discovered.

3 Shew Nothing to your Freind that may affright him.

4 In the Presence of Others Sing not to yourself with a humming Noise, nor Drum with your Fingers or Feet.

5 If You Cough, Sneeze, Sigh, or Yawn, do it not Loud but Privately; and Speak not in your Yawning, but put Your handkercheif or Hand before your face and turn aside.

6 Sleep not when others Speak, Sit not when others stand, Speak not when you Should hold your Peace, walk not on when others Stop.

7 Put not off your Cloths in the presence of Others, nor go out your Chamber half Drest.

8 At Play and at Fire its Good manners to Give Place to the last Commer, and affect not to Speak Louder than Ordinary.

9 Spit not in the Fire, nor Stoop low before it neither Put your Hands into the Flames to warm them, nor Set your Feet upon the Fire especially if there be meat before it.

10 When you Sit down, Keep your Feet firm and Even, without putting one on the other or Crossing them.

11 Shift not yourself in the Sight of others nor Gnaw your nails.

12 Shake not the head, Feet, or Legs rowl not the Eys lift not one eyebrow higher than the other wry not the mouth, and bedew

no mans face with your Spittle, by approaching too near him when you Speak.

13 Kill no Vermin as Fleas, lice ticks &c in the Sight of Others, if you See any filth or thick Spittle put your foot Dexteriously upon it if it be upon the Cloths of your Companions, Put it off privately, and if it be upon your own Cloths return Thanks to him who puts it off.

14 Turn not your Back to others especially in Speaking, Jog not the Table or Desk on which Another reads or writes, lean not upon any one.

15 Keep your Nails clean and Short, also your Hands and Teeth Clean yet without Shewing any great Concern for them.

16 Do not Puff up the Cheeks, Loll not out the tongue rub the Hands, or beard, thrust out the lips, or bite them or keep the Lips too open or too Close.

17 Be no Flatterer, neither Play with any that delights not to be Play'd Withal.

18 Read no Letters, Books, or Papers in Company but when there is a Necessity for the doing of it you must ask leave: come not near the Books or Writings of Another so as to read them unless desired or give your opinion of them unask'd also look not nigh when another is writing a Letter.

19 let your Countenance be pleasant but in Serious Matters Somewhat grave.

20 The Gestures of the Body must be Suited to the discourse you are upon.

21 Reproach none for the Infirmaties of Nature, nor Delight to Put them that have in mind thereof.

22 Shew not yourself glad at the Misfortune of another though he were your enemy.

23 When you see a Crime punished, you may be inwardly Pleased; but always shew Pity to the Suffering Offender.

24 Do not laugh too loud or too much at any Publick Spectacle.

25 Superfluous Complements and all Affectation of Ceremonie are to be avoided, yet where due they are not to be Neglected.

26 In Pulling off your Hat to Persons of Distinction, as Noblemen, Justices, Churchmen &c make a Reverence, bowing more or less according to the Custom of the Better Bred, and Quality of the Person. Amongst your equals expect not always that they Should begin with you first, but to Pull off the Hat when there is no need is Affectation, in the Manner of Saluting and resaluting in words keep to the most usual Custom.

27 Tis ill manners to bid one more eminent than yourself be covered as well as not to do it to whom it's due Likewise he that makes too much haste to Put on his hat does not well, yet he ought to Put it on at the first, or at most the Second time of being ask'd; now what is herein Spoken, of Qualification in behaviour in Saluting, ought also to be observed in taking of Place, and Sitting down for ceremonies without Bounds is troublesome.

28 If any one come to Speak to you while you are are Sitting Stand up tho he be your Inferiour, and when you Present Seats let it be to every one according to his Degree.

29 When you meet with one of Greater Quality than yourself, Stop, and retire especially if it be at a Door or any Straight place to give way for him to Pass.

30 In walking the highest Place in most Countrys Seems to be on the right hand therefore Place yourself on the left of him whom you desire to Honour: but if three walk together the middest Place is the most Honourable the wall is usually given to the most worthy if two walk together.

31 If any one far Surpassess others, either in age, Estate, or Merit yet would give Place to a meaner than himself in his own lodging or elsewhere the one ought not to except it, So he on the other part should not use much earnestness nor offer it above once or twice.

32 To one that is your equal, or not much inferior you are to give the cheif Place in your Lodging and he to who 'tis offered ought at the first to refuse it but at the Second to accept though not without acknowledging his own unworthiness.

33 They that are in Dignity or in office have in all places Preceedency but whilst they are Young they ought to respect those that are their equals in Birth or other Qualitys, though they have no Publick charge.

34 It is good Manners to prefer them to whom we Speak before ourselves especially if they be above us with whom in no Sort we ought to begin.

35 Let your Discourse with Men of Business be Short and Comprehensive.

36 Artificers & Persons of low Degree ought not to use many ceremonies to Lords, or Others of high Degree but Respect and highly Honour them, and those of high Degree ought to treat them with affibility & Courtesie, without Arrogancy.

37 In Speaking to men of Quality do not lean nor Look them full in the Face, nor approach too near them at lest Keep a full Pace from them.

38 In visiting the Sick, do not Presently play the Physicion if you be not Knowing therein.

39 In writing or Speaking, give to every Person his due Title According to his Degree & the Custom of the Place.

40 Strive not with your Superiers in argument, but always Submit your Judgment to others with Modesty.

41 Undertake not to Teach your equal in the art himself Proffesses; it Savours of arrogancy.

42 Let thy ceremonies in Courtesie be proper to the Dignity of his place with whom thou conversest for it is absurd to act the same with a Clown and a Prince.

43 Do not express Joy before one sick or in pain for that contrary Passion will aggravate his Misery.

44 When a man does all he can though it Succeeds not well blame not him that did it.

45 Being to advise or reprehend any one, consider whether it ought to be in publick or in Private; presently, or at Some other time in what terms to do it & in reproving Shew no Sign of Cholar but do it with all Sweetness and Mildness.

46 Take all Admonitions thankfully in what Time or Place Soever given but afterwards not being culpable take a Time & Place convenient to let him him know it that gave them.

47 Mock not nor Jest at any thing of Importance break no Jest that are Sharp Biting and if you Deliver any thing witty and Pleasent abstain from Laughing there at yourself.

48 Wherein wherein you reprove Another be unblameable yourself; for example is more prevalent than Precepts.

49 Use no Reproachfull Language against any one neither Curse nor Revile.

50 Be not hasty to beleive flying Reports to the Disparagement of any.

51 Wear not your Cloths, foul, unript or Dusty but See they be Brush'd once every day at least and take heed that you approach not to any Uncleaness.

52 In your Apparel be Modest and endeavour to accomodate Nature, rather than to procure Admiration keep to the Fashion of your equals Such as are Civil and orderly with respect to Times and Places.

53 Run not in the Streets, neither go too slowly nor with Mouth open go not Shaking yr Arms kick not the earth with yr feet, go not upon the Toes, nor in a Dancing fashion.

54 Play not the Peacock, looking every where about you, to See if you be well Deck't, if your Shoes fit well if your Stokings sit neatly, and Cloths handsomely.

55 Eat not in the Streets, nor in the House, out of Season.

56 Associate yourself with Men of good Quality if you Esteem your own Reputation; for 'tis better to be alone than in bad Company.

57 In walking up and Down in a House, only with One in Company if he be Greater than yourself, at the first give him the Right hand and Stop not till he does and be not the first that turns, and when you do turn let it be with your face towards him, if he be a Man of Great Quality, walk not with him Cheek by Joul but Somewhat behind him; but yet in Such a Manner that he may easily Speak to you.

58 Let your Conversation be without Malice or Envy, for 'tis a Sign of a Tractable and Commendable Nature: And in all Causes of Passion admit Reason to Govern.

59 Never express anything unbecoming, nor Act agst the Rules Moral before your inferiours.

60 Be not immodest in urging your Freinds to Discover a Secret.

61 Utter not base and frivilous things amongst grave and Learn'd Men nor very Difficult Questians or Subjects, among the Ignorant or things hard to be believed, Stuff not your Discourse with Sentences amongst your Betters nor Equals.

62 Speak not of doleful Things in a Time of Mirth or at the Table; Speak not of Melancholy Things as Death and Wounds, and if others Mention them Change if you can the Discourse tell not your Dreams, but to your intimate Friend.

63 A Man ought not to value himself of his Atchievements, or rare Qualities of wit; much less of his riches Virtue or Kindred.

64 Break not a Jest where none take pleasure in mirth Laugh not aloud, nor at all without Occasion, deride no mans Misfortune, tho' there Seem to be Some cause.

65 Speak not injurious Words neither in Jest nor Earnest Scoff at none although they give Occasion.

66 Be not forward but friendly and Courteous; the first to Salute hear and answer & be not Pensive when it's a time to Converse.

67 Detract not from others neither be excessive in Commanding.

68 Go not thither, where you know not, whether you Shall be Welcome or not. Give not Advice without being Ask'd & when desired do it briefly.

69 If two contend together take not the part of either unconstrained; and be not obstinate in your own Opinion, in Things indiferent be of the Major Side.

70 Reprehend not the imperfections of others for that belongs to Parents Masters and Superiours.

71 Gaze not on the marks or blemishes of Others and ask not how they came. What you may Speak in Secret to your Friend deliver not before others.

72 Speak not in an unknown Tongue in Company but in your own Language and that as those of Quality do and not as the Vulgar; Sublime matters treat Seriously.

73 Think before you Speak pronounce not imperfectly nor bring out your Words too hastily but orderly & distinctly.

74 When Another Speaks be attentive your Self and disturb not the Audience if any hesitate in his Words help him not nor Prompt him without desired, Interrupt him not, nor Answer him till his Speech be ended.

75 In the midst of Discourse ask not of what one treateth but if you Perceive any Stop because of your coming you may well intreat him gently to Proceed: If a Person of Quality comes in while your Conversing it's handsome to Repeat what was said before.

76 While you are talking, Point not with your Finger at him of Whom you Discourse nor Approach too near him to whom you talk especially to his face.

77 Treat with men at fit Times about Business & Whisper not in the Company of Others.

78 Make no Comparisons and if any of the Company be Commended for any brave act of Vertue, commend not another for the Same.

79 Be not apt to relate News if you know not the truth thereof. In Discoursing of things you Have heard Name not your Author always A Secret Discover not.

80 Be not Tedious in Discourse or in reading unless you find the Company pleased therewith.

81 Be not Curious to Know the Affairs of Others neither approach those that Speak in Private.

82 undertake not what you cannot perform but be carefull to keep your promise.

83 when you deliver a matter do it without passion & with discretion, however mean the person be you do it too.

84 When your Superiours talk to any Body hearken not neither Speak nor Laugh.

85 In Company of these of Higher Quality than yourself Speak not til you are ask'd a Question then Stand upright put of your Hat & Answer in few words.

86 In Disputes, be not So Desireous to Overcome as not to give Liberty to each one to deliver his Opinion and Submit to the Judgment of the Major Part especially if they are Judges of the Dispute.

87 Let thy carriage be such as becomes a Man Grave Settled and attentive to that which is spoken. Contradict not at every turn what others Say.

88 Be not tedious in Discourse, make not many Digressigns, nor repeat often the Same manner of Discourse.

89 Speak not Evil of the absent for it is unjust.

90 Being Set at meat Scratch not neither Spit Cough or blow your Nose except there's a Necessity for it.

91 Make no Shew of taking great Delight in your Victuals, Feed not with Greediness; cut your Bread with a Knife, lean not on the Table neither find fault with what you Eat.

92 Take no Salt or cut Bread with your Knife Greasy.

93 Entertaining any one at table it is decent to present him wt. meat, Undertake not to help others undesired by the Master.

94 If you Soak bread in the Sauce let it be no more than what you put in your Mouth at a time and blow not your broth at Table but Stay till Cools of it Self.

95 Put not your meat to your Mouth with your Knife in your hand neither Spit forth the Stones of any fruit Pye upon a Dish nor Cast anything under the table.

96 It's unbecoming to Stoop much to ones Meat Keep your Fingers clean & when foul wipe them on a Corner of your Table Napkin.

97 Put not another bit into your Mouth til the former be Swallowed let not your Morsels be too big for the Gowls.

98 Drink not nor talk with your mouth full neither Gaze about you while you are a Drinking.

99 Drink not too leisurely nor yet too hastily. Before and after Drinking wipe your Lips breath not then or Ever with too Great a Noise, for its uncivil.

100 Cleanse not your teeth with the Table Cloth Napkin Fork or Knife but if Others do it let it be done wt. a Pick Tooth.

101 Rince not your Mouth in the Presence of Others.

102 It is out of use to call upon the Company often to Eat nor need you Drink to others every Time you Drink.

103 In Company of your Betters be not longer in eating than they are lay not your Arm but only your hand upon the table.

104 It belongs to the Chiefest in Company to unfold his Napkin and fall to Meat first, But he ought then to Begin in time & to Dispatch with Dexterity that the Slowest may have time allowed him.

105 Be not Angry at Table whatever happens & if you have reason to be so, Shew it not but on a Chearfull Countenance especially if there be Strangers for Good Humour makes one Dish of Meat a Feast.

106 Set not yourself at the upper of the Table but if it Be your Due or that the Master of the house will have it So, Contend not, least you Should Trouble the Company.

107 If others talk at Table be attentive but talk not with Meat in your Mouth.

108 When you Speak of God or his Atributes, let it be Seriously & wt. Reverence. Honour & Obey your Natural Parents altho they be Poor.

109 Let your Recreations be Manfull not Sinfull.

110 Labour to keep alive in your Breast that Little Spark of Celestial fire Called Conscience.

(Translated from the French language by Francis Hawkins, published in England about 1640)

Correspondence between Committee of the United Baptist Churches the Baptists of Virginia and President George Washington

The Address of the Committee of the United Baptist Churches in Virginia assembled in the city of Richmond:

August 8, 1789

To the President of the United States of America:

SIR,— Among the many shouts of congratulation that you receive from cities, societies, States and the whole world, we wish to take an active part in the universal chorus by expressing our great satisfaction in your appointment to the first office in the nation. When America on a former occasion was reduced to the necessity of appealing to arms to defend her natural and civil rights, a WASHINGTON was found fully adequate to the exigencies of the dangerous attempt, who by the philanthropy of his heart and prudence of his head led forth her untutored troops into the field of battle, and by the skillfulness of his hands baffled the projects of the insulting foe and pointed out the road to independence, even at a time when the energy of the Cabinet was not sufficient to bring into action the natural aid of the association from its respective sources.

The grand object being obtained, the independence of the States acknowledged, free from ambition and devoid of a thirst for blood, our HERO returned with those he commanded and laid down his sword at the feet of those who gave it to him. *Such an example to the world is new.* Like other nations, we experience that it requires as great valor and wisdom to make an advantage of a conquest as to gain one.

The want of efficacy in the confederation, the redundancy of laws and their partial administration in the States, called aloud for a new arrangement of our system. The wisdom of the States for that purpose was collected in a grand convention, over which you, sir, had the honor to preside. A national government in all its parts was recommended as the only preservative of the Union, which plan of government is now actually in operation.

When the Constitution first made its appearance in Virginia, we, as a society, had unusual strugglings of mind, fearing that the liberty of conscience (dearer to us than property and life) was not sufficiently secured; perhaps our jealousies were heightened on account of the usage we received in Virginia under the British Government when mobs, bonds, fines and prisons were our frequent repast.

Convinced on the one hand that without an effective national government the States would fall into disunion and all the consequent evils; on the other hand it was feared we might be accessory to some religious oppression, should any one society in the Union preponderate all the rest. But amidst all the inquietudes of mind, our consolation arose from this consideration, the plan must be good, for it bears the signature of a *tried, trusty friend*; and if religious liberty is rather insecure in the Constitution, "the administration will prevent all oppression, for a WASHINGTON will preside." According to our wishes the unanimous voice of the Union has called you, sir, from your beloved retreat, to launch forth again into the faithless seas of human affairs, to guide the helm of the States. Should the horrid evils that have been so pestiferous in Asia and Europe — faction, ambition, war, perfidy, fraud and persecutions for conscience sake — ever approach the borders of our happy nation, may the name and administration of our beloved President, like the radiant source of day, scatter all those dark clouds from the American hemisphere.

And while we speak freely the language of our own hearts, we are satisfied that we express the sentiments of our brethren whom we represent. The very name of WASHINGTON is music in our ears; and although the great evil in the States is the want of mutual confidence between rulers and the people, yet we all have the utmost confidence in the President of the States, and it is our fervent prayer to Almighty God that the Federal Government and the government of the respective States, without rivalship, may so co-operate together as to make the numerous people over whom you preside the happiest nation on earth, and you, sir, the happiest man, in seeing the people whom, by the smiles of Providence, you saved from vassalage by your martial valor and made wise by your maxims, sitting securely under their vines and fig trees enjoying the perfection of human felicity. May God long preserve your life and health for a blessing to the world in general and the United States in particular; and when, like the sun, you have finished your course of great and unparalleled services, and you go the way of all the earth, may the Divine Being, who will reward every man according to his works, grant unto you a glorious admission into His everlasting kingdom through Jesus Christ. This, great sir, is the prayer of your happy admirers.

By order of the committee.
SAMUEL HARRISS, Chairman. Reuben Ford, Clerk.

George Washington's Reply the United Baptist Churches the Baptists of Virginia

To the General Committee representing the United Baptist Churches in Virginia:

GENTLEMEN, — I request that you will accept my best acknowledgments for your congratulation on my appointment to the first office in the nation. The kind manner in which you mention my past conduct equally claims the expression of my gratitude. After we had, by the smiles of Divine Providence on our exertions, obtained the object for which we contended, I retired at the conclusion of the war with the idea that my country could have no farther occasion for my services, and with the intention of never entering again into public life; but when the exigencies of my country seemed to require me once more to engage in public affairs, an honest conviction of duty superseded my former resolution and became my apology for deviating from the happy plan which I had adopted.

If I could have entertained the slightest apprehension that the Constitution framed in the convention where I had the honor to preside might possibly endanger the religious rights of any ecclesiastical society, certainly I would never have placed my signature to it; and if I could now conceive that the General Government might ever be so administered as to render the liberty of conscience insecure, I beg you will be persuaded that no one would be more zealous than myself to establish effectual barriers against the horrors of spiritual tyranny and every species of religious persecution. -- For you doubtless remember I have often expressed my sentiments that every man conducting himself as a good citizen, and being accountable to God alone for his religious opinions, ought to be protected in worshipping the Deity according to the dictates of his own conscience.

While I recollect with satisfaction that the religious society of which you are members have been throughout America, uniformly and almost unanimously, the firm friends to civil liberty, and the persevering promoters of our glorious revolution, I cannot hesitate to believe that they will be faithful supporters of a free yet efficient General Government. Under this pleasing expectation I rejoice to assure them that they may rely upon my best wishes and endeavors to advance their prosperity.

In the meantime be assured, gentlemen, that I entertain a proper sense of your fervent supplication to God for my temporal and eternal happiness.

I am, gentlemen, your most obedient servant,

G. WASHINGTON.

The letter from Moses Seixas to President George Washington

August 17, 1790

To the President of the United States of America,

Sir:

Permit the children of the stock of Abraham to approach you with the most cordial affection and esteem for your person and merits — and to join with our fellow citizens in welcoming you to NewPort.

With pleasure we reflect on those days — those days of difficulty, and danger, when the God of Israel, who delivered David from the peril of the sword, — shielded Your head in the day of battle: — and we rejoice to think, that the same Spirit, who rested in the Bosom of the greatly beloved Daniel enabling him to preside over the Provinces of the Babylonish Empire, rests and ever will rest, upon you, enabling you to discharge the arduous duties of Chief Magistrate in these States.

Deprived as we heretofore have been of the invaluable rights of free Citizens, we now with a deep sense of gratitude to the Almighty disposer of all events behold a Government, erected by the Majesty of the People — a Government, which to bigotry gives no sanction, to persecution no assistance — but generously affording to all Liberty of conscience, and immunities of Citizenship: — deeming every one, of whatever Nation, tongue, or language equal parts of the great governmental Machine: — This so ample and extensive Federal Union whose basis is Philanthropy, Mutual confidence and Public Virtue, we cannot but acknowledge to be the work of the Great God, who ruleth in the Armies of Heaven, and among the Inhabitants of the Earth, doing whatever seemeth him good.

For all these Blessings of civil and religious liberty which we enjoy under an equal and benign administration, we desire to send up our thanks to the Ancient of Days, the great preserver of Men — beseeching him, that the Angel who conducted our forefathers through the wilderness into the promised Land, may graciously conduct you through all the difficulties and dangers of this mortal life: — And, when, like Joshua full of days and full of honour, you are gathered to your Fathers, may you be admitted into the Heavenly Paradise to partake of the water of life, and the tree of immortality.

Done and Signed by order of the Hebrew Congregation in NewPort, Rhode Island August 17th 1790. Moses Seixas, Warden

George Washington's Letter to the Hebrew Congregation of Newport in response to Moses Seixas

August 21, 1790

To the Hebrew Congregation in Newport Rhode Island,

Gentlemen,

While I receive, with much satisfaction, your Address replete with expressions of affection and esteem; I rejoice in the opportunity of assuring you, that I shall always retain a grateful remembrance of the cordial welcome I experienced in my visit to Newport, from all classes of Citizens.

The reflection on the days of difficulty and danger which are past is rendered the more sweet, from a consciousness that they are succeeded by days of uncommon prosperity and security. If we have wisdom to make the best use of the advantages with which we are now favored, we cannot fail, under the just administration of a good Government, to become a great and happy people.

The Citizens of the United States of America have a right to applaud themselves for having given to mankind examples of an enlarged and liberal policy: a policy worthy of imitation. All possess alike liberty of conscience and immunities of citizenship. It is now no more that toleration is spoken of, as if it was by the indulgence of one class of people, that another enjoyed the exercise of their inherent natural rights. For happily the Government of the United States, which gives to bigotry no sanction, to persecution no assistance, requires only that they who live under its protection should demean themselves as good citizens, in giving it on all occasions their effectual support.

It would be inconsistent with the frankness of my character not to avow that I am pleased with your favorable opinion of my Administration, and fervent wishes for my felicity. May the children of the Stock of Abraham, who dwell in this land, continue to merit and enjoy the good will of the other Inhabitants; while every one shall sit in safety under his own vine and fig-tree, and there shall be none to make him afraid. May the father of all mercies scatter light and not darkness in our paths, and make us all in our several vocations useful here, and in his own due time and way everlastingly happy.

G. Washington

President George Washington's
Thanksgiving Proclamation

New York, 3 October 1789

By the President of the United States of America, a Proclamation

Whereas it is the duty of all Nations to acknowledge the Providence of Almighty God, to obey his will, to be grateful for his benefits, and humbly to implore his protection and favor-- and whereas both Houses of Congress have by their joint Committee requested me to recommend to the People of the United States a day of public thanksgiving and prayer to be observed by acknowledging with grateful hearts the many signal favors of Almighty God especially by affording them an opportunity peaceably to establish a form of government for their safety and happiness.

Now therefore I do recommend and assign Thursday the 26th day of November next to be devoted by the People of these States to the service of that great and glorious Being, who is the beneficent Author of all the good that was, that is, or that will be-- That we may then all unite in rendering unto him our sincere and humble thanks--for his kind care and protection of the People of this Country previous to their becoming a Nation--for the signal and manifold mercies, and the favorable interpositions of his Providence which we experienced in the course and conclusion of the late war--for the great degree of tranquility, union, and plenty, which we have since enjoyed--for the peaceable and rational manner, in which we have been enabled to establish constitutions of government for our safety and happiness, and particularly the national One now lately instituted--for the civil and religious liberty with which we are blessed; and the means we have of acquiring and diffusing useful knowledge; and in general for all the great and various favors which he hath been pleased to confer upon us.

And also that we may then unite in most humbly offering our prayers and supplications to the great Lord and Ruler of Nations and beseech him to pardon our national and other transgressions -- to enable us all, whether in public or private stations, to perform our several and relative duties properly and punctually--to render our national government a blessing to all the people, by constantly being a Government of wise, just, and constitutional laws, discreetly and faithfully executed and obeyed--to protect and guide all Sovereigns and Nations (especially such as have shewn kindness unto us) and to bless them with good government, peace, and concord--To promote the knowledge and practice of true religion and virtue, and the encrease of science among them and us--and generally to grant unto all Mankind such a degree of temporal prosperity as he alone knows to be best.

Given under my hand at the City of New York the third day of October in the year of our Lord 1789.

Geo: Washington

John Adams' Thoughts on Government, Applicable to the Present State of the American Colonies

A Pamphlet by John Adams
April, 1776

My dear Sir,

If I was equal to the task of forming a plan for the government of a colony, I should be flattered with your request, and very happy to comply with it; because as the divine science of politicks is the science of social happiness, and the blessings of society depend entirely on the constitutions of government, which are generally institutions that last for many generations, there can be no employment more agreeable to a benevolent mind, than a research after the best.

Pope flattered tyrants too much when he said,

> "For forms of government let fools contest,
> That which is best administered is best."

Nothing can be more fallacious than this: But poets read history to collect flowers not fruits—they attend to fanciful images, not the effects of social institutions. Nothing is more certain from the history of nations, and the nature of man, than that some forms of government are better fitted for being well administered than others.

We ought to consider, what is the end of government, before we determine which is the best form. Upon this point all speculative politicians will agree, that the happiness of society is the end of government, as all Divines and moral Philosophers will agree that the happiness of the individual is the end of man. From this principle it will follow, that the form of government, which communicates ease, comfort, security, or in one word happiness to the greatest number of persons, and in the greatest degree, is the best.

All sober enquiries after truth, ancient and modern, Pagan and Christian, have declared that the happiness of man, as well as his dignity consists in virtue. Confucius, Zoroaster, Socrates, Mahomet, not to mention authorities really sacred, have agreed in this.

If there is a form of government then, whose principle and foundation is virtue, will not every sober man acknowledge it better calculated to promote the general happiness than any other form?

Fear is the foundation of most governments; but is so sordid and brutal a passion, and renders men, in whose breasts it predominates, so stupid, and miserable, that Americans will not be likely to approve of any political institution which is founded on it.

Honor is truly sacred, but holds a lower rank in the scale of moral excellence than virtue. Indeed the former is but a part of the latter, and consequently has not equal pretensions to support a frame of government productive of human happiness.

The foundation of every government is some principle or passion in the minds of the people. The noblest principles and most generous affections in our nature then, have the fairest chance to support the noblest and most generous models of government.

A man must be indifferent to the sneers of modern Englishmen to mention in their company the names of Sidney, Harrington, Locke, Milton, Nedham, Neville, Burnet, and Hoadley. No small fortitude is necessary to confess that one has read them. The wretched condition of this country, however, for ten or fifteen years past, has frequently reminded me of their principles and reasonings. They will convince any candid mind, that there is no good government but what is Republican. That the only valuable part of the British constitution is so; because the very definition of a Republic, is "an Empire of Laws, and not of men." That, as a Republic is the best of governments, so that particular arrangement of the powers of society, or in other words that form of government, which is best contrived to secure an impartial and exact execution of the laws, is the best of Republics.

Of Republics, there is an inexhaustable variety, because the possible combinations of the powers of society, are capable of innumerable variations.

As good government, is an empire of laws, how shall your laws be made? In a large society, inhabiting an extensive country, it is impossible that the whole should assemble, to make laws: The first necessary step then, is, to depute power from the many, to a few of the most wise and good. But by what rules shall you chuse your Representatives? Agree upon the number and qualifications of persons, who shall have the benefit of choosing, or annex this priviledge to the inhabitants of a certain extent of ground.

The principal difficulty lies, and the greatest care should be employed in constituting this Representative Assembly. It should be in miniature, an exact portrait of the people at large. It should think, feel, reason, and act like them. That it may be the interest of this Assembly to do strict justice at all times, it should be an equal representation, or in other words equal interest among the people should have equal interest in it. Great care should be taken to effect this, and to prevent unfair, partial, and corrupt elections. Such regulations, however, may be better made in times of greater tranquility than the present, and they will spring up of themselves naturally, when all the powers of government come to be in the hands of the people's friends. At present it will be safest to proceed in all established modes to which the people have been familiarised by habit.

A representation of the people in one assembly being obtained, a question arises whether all the powers of government, legislative, executive, and judicial, shall be left in this body? I think a people cannot be long free, nor ever happy, whose government is in one Assembly. My reasons for this opinion are as follow.

A single Assembly is liable to all the vices, follies and frailties of an individual. Subject to fits of humour, starts of passion, flights of enthusiasm, partialities of prejudice, and consequently productive of hasty results and absurd judgments: And all these errors ought to be corrected and defects supplied by some controuling power.

A single Assembly is apt to be avaricious, and in time will not scruple to exempt itself from burthens which it will lay, without compunction, on its constituents.

A single Assembly is apt to grow ambitious, and after a time will not hesitate to vote itself perpetual. This was one fault of the long parliament, but more remarkably of Holland, whose Assembly first voted themselves from annual to septennial, then for life, and after a course of years, that all vacancies happening by death, or otherwise, should be filled by themselves, without any application to constituents at all.

A Representative Assembly, altho' extremely well qualified, and absolutely necessary as a branch of the legislature, is unfit to exercise the executive power, for want of two essential properties, secrecy and dispatch.

A Representative Assembly is still less qualified for the judicial power; because it is too numerous, too slow, and too little skilled in the laws.

Because a single Assembly, possessed of all the powers of government, would make arbitrary laws for their own interest, execute all laws arbitrarily for their own interest, and adjudge all controversies in their own favour.

But shall the whole power of legislation rest in one Assembly? Most of the foregoing reasons apply equally to prove that the legislative power ought to be more complex—to which we may add, that if the legislative power is wholly in one Assembly, and the executive in another, or in a single person, these two powers will oppose and enervate upon each other, until the contest shall end in war, and the whole power, legislative and executive, be usurped by the strongest.

The judicial power, in such case, could not mediate, or hold the balance between the two contending powers, because the legislative would undermine it. And this shews the necessity too, of giving the executive power a negative upon the legislative, otherwise this will be continually encroaching upon that.

To avoid these dangers let a [distinct] Assembly be constituted, as a mediator between the two extreme branches of the legislature, that which represents the people and that which is vested with the executive power.

Let the Representative Assembly then elect by ballot, from among themselves or their constituents, or both, a distinct

Assembly, which for the sake of perspicuity we will call a Council. It may consist of any number you please, say twenty or thirty, and should have a free and independent exercise of its judgment, and consequently a negative voice in the legislature.

These two bodies thus constituted, and made integral parts of the legislature, let them unite, and by joint ballot choose a Governor, who, after being stripped of most of those badges of domination called prerogatives, should have a free and independent exercise of his judgment, and be made also an integral part of the legislature. This I know is liable to objections, and if you please you may make him only President of the Council, as in Connecticut: But as the Governor is to be invested with the executive power, with consent of Council, I think he ought to have a negative upon the legislative. If he is annually elective, as he ought to be, he will always have so much reverence and affection for the People, their Representatives and Councillors, that although you give him an independent exercise of his judgment, he will seldom use it in opposition to the two Houses, except in cases the public utility of which would be conspicuous, and some such cases would happen.

In the present exigency of American affairs, when by an act of Parliament we are put out of the royal protection, and consequently discharged from our allegiance; and it has become necessary to assume government for our immediate security, the Governor, Lieutenant-Governor, Secretary, Treasurer, Commissary, Attorney-General, should be chosen by joint Ballot, of both Houses. And these and all other elections, especially of Representatives, and Councillors, should be annual, there not being in the whole circle of the sciences, a maxim more infallible than this,

"Where annual elections end, there slavery begins."

These great men, in this respect, should be, once a year

"Like bubbles on the sea of matter borne,
They rise, they break, and to that sea return."

This will teach them the great political virtues of humility, patience, and moderation, without which every man in power becomes a ravenous beast of prey.

This mode of constituting the great offices of state will answer very well for the present, but if, by experiment, it should be found inconvenient, the legislature may at its leisure devise other methods of creating them, by elections of the people at large, as in Connecticut, or it may enlarge the term for which they shall be chosen to seven years, or three years, or for life, or make any other alterations which the society shall find productive of its ease, its safety, its freedom, or in one word, its happiness.

A rotation of all offices, as well as of Representatives and Councillors, has many advocates, and is contended for with many plausible arguments. It would be attended no doubt with many advantages, and if the society has a sufficient number of suitable characters to supply the great number of vacancies which would be made by such a rotation, I can see no objection to it. These persons may be allowed to serve for three years, and then excluded three years, or for any longer or shorter term.

Any seven or nine of the legislative Council may be made a Quorum, for doing business as a Privy Council, to advise the Governor in the exercise of the executive branch of power, and in all acts of state.

The Governor should have the command of the militia, and of all your armies. The power of pardons should be with the Governor and Council.

Judges, Justices and all other officers, civil and military, should be nominated and appointed by the Governor, with the advice and consent of Council, unless you choose to have a government more popular; if you do, all officers, civil and military, may be chosen by joint ballot of both Houses, or in order to preserve the independence and importance of each House, by ballot of one House, concurred by the other. Sheriffs should be chosen by the freeholders of counties—so should Registers of Deeds and Clerks of Counties.

All officers should have commissions, under the hand of the Governor and seal of the Colony.

The dignity and stability of government in all its branches, the morals of the people and every blessing of society, depends so much upon an upright and skillful administration of justice, that the judicial power ought to be distinct from both the legislative and executive, and independent upon both, that so it may be a check upon both, as both should be checks upon that. The Judges therefore should always be men of learning and experience in the laws, of exemplary morals, great patience, calmness, coolness and attention. Their minds should not be distracted with jarring interests; they should not be dependant upon any man or body of men. To these ends they should hold estates for life in their offices, or in other words their commissions should be during good behaviour, and their salaries ascertained and established by law. For misbehaviour the grand inquest of the Colony, the House of Representatives, should impeach them before the Governor and Council, where they should have time and opportunity to make their defence, but if convicted should be removed from their offices, and subjected to such other punishment as shall be thought proper.

A Militia Law requiring all men, or with very few exceptions, besides cases of conscience, to be provided with arms and ammunition, to be trained at certain seasons, and requiring counties, towns, or other small districts to be provided with public stocks of ammunition and entrenching utensils, and with some settled plans for transporting provisions after the militia, when marched to defend their country against sudden invasions, and requiring certain districts to be provided with field-pieces, companies of matrosses and perhaps some regiments of light horse, is always a wise institution, and in the present circumstances of our country indispensible.

Laws for the liberal education of youth, especially of the lower class of people, are so extremely wise and useful, that to a humane and generous mind, no expence for this purpose would be thought extravagant.

The very mention of sumptuary laws will excite a smile. Whether our countrymen have wisdom and virtue enough to submit to them I know not. But the happiness of the people might be greatly promoted by them, and a revenue saved sufficient to carry on this war forever. Frugality is a great revenue, besides curing us of vanities, levities and fopperies which are real antidotes to all great, manly and warlike virtues.

But must not all commissions run in the name of a king? No. Why may they not as well run thus,

"The Colony of _____ to A. B. greeting," and be tested by the Governor? Why may not writs, instead of running in the name of a King, run thus,

"The Colony of _____ to the Sheriff, &c." and be tested by the Chief Justice. Why may not indictments conclude,

"against the peace of the Colony of _____ and the dignity of the same?"

A Constitution, founded on these principles, introduces knowledge among the People, and inspires them with a conscious dignity, becoming Freemen. A general emulation takes place, which causes good humour, sociability, good manners, and good morals to be general. That elevation of sentiment, inspired by such a government, makes the common people brave and enterprizing. That ambition which is inspired by it makes them sober, industrious and frugal. You will find among them some elegance, perhaps, but more solidity; a little pleasure, but a great deal of business—some politeness, but more civility. If you compare such a country with the regions of domination, whether Monarchial or Aristocratical, you will fancy yourself in Arcadia or Elisium.

If the Colonies should assume governments separately, they should be left entirely to their own choice of the forms, and if a Continental Constitution should be formed, it should be a Congress, containing a fair and adequate Representation of the Colonies, and its authority should sacredly be confined to these cases, viz. war, trade, disputes between Colony and Colony, the Post-Office, and the unappropriated lands of the Crown, as they used to be called.

These Colonies, under such forms of government, and in such a union, would be unconquerable by all the Monarchies of Europe.

You and I, my dear Friend, have been sent into life, at a time when the greatest law-givers of antiquity would have wished to have lived. How few of the human race have ever enjoyed an opportunity of making an election of government more than of air, soil, or climate, for themselves or their children. When! Before the present epocha, had three millions of people full power and a fair opportunity to form and establish the wisest and happiest government that human wisdom can contrive? I hope you will avail yourself and your country of that extensive learning and indefatigable industry which you possess, to assist her in the formations of the happiest governments, and the best character of a great People. For myself, I must beg you to keep my name out of sight, for this feeble attempt, if it should be known to be mine, would oblige me to apply to myself those lines of the immortal John Milton, in one of his sonnets,

> "I did but teach the age to quit their cloggs
> By the plain rules of ancient Liberty,
> When lo! a barbarous noise surrounded me,
> Of owls and cuckoos, asses, apes and dogs."

A letter from John Adams to Thomas Jefferson with a postscript by Abigail Adams, 20 June 1815

Quincy June 20. 1815

Dear Sir

The fit of recollection came upon both of Us, So nearly at the same time that I may, Sometime or other, begin to think there is Some thing in Priestleys and Hartleys vibrations. The day before Yesterday I Sent to the Post office a letter to you and last night I received your kind favour of the 10th.

The question before the human race is, Whether the God of nature Shall govern the World by his own laws, or Whether Priests and Kings Shall rule it by fictitious Miracles.? Or, in other Words, whether Authority is originally in the People? or whether it has descended for 1800 Years in a Succession of Popes and Bishops, or brought down from Heaven by the holy Ghost in the form of a Dove, in a Phyal of holy Oil?

Who shall take the side of God and Nature? Brackmans,? Mandarins? Druids? Or Tecumseh and his Brother the Prophet? or Shall We become Disciples of the Phylosophers? And who are the Phylosophers? Frederick? Voltaire? Rousseau? Buffon? Diderot? or Condorcet? These Phylosophers have Shewn them Selves as incapable of governing man kind, as the Bourbons or the Guelphs.

Condorcet has let the Cat out of the Bag. He has made precious confessions. I regret that I have only an English Translation of his "Outlines of an historical View of the progress of the human Mind." But in pages 247. 248 and 249 you will find it frankly acknowledged that the Phylosophers of the 18th Century, adopted all the Maxims and practiced all the Arts of the Pharisees, the ancient Priests of all Countries, the Jesuits, the Machiavillians &c &c to overthrow the Institutions that Such Arts had established. This new Phylosophy, was by his own Account, as insideous, fraudulent hypocritical and cruel, as the old Policy of Priests, Nobles and Kings. When and where were ever found or will be found, Sincerity, Honesty or Veracity in any Sect or Party in Religion Government or Phylosophy? Johnson and Burke were more of Catholicks than Protestants at Heart and Gibbon became an Advocate for the Inquisition. There is no Act of Uniformity in the Church or State phylosophick. As many Sects and Systems among them as among Quakers and Baptists.

Bona. will not revive Inquisitions Jesuits or Slave Trade for which hebetudes, Bourbons have been driven again into Exile.

We Shall get along, with or without War.

I have at last procured the Marquis D'Argens's Ocellus Timæus and Julian. Three Such Volumes I never read. They are a most perfect exemplification of Condorcetts precious Confessions. It is astonishing they have not made more Noise in the World.

Our Athanasians have printed in a Pamphlet in Boston Your Letters and Priestleys from Belshams Lindsey. It will do you no harm. Our Correspondence Shall not again be So long interrupted. Affectionately

John Adams

[In Abigail Adams's hand:]

Mrs Adams thanks mr Jefferson for his friendly remembrance of her, and reciprocates to him a thousand good wishes.

[In John Adams's hand:]

P.S. Tickner and Gray were highly delighted with their Visit; charmed with the whole Family.

Have you read Carnot? Is it not afflicting to See a Man of Such large Views So many noble Sentiments and Such exalted integrity, groping in the dark for a Remedy? a ballance or a mediator between Independence and Despotism? How Shall his "Love of Country," his "Honor" and his "national Spirit" be produced.

I cannot write a hundreth part of what I wish to Say to you

J. A.

A Bill Establishing A Provision for Teachers of the Christian Religion, Submitted by Patrick Henry

Whereas the general diffusion of Christian knowledge hath a natural tendency to correct the morals of men, restrain their vices, and preserve the peace of society; which cannot be effected without a competent provision for learned teachers, who may be thereby enabled to devote their time and attention to the duty of instructing such citizens, as from their circumstances and want of education, cannot otherwise attain such knowledge; and it is judged that such provision may be made by the Legislature, without counteracting the liberal principle heretofore adopted and intended to be preserved by abolishing all distinctions of pre-eminence amongst the different societies or communities of Christians;

Be it therefore enacted by the General Assembly, that for the support of Christian teachers, — per centum on the amount, or — in the pound on the sum payable for tax on the property within this Commonwealth, is hereby assessed, and shall be paid by every person chargeable with the said tax at the time the same shall become due; and the Sheriffs of the several Counties shall have power to levy and collect the same in the same manner and under the like restrictions and limitations, as are or may be prescribed by the laws for raising the Revenues of this State.

And be it enacted, That for every sum so paid, the Sheriff or Collector shall give a receipt, expressing therein to what socity of Christians the person from whom he may receive the same shall direct the money to be paid, keeping a distinct account thereof in his books. The Sheriff of every County, shall, on or before the _ _ day of _ _ in every year, return to the Court, upon oath, two alphabetical lists of the payments to him made, distinguishing in columns opposite to the names of the persons who shall have paid the same, the society to which the money so paid was by them appropriated; and one column for the names where no appropriation shall be made. One of which lists, after being recorded in a book to be kept for that purpose, shall be filed by the

Clerk in his office; the other shall be the Sheriff be fixed up in the Court-house, there to remain for the inspection of all concerned.

And the Sheriff, after deducting five per centum for the collection, shall forthwith pay to such person or persons as shall be appointed to receive the same by the Vestry, Elders, or Directors, however, denominated of each such society, the sum so stated to be due to that society; or in default thereof, upon the motion of such person or persons to the next or any succeeding Court, execution shall be awarded for the same against the Sheriff and his security, his and their executors or administrators; provided that ten days previous notice be given of such motion. An upon every such execution, the Officer serving the same shall proceed to immediate sale of the estate taken, and shall not accept of security for payment at the end of three months, nor to have the goods forthcoming at the day of sale; for his better direction wherein, the Clerk shall endorse upon every such execution that no security of any kind shall be taken.

And be it further enacted, That the money to be raised by virtue of this Act, shall be by the Vestres, Elders, or Directors of each religious society, appropriated to a provision for a Minister or Teacher of the Gospel of their denomination, or the providing place of divine worship, and to none other use whatsoever; except in the denominations of Quakers and Menonists, who may receive what is collected from their members, and place it in their general fund, to be disposed of in a manner which they shall think best calculated to promote their particular mode of worship.

And be it enacted, That all sums which at the time of payment to the Sheriff or Collector may not be appropriated by the person paying the same, shall be accounted for with the Court in manner as by this Act is directed; and after deducting for his collection, the Sheriff shall pay the amount thereof (upon account certified by the Court to the Auditors of Public Accounts, and by them to the Treasurer) into the public Treasury, to be disposed of under the direction of the General Assembly, for the encouragement of seminaries of learning within the Counties whence such sums shall arise, and to no other use or purpose whatsoever.

James Madison, Memorial and Remonstrance against Religious Assessments

20 June 1785

To the Honorable the General Assembly of the Commonwealth
of Virginia
A Memorial and Remonstrance

We the subscribers, citizens of the said Commonwealth, having taken into serious consideration, a Bill printed by order of the last Session of General Assembly, entitled "A Bill establishing a provision for Teachers of the Christian Religion," and conceiving that the same if finally armed with the sanctions of a law, will be a dangerous abuse of power, are bound as faithful members of a free State to remonstrate against it, and to declare the reasons by which we are determined. We remonstrate against the said Bill,

1. Because we hold it for a fundamental and undeniable truth, "that Religion or the duty which we owe to our Creator and the manner of discharging it, can be directed only by reason and conviction, not by force or violence." (Virginia Declaration of Rights, art. 16) The Religion then of every man must be left to the conviction and conscience of every man; and it is the right of every man to exercise it as these may dictate. This right is in its nature an unalienable right. It is unalienable, because the opinions of men, depending only on the evidence contemplated by their own minds cannot follow the dictates of other men: It is unalienable also, because what is here a right towards men, is a duty towards the Creator. It is the duty of every man to render to the Creator such homage and such only as he believes to be acceptable to him. This duty is precedent, both in order of time and in degree of obligation, to the claims of Civil Society. Before any man can be considered as a member of Civil Society,

he must be considered as a subject of the Governour of the Universe: And if a member of Civil Society, who enters into any subordinate Association, must always do it with a reservation of his duty to the General Authority; much more must every man who becomes a member of any particular Civil Society, do it with a saving of his allegiance to the Universal Sovereign. We maintain therefore that in matters of Religion, no mans right is abridged by the institution of Civil Society and that Religion is wholly exempt from its cognizance. True it is, that no other rule exists, by which any question which may divide a Society, can be ultimately determined, but the will of the majority; but it is also true that the majority may trespass on the rights of the minority.

2. Because if Religion be exempt from the authority of the Society at large, still less can it be subject to that of the Legislative Body. The latter are but the creatures and vicegerents of the former. Their jurisdiction is both derivative and limited: it is limited with regard to the co-ordinate departments, more necessarily is it limited with regard to the constituents. The preservation of a free Government requires not merely, that the metes and bounds which separate each department of power be invariably maintained; but more especially that neither of them be suffered to overleap the great Barrier which defends the rights of the people. The Rulers who are guilty of such an encroachment, exceed the commission from which they derive their authority, and are Tyrants. The People who submit to it are governed by laws made neither by themselves nor by an authority derived from them, and are slaves.

3. Because it is proper to take alarm at the first experiment on our liberties. We hold this prudent jealousy to be the first duty of Citizens, and one of the noblest characteristics of the late Revolution. The free men of America did not wait till usurped power had strengthened itself by exercise, and entangled the question in precedents. They saw all

the consequences in the principle, and they avoided the consequences by denying the principle. We revere this lesson too much soon to forget it. Who does not see that the same authority which can establish Christianity, in exclusion of all other Religions, may establish with the same ease any particular sect of Christians, in exclusion of all other Sects? that the same authority which can force a citizen to contribute three pence only of his property for the support of any one establishment, may force him to conform to any other establishment in all cases whatsoever?

4. Because the Bill violates that equality which ought to be the basis of every law, and which is more indispensible, in proportion as the validity or expediency of any law is more liable to be impeached. If "all men are by nature equally free and independent," [Virginia Declaration of Rights, art. 1] all men are to be considered as entering into Society on equal conditions; as relinquishing no more, and therefore retaining no less, one than another, of their natural rights. Above all are they to be considered as retaining an "*equal* title to the free exercise of Religion according to the dictates of Conscience." (Virginia Declaration of Rights, art. 16) Whilst we assert for ourselves a freedom to embrace, to profess and to observe the Religion which we believe to be of divine origin, we cannot deny an equal freedom to those whose minds have not yet yielded to the evidence which has convinced us. If this freedom be abused, it is an offence against God, not against man: To God, therefore, not to man, must an account of it be rendered. As the Bill violates equality by subjecting some to peculiar burdens, so it violates the same principle, by granting to others peculiar exemptions. Are the Quakers and Menonists the only sects who think a compulsive support of their Religions unnecessary and unwarrantable? Can their piety alone be entrusted with the care of public worship? Ought their Religions to be endowed above all others with extraordinary privileges

by which proselytes may be enticed from all others? We think too favorably of the justice and good sense of these denominations to believe that they either covet pre-eminences over their fellow citizens or that they will be seduced by them from the common opposition to the measure.

5. Because the Bill implies either that the Civil Magistrate is a competent Judge of Religious Truth; or that he may employ Religion as an engine of Civil policy. The first is an arrogant pretension falsified by the contradictory opinions of Rulers in all ages, and throughout the world: the second an unhallowed perversion of the means of salvation.

6. Because the establishment proposed by the Bill is not requisite for the support of the Christian Religion. To say that it is, is a contradiction to the Christian Religion itself, for every page of it disavows a dependence on the powers of this world: it is a contradiction to fact; for it is known that this Religion both existed and flourished, not only without the support of human laws, but in spite of every opposition from them, and not only during the period of miraculous aid, but long after it had been left to its own evidence and the ordinary care of Providence. Nay, it is a contradiction in terms; for a Religion not invented by human policy, must have pre-existed and been supported, before it was established by human policy. It is moreover to weaken in those who profess this Religion a pious confidence in its innate excellence and the patronage of its Author; and to foster in those who still reject it, a suspicion that its friends are too conscious of its fallacies to trust it to its own merits.

7. Because experience witnesseth that ecclesiastical establishments, instead of maintaining the purity and efficacy of Religion, have had a contrary operation. During almost fifteen centuries has the legal establishment of Christianity been on trial. What have been its fruits? More or less in all places, pride and indolence in the Clergy,

ignorance and servility in the laity, in both, superstition, bigotry and persecution. Enquire of the Teachers of Christianity for the ages in which it appeared in its greatest lustre; those of every sect, point to the ages prior to its incorporation with Civil policy. Propose a restoration of this primitive State in which its Teachers depended on the voluntary rewards of their flocks, many of them predict its downfall. On which Side ought their testimony to have greatest weight, when for or when against their interest?

8. Because the establishment in question is not necessary for the support of Civil Government. If it be urged as necessary for the support of Civil Government only as it is a means of supporting Religion, and it be not necessary for the latter purpose, it cannot be necessary for the former. If Religion be not within the cognizance of Civil Government how can its legal establishment be necessary to Civil Government? What influence in fact have ecclesiastical establishments had on Civil Society? In some instances they have been seen to erect a spiritual tyranny on the ruins of the Civil authority; in many instances they have been seen upholding the thrones of political tyranny: in no instance have they been seen the guardians of the liberties of the people. Rulers who wished to subvert the public liberty, may have found an established Clergy convenient auxiliaries. A just Government instituted to secure& perpetuate it needs them not. Such a Government will be best supported by protecting every Citizen in the enjoyment of his Religion with the same equal hand which protects his person and his property; by neither invading the equal rights of any Sect, nor suffering any Sect to invade those of another.

9. Because the proposed establishment is a departure from that generous policy, which, offering an Asylum to the persecuted and oppressed of every Nation and Religion, promised a lustre to our country, and an accession to the number of its citizens. What a melancholy mark is the Bill of sudden degeneracy? Instead of holding forth an Asylum

to the persecuted, it is itself a signal of persecution. It degrades from the equal rank of Citizens all those whose opinions in Religion do not bend to those of the Legislative authority. Distant as it may be in its present form from the Inquisition, it differs from it only in degree. The one is the first step, the other the last in the career of intolerance. The magnanimous sufferer under this cruel scourge in foreign Regions, must view the Bill as a Beacon on our Coast, warning him to seek some other haven, where liberty and philanthrophy in their due extent, may offer a more certain repose from his Troubles.

10. Because it will have a like tendency to banish our Citizens. The allurements presented by other situations are every day thinning their number. To superadd a fresh motive to emigration by revoking the liberty which they now enjoy, would be the same species of folly which has dishonoured and depopulated flourishing kingdoms.

11. Because it will destroy that moderation and harmony which the forbearance of our laws to intermeddle with Religion has produced among its several sects. Torrents of blood have been spilt in the old world, by vain attempts of the secular arm, to extinguish Religious discord, by proscribing all difference in Religious opinion. Time has at length revealed the true remedy. Every relaxation of narrow and rigorous policy, wherever it has been tried, has been found to assuage the disease. The American Theatre has exhibited proofs that equal and compleat liberty, if it does not wholly eradicate it, sufficiently destroys its malignant influence on the health and prosperity of the State. If with the salutary effects of this system under our own eyes, we begin to contract the bounds of Religious freedom, we know no name that will too severely reproach our folly. At least let warning be taken at the first fruits of the threatened innovation. The very appearance of the Bill has transformed "that Christian forbearance, love and charity," [Virginia Declaration of Rights, art. 16] which of late mutually

prevailed, into animosities and jealousies, which may not soon be appeased. What mischiefs may not be dreaded, should this enemy to the public quiet be armed with the force of a law?

12. Because the policy of the Bill is adverse to the diffusion of the light of Christianity. The first wish of those who enjoy this precious gift ought to be that it may be imparted to the whole race of mankind. Compare the number of those who have as yet received it with the number still remaining under the dominion of false Religions; and how small is the former! Does the policy of the Bill tend to lessen the disproportion? No; it at once discourages those who are strangers to the light of revelation from coming into the Region of it; and countenances by example the nations who continue in darkness, in shutting out those who might convey it to them. Instead of Levelling as far as possible, every obstacle to the victorious progress of Truth, the Bill with an ignoble and unchristian timidity would circumscribe it with a wall of defence against the encroachments of error.

13. Because attempts to enforce by legal sanctions, acts obnoxious to so great a proportion of Citizens, tend to enervate the laws in general, and to slacken the bands of Society. If it be difficult to execute any law which is not generally deemed necessary or salutary, what must be the case, where it is deemed invalid and dangerous? And what may be the effect of so striking an example of impotency in the Government, on its general authority?

14. Because a measure of such singular magnitude and delicacy ought not to be imposed, without the clearest evidence that it is called for by a majority of citizens, and no satisfactory method is yet proposed by which the voice of the majority in this case may be determined, or its influence secured. "The people of the respective counties are indeed requested to signify their opinion respecting the adoption of the Bill to the next Session

of Assembly." But the representation must be made equal, before the voice either of the Representatives or of the Counties will be that of the people. Our hope is that neither of the former will, after due consideration, espouse the dangerous principle of the Bill. Should the event disappoint us, it will still leave us in full confidence, that a fair appeal to the latter will reverse the sentence against our liberties.

15. Because finally, "the equal right of every citizen to the free exercise of his Religion according to the dictates of conscience" is held by the same tenure with all our other rights. If we recur to its origin, it is equally the gift of nature; if we weigh its importance, it cannot be less dear to us; if we consult the "Declaration of those rights which pertain to the good people of Virginia, as the basis and foundation of Government," it is enumerated with equal solemnity, or rather studied emphasis. Either then, we must say, that the Will of the Legislature is the only measure of their authority; and that in the plenitude of this authority, they may sweep away all our fundamental rights; or, that they are bound to leave this particular right untouched and sacred: Either we must say, that they may controul the freedom of the press, may abolish the Trial by Jury, may swallow up the Executive and Judiciary Powers of the State; nay that they may despoil us of our very right of suffrage, and erect themselves into an independent and hereditary Assembly or, we must say, that they have no authority to enact into law the Bill under consideration. We the Subscribers say, that the General Assembly of this Commonwealth have no such authority: And that no effort may be omitted on our part against so dangerous an usurpation, we oppose to it, this remonstrance; earnestly praying, as we are in duty bound, that the Supreme Lawgiver of the Universe, by illuminating those to whom it is addressed, may on the one hand, turn their Councils from every act which would affront his holy prerogative, or violate the trust

223

committed to them: and on the other, guide them into every measure which may be worthy of his blessing, may redound to their own praise, and may establish more firmly the liberties, the prosperity and the happiness of the Commonwealth.

An Act for establishing religious Freedom

drafted in 1777 Thomas Jefferson

Whereas, Almighty God hath created the mind free;

That all attempts to influence it by temporal punishments or burthens, or by civil incapacitations tend only to beget habits of hypocrisy and meanness, and therefore are a departure from the plan of the holy author of our religion, who being Lord, both of body and mind yet chose not to propagate it by coercions on either, as was in his Almighty power to do,

That the impious presumption of legislators and rulers, civil as well as ecclesiastical, who, being themselves but fallible and uninspired men have assumed dominion over the faith of others, setting up their own opinions and modes of thinking as the only true and infallible, and as such endeavouring to impose them on others, hath established and maintained false religions over the greatest part of the world and through all time;

That to compel a man to furnish contributions of money for the propagation of opinions, which he disbelieves is sinful and tyrannical;

That even the forcing him to support this or that teacher of his own religious persuasion is depriving him of the comfortable liberty of giving his contributions to the particular pastor, whose morals he would make his pattern, and whose powers he feels most persuasive to righteousness, and is withdrawing from the Ministry those temporary rewards, which, proceeding from an approbation of their personal conduct are an additional incitement to earnest and unremitting labours for the instruction of mankind;

That our civil rights have no dependence on our religious opinions any more than our opinions in physics or geometry,

That therefore the proscribing any citizen as unworthy the public confidence, by laying upon him an incapacity of being called to offices of trust and emolument, unless he profess or renounce this or that religious opinion, is depriving him injuriously of those privileges and advantages, to which, in common with his fellow citizens, he has a natural right,

That it tends only to corrupt the principles of that very Religion it is meant to encourage, by bribing with a monopoly of worldly honours and emoluments those who will externally profess and conform to it;

That though indeed, these are criminal who do not withstand such temptation, yet neither are those innocent who lay the bait in their way;

That to suffer the civil magistrate to intrude his powers into the field of opinion and to restrain the profession or propagation of principles on supposition of their ill tendency is a dangerous fallacy which at once destroys all religious liberty because he being of course judge of that tendency will make his opinions the rule of judgment and approve or condemn the sentiments of others only as they shall square with or differ from his own;

That it is time enough for the rightful purposes of civil government, for its officers to interfere when principles break out into overt acts against peace and good order;

And finally, that Truth is great, and will prevail if left to herself, that she is the proper and sufficient antagonist to error, and has nothing to fear from the conflict, unless by human interposition disarmed of her natural weapons free argument and debate, errors ceasing to be dangerous when it is permitted freely to contradict them:

Be it enacted by General Assembly that no man shall be compelled to frequent or support any religious worship, place, or ministry whatsoever, nor shall be enforced, restrained, molested, or burthened in his body or goods, nor shall otherwise suffer on account of his religious opinions or belief, but that all men shall be free to profess, and by argument to maintain, their opinions in matters of Religion, and that the same shall in no wise diminish, enlarge or affect their civil capacities. And though we well know that this Assembly elected by the people for the ordinary purposes of Legislation only, have no power to restrain the acts of succeeding Assemblies constituted with powers equal to our own, and that therefore to declare this act irrevocable would be of no effect in law; yet we are free to declare, and do declare that the rights hereby asserted, are of the natural rights of mankind, and that if any act shall be hereafter passed to repeal the present or to narrow its operation, such act will be an infringement of natural right.

(Introduced by James Madison and passed by the Virginia General Assembly on January 16, 1786.

A Letter To Peter Carr From Thomas Jefferson

Paris, Aug. 10, 1787

DEAR PETER,

— I have received your two letters of Decemb. 30 and April 18, and am very happy to find by them, as well as by letters from Mr. Wythe, that you have been so fortunate as to attract his notice & good will; I am sure you will find this to have been one of the most fortunate events of your life, as I have ever been sensible it was of mine. I inclose you a sketch of the sciences to which I would wish you to apply in such order as Mr. Wythe shall advise; I mention also the books in them worth your reading, which submit to his correction. Many of these are among your father's books, which you should have brought to you. As I do not recollect those of them not in his library, you must write to me for them, making out a catalogue of such as you think you shall have occasion for in 18 months from the date of your letter, & consulting Mr. Wythe on the subject. To this sketch I will add a few particular observations.

Italian. I fear the learning this language will confound your French and Spanish. Being all of them degenerated dialects of the Latin, they are apt to mix in conversation. I have never seen a person speaking the three languages who did not mix them. It is a delightful language, but late events having rendered the Spanish more useful, lay it aside to prosecute that.

Spanish. Bestow great attention on this, & endeavor to acquire an accurate knowlege of it. Our future connections with Spain & Spanish America will render that language a valuable acquisition. The antient history of a great part of America, too, is written in that language. I send you a dictionary.

Moral philosophy. I think it lost time to attend lectures in this branch. He who made us would have been a pitiful bungler if he had made the rules of our moral conduct a matter of science. For one man of science, there are thousands who are not. What would have become of them? Man was destined for society. His morality therefore was to be formed to this object. He was endowed with a sense of right & wrong merely relative to this. This sense is as much a part of his nature as the sense of hearing, seeing, feeling; it is the true foundation of morality, & not the {to kalon}, truth,& c. as fanciful writers have imagined. The moral sense, or conscience, is as much a part of man as his leg or arm. It is given to all human beings in a stronger or weaker degree, as force of members is given them in a greater or less degree. It may be strengthened by exercise, as may any particular limb of the body. This sense is submitted indeed in some degree to the guidance of reason; but it is a small stock which is required for this: even a less one than what we call common sense. State a moral case to a ploughman & a professor. The former will decide it as well, & often better than the latter, because he has not been led astray by artificial rules. In this branch therefore read good books because they will encourage as well as direct your feelings. The writings of Sterne particularly form the best course of morality that ever was written. Besides these read the books mentioned in the enclosed paper; and above all things lose no occasion of exercising your dispositions to be grateful, to be generous, to be charitable, to be humane, to be true, just, firm, orderly, courageous &c. Consider every act of this kind as an exercise which will strengthen your moral faculties, & increase your worth.

Religion. Your reason is now mature enough to examine this object. In the first place divest yourself of all bias in favour of novelty & singularity of opinion. Indulge them in any other subject rather than that of religion. It is too important, & the consequences of error may be too serious. On the other hand shake off all the fears & servile prejudices under which weak minds are servilely crouched. Fix reason firmly in her seat, and call to her tribunal every fact, every opinion. Question with boldness even the existence of a god; because, if there be one, he must more approve of the homage of reason, than that of blindfolded fear. You will naturally examine first the religion of your own country. Read the bible then, as you would read Livy or Tacitus. The facts which are within the ordinary course of nature you will believe on the authority of the writer, as you do those of the same kind in Livy & Tacitus. The testimony of the writer weighs in their favor in one scale, and their not being against the laws of nature does not weigh against them. But those facts in the bible which contradict the laws of nature, must be examined with more care, and under a variety of faces. Here you must recur to the pretensions of the writer to inspiration from god. Examine upon what evidence his pretensions are founded, and whether that evidence is so strong as that its falsehood would be more improbable than a change in the laws of nature in the case he relates. For example in the book of Joshua we are told the sun stood still several hours. Were we to read that fact in Livy or Tacitus we should class it with their showers of blood, speaking of statues, beasts, &c. But it is said that the writer of that book was inspired. Examine therefore candidly what evidence there is of his having been inspired. The pretension is entitled to your inquiry, because millions believe it. On the other hand you are astronomer enough to know how contrary it is to the law of nature that a body revolving on its axis as the earth does, should have stopped, should not by that sudden stoppage have prostrated animals, trees, buildings, and should after a certain time have resumed its revolution, & that without a second general prostration. Is this arrest of the earth's motion, or the evidence which affirms it, most within the law of probabilities? You will next read the new testament. It is the history of a personage called Jesus. Keep in your eye the opposite pretensions of those who say he was begotten by god, born of a virgin, suspended & reversed the laws of nature at will, & ascended bodily into heaven: and of those who say he was a man of illegitimate birth, of a benevolent heart, enthusiastic mind, who set out without pretensions to divinity, ended in believing them,& was punished capitally for sedition by being gibbeted according to the Roman law which punished the first commission of that offence by whipping, & the second by exile or death in furca.

See this law in the Digest Lib. 48. tit. 19. 28. 3. & Lipsius Lib. 2. de cruce. cap. 2. These questions are examined in the books I have mentioned under the head of religion, & several others. They will assist you in your inquiries, but keep your reason firmly on the watch in reading them all. Do not be frightened from this inquiry by any fear of it's consequences. If it ends in a belief that there is no god, you will find incitements to virtue in the comfort & pleasantness you feel in it's exercise, and the love of others which it will procure you. If you find reason to believe there is a god, a consciousness that you are acting under his eye, & that he approves you, will be a vast additional incitement; if that there be a future state, the hope of a happy existence in that increases the appetite to deserve it; if that Jesus was also a god, you will be comforted by a belief of his aid and love. In fine, I repeat that you must lay aside all prejudice on both sides, & neither believe nor reject anything because any other persons, or description of persons have rejected or believed it. Your own reason is the only oracle given you by heaven, and you are answerable not for the rightness but uprightness of the decision. I forgot to observe when speaking of the new testament that you should read all the histories of Christ, as well of those whom a council of ecclesiastics have decided for us to be Pseudo-evangelists, as those they named Evangelists. Because these Pseudo-evangelists pretended to inspiration as much as the others, and you are to judge their pretensions by your own reason, & not by the reason of those ecclesiastics. Most of these are lost. There are some however still extant, collected by Fabricius which I will endeavor to get & send you.

Travelling. This makes men wiser, but less happy. When men of sober age travel, they gather knolege which they may apply usefully for their country, but they are subject ever after to recollections mixed with regret, their affections are weakened by being extended over more objects, & they learn new habits which cannot be gratified when they return home. Young men who travel are exposed to all these inconveniences in a higher degree, to others still more serious, and do not acquire that wisdom for which a previous foundation is requisite by repeated & just observations at home. The glare of pomp & pleasure is analogous to the motion of their blood, it absorbs all their affection & attention, they are torn from it as from the only good in this world, and return to their home as to a place of exile & condemnation. Their eyes are for ever turned back to the object they have lost, & it's recollection poisons the residue of their lives. Their first & most delicate passions are hackneyed on unworthy objects here, & they carry home only the dregs, insufficient to make themselves or anybody else happy. Add to this that a habit of idleness, an inability to apply themselves to business is acquired & renders them useless to themselves & their country. These observations are founded in experience. There is no place where your pursuit of knolege will be so little obstructed by foreign objects as in your own country, nor any wherein the virtues of the heart will be less exposed to be weakened. Be good, be learned, & be industrious, & you will not want the aid of travelling to render you precious to your country, dear to your friends, happy within yourself. I repeat my advice to take a great deal of exercise, & on foot. Health is the first requisite after morality. Write to me often & be assured of the interest I take in your success, as well as of the warmth of those sentiments of attachment with which I am, dear Peter,

> your affectionate friend.
> TH: JEFFERSON

P.S. Let me know your age in your next letter. Your cousins here are well & desire to be remembered to you.

A Letter From Thomas Jefferson to James Monroe

Eppington May 26. 1800.

Dear Sir

I am sorry your servant had such a chase to find me. I came to this place on Saturday. he got here in the night last night. further reflection on the matter which had been proposed in conversation the evening before I left you, convinced me that it could not succeed, that obstacles must arise to it, and that these would give rise to disagreeable incidents. could I have seen you therefore in the morning of my leaving Richmond I should have dissuaded the attempt. however as it has been made it shews who are the Anti-unionists in principle. my only anxiety is that the friends of our principle may take no umbrage at my declining their proffered civility. I will thank you to express my particular respect to Doctr Foushee to whom it happened that I had not an opportunity of doing it sufficiently while we were together at your house.—as to the calumny of atheism, I am so broken to calumnies of every kind, from every department of government Executive, Legislative, & Judiciary, & from every minion of theirs holding office or seeking it, that I entirely disregard it; and from Chace it will have less effect than from any other man in the United States. it has been so impossible to contradict all their lies, that I have determined to contradict none; for while I should be engaged with one, they would publish twenty new ones. thirty years of public life have enabled most of those who read newspapers to judge of me for themselves.

I think it essentially just and necessary that Callendar should be substantially defended. whether in the first stages by publick interference, or private contribution, may be a question. perhaps it might be as well that it should be left to the legislature who will meet in time, & before whom you can lay the matter so as to bring it before them. it is become peculiarly their cause and may furnish them a fine opportunity of shewing their respect to the union & at the same time of doing justice in another way to those whom they can protect without committing the publick tranquility.

I leave this place tomorrow for Monticello, and shall be three days on the road. I think it possible that in the course of a month or two the Senate may be called to the Federal city by the arrival of a treaty with France. however I presume it will be a very short call. I shall give you notice when Dupont arrives at Monticello, as you may perhaps so time your visits of business to that quarter as to see him. present my friendly respects to mrs Monroe, & accept yourself assurances of constant & affectionate attachment from Dear Sir

Your friend & servt
TH: JEFFERSON

Thomas Jefferson's letter To Dr. Benjamin Rush

Monticello, September 23, 1800

DEAR SIR,

— I have to acknowledge the receipt of your favor of Aug. 22, and to congratulate you on the healthiness of your city. Still Baltimore, Norfolk & Providence admonish us that we are not clear of our new scourge. When great evils happen, I am in the habit of looking out for what good may arise from them as consolations to us, and Providence has in fact so established the order of things, as that most evils are the means of producing some good. The yellow fever will discourage the growth of great cities in our nation, & I view great cities as pestilential to the morals, the health and the liberties of man. True, they nourish some of the elegant arts, but the useful ones can thrive elsewhere, and less perfection in the others, with more health, virtue & freedom, would be my choice.

I agree with you entirely, in condemning the mania of giving names to objects of any kind after persons still living. Death alone can seal the title of any man to this honor, by putting it out of his power to forfeit it. There is one other mode of recording merit, which I have often thought might be introduced, so as to gratify the living by praising the dead. In giving, for instance, a commission of chief justice to Bushrod Washington, it should be in consideration of his integrity, and science in the laws, and of the services rendered to our country by his illustrious relation, &c. A commission to a descendant of Dr. Franklin, besides being in consideration of the proper qualifications of the person, should add that of the great services rendered by his illustrious ancestor, Bn Fr, by the advancement of science, by inventions useful to man, &c. I am not sure that we ought to change all our names. And during the regal government, sometimes, indeed, they were given through adulation; but often also as the reward of the merit of the times, sometimes for services rendered the colony. Perhaps, too, a name when given, should be deemed a sacred property.

I promised you a letter on Christianity, which I have not forgotten. On the contrary, it is because I have reflected on it, that I find much more time necessary for it than I can at present dispose of. I have a view of the subject which ought to displease neither the rational Christian nor Deists, and would reconcile many to a character they have too hastily rejected. I do not know that it would reconcile the _genus irritabile vatum_ who are all in arms against me. Their hostility is on too interesting ground to be softened. The delusion into which the X. Y. Z. plot shewed it possible to push the people; the successful experiment made under the prevalence of that delusion on the clause of the constitution, which, while it secured the freedom of the press, covered also the freedom of religion, had given to the clergy a very favorite hope of obtaining an establishment of a particular form of Christianity thro' the U. S.; and as every sect believes its own form the true one, every one perhaps hoped for his own, but especially the Episcopalians& Congregationalists. The returning good sense of our country threatens abortion to their hopes, & they believe that any portion of power confided to me, will be exerted in opposition to their schemes. And they believe rightly; for I have sworn upon the altar of god, eternal hostility against every form of tyranny over the mind of man. But this is all they have to fear from me: & enough too in their opinion, & this is the cause of their printing lying pamphlets against me, forging conversations for me with Mazzei, Bishop Madison,& c., which are absolute falsehoods without a circumstance of truth to rest on; falsehoods, too, of which I acquit Mazzei & Bishop Madison, for they are men of truth.

But enough of this: it is more than I have before committed to paper on the subject of all the lies that has been preached and printed against me. I have not seen the work of Sonnoni which you mention, but I have seen another work on Africa, (Parke's,) which I fear will throw cold water on the hopes of the friends of freedom. You will hear an account of an attempt at insurrection in this state. I am looking with anxiety to see what will be it's effect on our state. We are truly to be pitied. I fear we have little chance to see you at the Federal city or in Virginia, and as little at Philadelphia. It would be a great treat to receive you here. But nothing but sickness could effect that; so I do not wish it. For I wish you health and happiness, and think of you with affection.

Adieu.
Thomas Jefferson

A Letter From Thomas Jefferson to Timothy Pickering

Monticello Feb. 27. 21.

I have recieved, Sir, your favor of the 12th and I assure you I recieved it with pleasure. it is true as you say that we have differed in political opinions; but I can say with equal truth, that I never suffered a political to become a personal difference. I have been left on this ground by some friends whom I dearly loved, but I was never the first to separate. with some others, of politics different from mine, I have continued in the warmest friendship to this day, and to all, and to yourself particularly, I have ever done moral justice.

I thank you for mr Channing's discourse, which you have been so kind as to forward me. it is not yet hand, but is doubtless on it's way. I had recieved it thro' another channel, and read it with high satisfaction. no one sees with greater pleasure than myself the progress of reason in it's advances towards rational Christianity. when we shall have done away the incomprehensible jargon of the Trinitarian arithmetic, that three are one, and one is three; when we shall have knocked down the artificial scaffolding, reared to mask from view the simple structure of Jesus, when, in short, we shall have unlearned every thing which has been taught since his day, and got back to the pure and simple doctrines he inculcated, we shall then be truly and worthily his disciples: and my opinion is that if nothing had ever been added to what flowed purely from his lips, the whole world would at this day have been Christian. I know that the case you cite, of Dr Drake, has been a common one. the religion-builders have so distorted and deformed the doctrines of Jesus, so muffled them in mysticisms, fancies and falsehoods, have caricatured them into forms so monstrous and inconcievable, as to shock reasonable thinkers, to revolt them against the whole, and drive them rashly to pronounce it's founder an imposter. had there never been a Commentator, there never would have been an infidel. in the present advance of truth, which we both approve, I do not know that you and I may think alike on all points. as the Creator has made no two faces alike, so no two minds, and probably no two creeds. we well know that among Unitarians themselves there are strong shades of difference, as between Doctors Price and Priestley for example. so there may be peculiarities in your creed and in mine. they are honestly formed without doubt. I do not wish to trouble the world with mine, nor to be troubled for them. these accounts are to be settled only with him who made us; and to him we leave it, with charity for all others, of whom also he is the only rightful and competent judge. I have little doubt that the whole of our country will soon be rallied to the Unity of the Creator, and, I hope, to the pure doctrines of Jesus also.

In saying to you so much, and without reserve, on a subject on which I never permit myself to go before the public, I know that I am safe against the infidelities which have so often betrayed my letters to the strictures of those for whom they were not written, and to whom I never meant to commit my peace. to yourself I wish every happiness, and will conclude, as you have done, in the same simple style of antiquity, da operam ut Valeas. hoc mihi gratius facere nihil potes.

TH: JEFFERSON

A letter from Thomas Jefferson to Horatio G. Spafford

Monticello Mar. 17. 14.

Dear Sir,

I am an unpunctual correspondent at best. while my affairs permit me to be within doors, I am too apt to take up a book, and to forget the calls of the writing table. besides this I pass a considerable portion of my time at a possession so distant, and uncertain as to it's mails that my letters always await my return here. this must apologise for my being so late in acknoleging your two favors of Dec. 17.1 and Jan. 28. as also that of the gazetteer which came safely to hand. I have read it with pleasure, and derived from it much information which I did not possess before. I wish we had as full a statement as to all our states. we should know ourselves better our circumstances and resources, and the advantageous ground we stand on as a whole. we are certainly much in debted to you for this fund of valuable information.—I join in your reprobation of our merchants, priests and lawyers for their adherence to England & monarchy in preference to their own country and it's constitution. but merchants have no country. the mere spot they stand on does not constitute so strong an attachment as that from which they draw their gains. in every country and in every age, the priest has been hostile to liberty. he is always in alliance with the Despot abetting his abuses in return for protection to his own. it is easier to acquire wealth and power by this combination than by deserving them: and to effect this they have perverted the purest religion ever preached to man, into mystery & jargon unintelligible to all mankind & therefore the safer engine for their purposes. with the lawyers it is a new thing. they have in the mother country been generally the firmest supporters of the free principles of their constitution. but there too they have changed. I ascribe much of this to the substitution of Blackstone for my Lord Coke, as an elementary work. in truth Blackstone and Hume have made tories of all England, and are making tories of those young Americans whose native feelings of independance do not place them above the wily sophistries of a Hume or a Blackstone. these two books, but especially the former have done more towards the suppression of the liberties of man, than all the million of men in arms of Bonaparte and the millions of human lives with the sacrifice of which he will stand loaded before the judgment seat of his maker. I fear nothing for our liberty from the assaults of force; but I have seen and felt much, and fear more from English books, English prejudices, English manners, and the apes, the dupes, and designs among our professional crafts. when I look around me for security against these seductions, I find it in the wide spread of our Agricultural citizens, in their unsophisticated minds, their independance and their power if called on to crush the Humists of our cities, and to maintain the principles which severed us from England. I see our safety in the extent of our confederacy, and in the probability3 that in the proportion of that the sound parts will always be sufficient to crush local poisons. in this hope I rest, and tender you the assurance of my esteem and respect.

Th: Jefferson

Jefferson's letter To Charles Thomson on January 9, 1816

MY DEAR AND ANCIENT FRIEND,

— An acquaintance of fifty-two years, for I think ours dates from 1764, calls for an interchange of notice now and then, that we remain in existence, the monuments of another age, and examples of a friendship unaffected by the jarring elements by which we have been surrounded, of revolutions of government, of party and of opinion. I am reminded of this duty by the receipt, through our friend Dr. Patterson, of your synopsis of the four Evangelists. I had procured it as soon as I saw it advertised, and had become familiar with its use; but this copy is the more valued as it comes from your hand. This work bears the stamp of that accuracy which marks everything from you, and will be useful to those who, not taking things on trust, recur for themselves to the fountain of pure morals. I, too, have made a wee-little book from the same materials, which I call the Philosophy of Jesus; it is a paradigma of his doctrines, made by cutting the texts out of the book, and arranging them on the pages of a blank book, in a certain order of time or subject. A more beautiful or precious morsel of ethics I have never seen; it is a document in proof that I am a real Christian, that is to say, a disciple of the doctrines of Jesus, very different from the Platonists, who call me infidel and themselves Christians and preachers of the gospel, while they draw all their characteristic dogmas from what its author never said nor saw. They have compounded from the heathen mysteries a system beyond the comprehension of man, of which the great reformer of the vicious ethics and Deismof the Jews, were he to return on earth, would not recognize one feature. If I had time I would add to my little book the Greek, Latin and French texts, in columns side by side. And I wish I could subjoin a translation of Gosindi's Syntagma of the doctrines of Epicurus, which, notwithstanding the calumnies of the Stoics and caricatures of Cicero, is the most rational system remaining of the philosophy of the ancients, as frugal of vicious indulgence, and fruitful of virtue as the hyperbolical extravagances of his rival sects.

I retain good health, am rather feeble to walk much, but ride with ease, passing two or three hours a day on horseback, and every three or four months taking in a carriage a journey of ninety miles to a distant possession, where I pass a good deal of my time. My eyes need the aid of glasses by night, and with small print in the day also; my hearing is not quite so sensible as it used to be; no tooth shaking yet, but shivering and shrinking in body from the cold we now experience, my thermometer having been as low as 12 degrees this morning. My greatest oppression is a correspondence afflictingly laborious, the extent of which I have been long endeavoring to curtail. This keeps me at the drudgery of the writing-table all the prime hours of the day, leaving for the gratification of my appetite for reading, only what I can steal from the hours of sleep. Could I reduce this epistolary corvee within the limits of my friends and affairs, and give the time redeemed from it to reading and reflection, to history, ethics, mathematics, my life would be as happy as the infirmities of age would admit, and I should look on its consummation with the composure of one "qui summum nec me tuit diem nec optat." *(who is the supreme ; nor did I tuit day, nor desires it.)* So much as to myself, and I have given you this string of egotisms in the hope of drawing a similar one from yourself. I have heard from others that you retain your health, a good degree of activity, and all the vivacity and cheerfulness of your mind, but I wish to learn it more minutely from yourself. How has time affected your health and spirits? What are your amusements, literary and social?

Tell me everything about yourself, because all will be interesting to me who retains for you ever the same constant and affectionate friendship and respect.

Th: Jefferson

Thomas Jefferson's Essay on New England Religious Intolerance (Draft), [ca. 10 January 1816]

Monticello, January 21, 1816.

The letter fro Jefferson to Thomas Ritchie, editor of the Richmond *Enquirer*:

Dear Sir, - in answering the letter of a northern correspondent lately, I indulged in a tirade against a pamphlet recently published in this quarter. On revising my letter, however, I thought it unsafe to commit myself so far to a stranger. I struck out the passage therefore, yet I think the pamphlet of such a character as not to be unknown or unnoticed by the people of the United States. It is the most bold and impudent stride New England has ever made in arroganting an ascendency of the rest of the Union. The first form of the pamphlet was an address from the Reverend Lyman Beecher, chairman of the Connecticut Society for the education of *pious* young men for the ministry. Its matter was then adopted and published in a sermon by Reverend Mr. Person of Andover in Massachusetts, where they have a *theological* college; and where the address "with circumstantial variations to adapt it to more general use" is reprinted on a sheet and a half of paper, in so cheap a form as to be distributed, I imagine, gratis, for it has a final note indicating six thousand copies of the first edition printed. So far as it respects Virginia, the extract of my letter gives the outline. I therefore send it to you to publish of burn, abridge or alter, as you think best. You understand the public palate better than I do. Only give it such a title as may lead to no suspicion from whom you receive it. I am the more induced to offer it to you because it is possible mine may be the only copy in the state, and because, to it may be [sic] *a' propos** for the petition for the establishment of *a theological society* now before the legislature, and to witch they have shown the unusual respect of hearing an advocate for it at their bar. From what quarter this theological society comes I know not; perhaps from our own tramontaine cherty, of New England religion and politics; perhaps is is the entering wedge from its *theological* sister in Andover, for the body of 'qualified religious instructors' proposed by their pious brethren of the East 'to evangelize and catechize', to edify our daughters by weekly lectures and our wives by 'family visits' fro these pious young monks fro Harvard and Yale. However, do with this what you please, and be assured of my friendship and respect.

(*French for *opportunity* or *to the purpose*)

The deleted paragraph of the letter to Spafford:

you judge truly that I am not afraid of the priests. they have tried upon me all their various batteries, of pious whining, hypocritical canting, lying & slandering, without being able to give me one moment of pain. I have contemplated their order from the Magi of the East to the Saints of the West, and I have found no difference of character, but of more or less caution, in proportion to the information or ignorance of those on whom their interested duperies were to be plaid off. their sway in New England is indeed formidable. no mind beyond mediocrity dares there to develope itself. if it does, they excite against it the public opinion which they command, & by little, but incessant and teazing persecutions, drive it from among them. their present great emigrations to the Western country are real flights from persecution, religious & political. but the abandonment of the country by those who wish to enjoy freedom of opinion leaves the despotism over the residue more intense, more oppressive. they are now looking to the fleshpots of the South, and aiming at foothold there by their missionary teachers. they have lately come forward boldly with their plan to establish 'a qualified religious instructor over every thousand souls in the US.' and they seem to consider none as qualified but their own sect. thus, in Virginia, they say there are but 60. qualified, and that 914. are still wanting of the full quota. all besides the 60. are 'mere nominal ministers unacquainted with theology.' now the 60. they allude to are exactly in the string of counties at the Western foot of the Blue ridge, settled originally by Irish presbyterians, and composing precisely the tory district of the state. there indeed is found, in full vigor, the hypocrisy, the despotism, and anti-civism of the New England qualified religious instructors. the country below the mountains, inhabited by Episcopalians, Methodists & Baptists (under mere nominal ministers unacquainted with theology) are pronounced 'destitute of the means of grace, and as sitting in darkness and under the shadow of death.' they are quite in despair too at the insufficient means of New England to fill this fearful void 'with Evangelical light, with catechetical instructions, weekly lectures, & family visiting. that Yale cannot furnish above 80. graduates annually, and Harvard perhaps not more. that there must therefore be an immediate, universal, vigorous & systematic effort made to evangelize the nation to see that there is a bible for every family, a school for every district, and a qualifi[ed'] (i.e. Presbyterian) 'pastor for every thousand souls; that newspapers, tracts, magazines, must be employed; the press be made to groan, & every pulpit in the land to sound it's trumpet long and loud. a more homogeneous' (i.e. New-England) 'character must be produced thro' the nation.' that section then of our union having lost it's political influence by disloyalty to it's country is now to recover it under the mask of religion. it is to send among us their Gardiners, their Osgoods, their Parishes & Pearsons, as apostles to teach us their orthodoxy. this is the outline of the plan as published by messrs Beecher, Pearson & co. it has uttered however one truth. 'that the nation must be awaked to save itself by it's own exertions, or we are undone.' and I trust that this publication will do not a little to awaken it; and that in aid of it newspapers, tracts and magazines must sound the trumpet. yours I hope will make itself heard. and the louder as yours is the nearest house in the course of conflagration

A Letter from James Madison to Edward Livingston

Montpr., July 10, 1822

To Edward fLivingston

Dear Sir,

I observe with particular pleasure the view you have taken of the immunity of Religion from civil jurisdiction, in every case where it does not trespass on private rights or the public peace. This has always been a favorite principle with me; and it was not with my approbation, that the deviation from it took place in Congs., when they appointed Chaplains, to be paid from the Natl. Treasury. It would have been a much better proof to their Constituents of their pious feeling if the members had contributed for the purpose, a pittance from their own pockets. As the precedent is not likely to be rescinded, the best that can now be done, may be to apply to the Constn. the maxim of the law, de minimis non curat.

There has been another deviation from the strict principle in the Executive Proclamations of fasts & festivals, so far, at least, as they have spoken the language of injunction, or have lost sight of the equality of all religious sects in the eye of the Constitution. Whilst I was honored with the Executive Trust I found it necessary on more than one occasion to follow the example of predecessors. But I was always careful to make the Proclamations absolutely indiscriminate, and merely recommendatory; or rather mere designations of a day, on which all who thought proper might unite in consecrating it to religious purposes, according to their own faith & forms. In this sense, I presume you reserve to the Govt. a right to appoint particular days for religious worship throughout the State, without any penal sanction enforcing the worship. I know not what may be the way of thinking on this subject in Louisiana. I should suppose the Catholic portion of the people, at least, as a small & even unpopular sect in the U. S., would rally, as they did in Virga. when religious liberty was a Legislative topic, to its broadest principle. Notwithstanding the general progress made within the two last centuries in favour of this branch of liberty, & the full establishment of it, in some parts of our Country, there remains in others a strong bias towards the old error, that without some sort of alliance or coalition between Govt. & Religion neither can be duly supported. Such indeed is the tendency to such a coalition, and such its corrupting influence on both the parties, that the danger cannot be too carefully guarded agst. And in a Govt. of opinion, like ours, the only effectual guard must be found in the soundness and stability of the general opinion on the subject. Every new& successful example therefore of a perfect separation between ecclesiastical and civil matters, is of importance. And I have no doubt that every new example, will succeed, as every past one has done, in shewing that religion & Govt. will both exist in greater purity, the less they are mixed together. It was the belief of all sects at one time that the establishment of Religion by law, was right & necessary; that the true religion ought to be established in exclusion of every other; And that the only question to be decided was which was the true religion. The example of Holland proved that a toleration of sects, dissenting from the established sect, was safe & even useful. The example of the Colonies, now States, which rejected religious establishments altogether, proved that all Sects might be safely & advantageously put on a footing of equal & entire freedom; and a continuance of their example since the declaration of Independence, has shewn that its success in Colonies was not to be ascribed to their connection with the parent Country. If a further confirmation of the truth could be wanted, it is to be found in the examples furnished by the States, which have abolished their religious establishments. I cannot speak particularly of any of the cases excepting that of Virga. where it is impossible to deny that Religion prevails with more zeal, and a more exemplary priesthood than it ever did when established and patronised by Public authority. We are teaching the world the great truth that Govts. do better without Kings& Nobles than with them. The merit will be doubled by the other lesson that Religion flourishes in greater purity, without than with the aid of Govt.

My pen I perceive has rambled into reflections for which it was not taken up. I recall it to the proper object of thank you for your very interesting pamphlet, and of tendering you my respects and good wishes.

J. M. presents his respects to Mr. Livingston and requests the favor of him to forward the above inclosed letter to N. Orleans or to retain it as his brother may or may not be expected at N. York.

Ben Franklin's Letter to Ezra Stiles, March 9,1790

Philadelphia March 9. 1790

Reverend and Dear Sir,

I received your kind Letter of Jany 28, and am glad you have at length received the Portraits of Govr Yale from his Family, and deposited it in the College Library. He was a great and good Man, and has the Merit of doing infinite Service to your Country by his Munificence to that Institution. The Honour you propose doing me by placing in the same Room with his, is much too great for my Deserts; but you always had a Partiality for me, and to that it must be ascribed. I am however too much obliged to Yale College, the first learned Society that took Notice of me, and adorned me with its Honours, to refuse a Request that comes from it thro' so esteemed a Friend. But I do not think any one of the Portraits you mention as in my Possession worthy of the Place and Company you propose to place it in. You have an excellent Artist lately arrived. If he will undertake to make one for you, I shall chearfully pay the Expence: But he must not long delay setting about it, or I may slip thro' his Fingers, for I am now in my 85th Year's and very infirm.

I send with this a very learned Work, (as it seems to me) on the antient Samaritan Coins, lately printed in Spain, and at least curious for the Beauty of the Impression. Please to accept it for your College Library. I have subscribed for the Encyclopedia now printing here, with the Intention of presenting it to the College; I shall probably depart before the Work is finished, but shall leave Directions for its Continuance to the End. With this you will receive some of the first Numbers.

You desire to know something of my Religion. It is the first time I have been questioned upon it: But I do not take your Curiosity amiss, and shall endeavour in a few Words to gratify it.

Here is my Creed: I believe in one God, Creator of the Universe. That He governs it by his Providence. That he ought to be worshipped. That the most acceptable Service we can render to him, is doing Good to his other Children. That the Soul of

Man is immortal, and will be treated with Justice in another Life respecting its Conduct in this. These I take to be the fundamental Principles of all sound Religion, and I regard them as you do, in whatever Sect I meet with them.

As to Jesus of Nazareth, my Opinion of whom you particularly desire, I think the System of Morals and his Religion as he left them to us, the best the World ever saw, or is likely to see; but I apprehend it has received various corrupting Changes, and I have with most of the present Dissenters in England, some Doubts as to his Divinity: tho' it is a Question I do not dogmatise upon, having never studied it, and think it needless to busy myself with it now, when I expect soon an Opportunity of knowing the Truth with less Trouble. I see no harm however in its being believed, if that Belief has the good Consequence as probably it has, of making his Doctrines more respected and better observed, especially as I do not perceive that the Supreme takes it amiss, by distinguishing the Believers, in his Government of the World, with any particular Marks of his Displeasure. I shall only add respecting myself, that having experienced the Goodness of that Being, in conducting me prosperously thro' a long Life, I have no doubt of its Continuance in the next, tho' without the smallest Conceit of meriting such Goodness. My Sentiments in this Head you will see in the Copy of an old Letter enclosed, which I wrote in answer to one from a zealous Religionist whom I had relieved in a paralitic Case by Electricity, and who being afraid I should grow proud upon it, sent me his serious, tho' rather impertinent, Cautions. I send you also the Copy of another Letter, which will shew something of my Disposition relating to Religion. With great and sincere Esteem and Affection, I am, Dear Sir, Your obliged old Friend and most obedient humble Servant

B Franklin

p.s. Had not your College some Present of Books from the King of France? Please to let me know if you had an Expectation given you of more, and the Nature of that Expectation. I have a Reason for the Enquiry. (I confide, that you will not expose me to Criticism and Censure by publishing any part of this Communication to you. I have ever let others enjoy their religious Sentiments, without reflecting on them for those that appeared to me insupportable and even absurd. All Sects here, and we have a great Variety, have experienced my Good will in assisting them with Subscriptions for building their new Places of Worship, and as I have never opposed any of their Doctrines I hope to go out of the World in Peace with them all.)

Religious Measures Introduced in Congress Since 1888

50th Congress – First Session: 1887 – 1888

S. 2983, introduced by Senator Blair of New Hampshire, May 21, 1888; a bill "To secure to the people the enjoyment of the first day of the week, commonly known as the Lord's Day, as a day of rest, and to promote its observance as a day of worship." Referred to Committee on Education and Labor; hearing on bill December 13, 1888, report of hearing Miscellaneous Document No. 43; not reported out of committee. C. R. 19.4155.

S. R. 86: introduced by Senator Blair of New Hampshire, May 25, 1888; a bill "Proposing an amendment to the Constitution of the United States respecting establishments of religion and free public schools." Amendment ordered to lie on table; later referred to Committee on Education and Labor; hearing on measure February 15 and February 22, 1889, not reported out of committee. C. R. 19:4615.

51st Congress – First Session: 1889 – 1890

S. 946 introduced by Senator Blair of New Hampshire, December 9, 1889, a bill "To secure to the people the privileges of rest and religious worship, free from disturbance by others, on the first day of the week." Sent to Committee on Education and Labor; not reported out of committee. C. R. 21:124.

S. R. 17, introduced by Senator Blair of New Hampshire, December 9, 1889, a bill "Proposing an amendment to The Constitution of the United States respecting establishments of religion and free public schools." Sent to Committee on Education and Labor; not reported out of committee. C. R. 21: 125.

H. R. 3854, W. C. P. Breckinridge of Kentucky, January 6, 1890; a bill "To prevent persons from being forced to labor on

Sunday." (in the District of Columbia). Sent to Committee on District of Columbia; hearing on bill before subcommittee, February 18, 1890; not reported out of committee. C. R. 21:403.

52ⁿᵈ Congress – First Session: 1891 – 1892

H. R. 194, introduced by Elijah Morse of Massachusetts, January 5, 1892; a bill "To prohibit opening on Sunday any exhibition or exposition for which the United States government makes appropriations." Sent to Committee on Judiciary; not reported out of committee. C. R. 23:130.

H. R. 540, introduced by William Breckinridge, of Kentucky, January 7, 1892; a bill "To prevent persons from being forced to labor on Sunday in the District of Columbia." Sent to Committee on District of Columbia; not reported out of committee. C. R. 23:203.

S. 2168, introduced by Alfred H. Colquitt of Georgia, February 11, 1892; a bill "To prohibit opening on Sunday any exhibition or exposition for which the United States government makes appropriations." Sent to Committee on Education and Labor; not reported out of committee. C. R. 23:1047.

S. 2994, introduced by James McMillan of Michigan, April 25, 1892; a bill "To prevent the sale or delivery of ice within the District of Columbia on the Sabbath day, commonly known as Sunday." Sent to Committee on District of Columbia; reported with amendments; not acted on in Senate. C. R. 23 : 3607, 4480

H. R. 8367, introduced by John J. Hemphill of South Carolina, April 25, 1892; a bill "Prohibiting the sale and delivery of ice within the District of Columbia on the Sabbath day, commonly known as Sunday." Sent to Committee on District of Columbia: reported back with amendments; passed House, not acted on in Senate. C. R. 23:3639, 4480

H. R. 7520. Sunday Civil bill, loaning $5,000,000 to Chicago World's Fair, conditioned on a Sunday closing. Approved August 5, 1892.

Gift of 2,500,000, H. R. 9710, introduced by James B. Reilly of Pennsylvania, August 4, 1892; "To aid in carrying out an act of Congress to provide for celebrating the discovery of America", with proviso for closing Columbian Exposition on Sundays. Sent to Committee of the Whole House; passed House and Senate and received President Harrison's signature August 5, 1892. C. R. 23: 7940, 7064-7, 7086, 7102.

53ʳᵈ Congress – Second Session: 1894 – 1895

S. 56, introduced by Senator William P. Frye of Maine, January 25, 1894; a bill "Proposing an amendment to the Constitution of the United States inserting God in the Constitution". Sent to Committee on Judiciary; not reported out of committee. C. R. 26: 1374

S. 1628, introduced by Jacob H. Gallinger of New Hampshire, February 15, 1894; a bill "To further protect the first day of the week, commonly called Sunday as a day of rest and worship in the District of Columbia." Sent to Committee on District of Columbia; not reported out of committee. C. R. 26:2211.

H. R. 6215, introduced by Elijah A. Morse of Massachusetts, March 10, 1894; a bill "To protect the first day of the week, commonly called Sunday, as a day of rest and worship in the District of Columbia." Sent to Committee on District of Columbia; not reported out of committee. C. R. 26:2827.

S. 1890, introduced by Jams H. Kyle of South Dakota, April 12, 1894; a bill "For Sunday rest in any territory, district, or place subject to the exclusive jurisdiction of the United States." Sent to Committee on Education and Labor; not reported out of committee. C. R. 26: 3688

54ᵗʰ Congress – First Session: 1895 – 1896

H. R. 167, introduced by Elijah A. Morse of Massachusetts, December 6, 1895; a bill "To protect the first day of the week, commonly called Sunday, as a day of rest and worship in the District of Columbia." Sent to worship Committee on District of Columbia; not reported out of committee. C. R. 28:48.

S. 1441, introduced by McMillan of Michigan, January 9, 1896; a bill "To protect the first day of the week, commonly called Sunday, as a day of rest and worship in the District of Columbia." Sent to Committee on District of Columbia; not reported out of committee. C. R. 28:526

H. R. 6893, introduced by George L. Wellington of Maryland, March 5, 1896; "For Sunday as a day of rest in the District of Columbia." Sent to Committee on District of Columbia; not reported out of committee. C. R. 28: 2516.

S. R. 2485, introduced by James McMillan of Michigan, March 11, 1896, a bill "To further protect the first day of the week as a day of rest in the District of Columbia." Sent to Committee on District of Columbia; not reported out of committee. C. R. 28: 2678.

S. 3136, introduced by James H. Kyle of South Dakota, May 13, 1896; a bill to make "Sunday as a day of rest in District of Columbia". Sent to Committee on District of Columbia; not reported out of committee. C. R. 28.5154.

S. 3235, introduced by James H. Kyle of South Dakota, May 28, 1896; a bill "To regulate labor and business in the District of Columbia." Sent to Committee on District of Columbia; not reported out of committee. C. R. 28:5827.

54ᵗʰ Congress – Second Session: 1896 – 1897

H. R. 9679, introduced by Joseph E. Washington of Tennessee, December 16, 1896 "To further protect the first day of the week as a day of rest in the District of Columbia." Sent to Committee on District of Columbia; not reported out of committee. C. R. 29:229.

55ᵗʰ Congress – First Session: 1897 – 1898

S. 920, introduced by James McMillan of Michigan, March 19, 1897, a bill "To further protect the first day of the week as a day of rest ill the District of Columbia." Sent to Committee on District of Columbia; not reported out of committee. C. Ii. 30:68.

H. R. 1075, introduced by Alfred C. Harmer of Pennsylvania, March 19, 1897; a bill "To further protect the first day of the week as a day of rest in the District of Columbia." Sent to Committee on District of Columbia; not reported out of committee. C. R. 30:91.

56ᵗʰ Congress – First Session: 1899 – 1900

H. R. 9829, introduced by Joseph R. Lane of Iowa, March 21, 1900; "To provide for celebrating 100th anniversary of the purchase of the Louisiana territory in St. Louis." Sent to Special Committee on Centennial of the Louisiana Purchase; amended and favorably reported; passed House Feb. 18, 1901, without Sunday-closing condition; referred to Senate Committee on Industrial Expositions; reported favorably (Senate Report 2382); passed Senate February 28, 1901, with Senator Teller's amendment: "That as a condition precedent to the payment of this appropriation the directors shall contract to close the gates to visitors on Sundays during the whole duration of the fair;" went to conference, House non-concurring in Sunday-closing amendment (H. R. Report 2976); went to second conference, House receding from non-concurrence, and both houses agreeing, March I, 1901, to bill as passed by Senate. C. R. 34:2872-4.

H. R. 10592, introduced by Amos L. Allen of Maine, April 10, 1900; a bill "To further protect the first day of the week as a day of rest in the District of Columbia." Sent to Committee on District of Columbia; not reported out of committee. C.R. 33: 3995.

57ᵗʰ Congress – First Session: 1901 – 1902

S. 5334, introduced by James McMillan of Michigan. April 19, 1902; a bill "Requiring places of business in the Dist. of Columbia to he closed on Sunday." Sent to Corn. on Dist. of Columbia; not reported out of committee. C. R. 35:4422.

H. R. 13970, introduced by John J. Jenkins of Wisconsin, April 24, 1902; a bill "Requiring places of business in the District of Columbia to be closed on Sunday." Sent to Committee on District of Columbia; not reported out of committee. C. R. 35: 4655.

H. R. 14110, introduced by Amos L. Allen of Maine, April 30.'902; a bill "To further protect the first day of the week as a day of rest in the District of Columbia." Sent to Committee on District of Columbia; not reported out of committee. C. R. 35:4905.

S. 5563, introduced by William P. Dillingham of Vermont, May I, 1902; a bill "To further protect the first day of the week as a day of rest in the District Of Columbia." Sent to Committee on District of Columbia; not reported out of committee. C. R. 35: 4909.

58ᵗʰ Congress – First Session: 1903 – 1904

H. R 4859, introduced by Amos L. Allen of Maine, November 24, 1903, a bill "To further protect the first day of the week as a day of rest in the District of Columbia." Sent to Committee on District of Columbia; not reported out of committee. C. R. 37:472.

H. R. 11819, introduced by James W. Wadsworth of New York, February 4, 1904; a bill "Requiring certain places of business in the

District of Columbia to be closed on Sunday." Sent to Committee on District of Columbia; reported favorably; amended and passed House; referred to Senate Committee 017 District of Columbia; not reported out of committee. C. R. 38: 1646, 4077, 4375, 4414

59ᵗʰ Congress – First Session: 1905 – 1906

H. R. 3022. LL, introduced by Joseph C. Sibley of Pennsylvania, December 5, 1905; a bill "To prevent Sunday banking in post-offices in the handling of money-orders and registered letters." Sent to Committee of Post-Offices and Post-Roads; not reported out of committee. C. R. 40: 112

S. 1653, introduced by Boies Penrose of Pennsylvania, December 14, 1905; a bill "To prevent Sunday banking in post offices in the handling of money-orders and registered letters." Sent to Committee on Post Offices and Post Roads; reported adversely and indefinitely postponed. C. R. 40.385, 2747.

H. R. 10510, introduced by Alien of Maine, January 5, 1906; a bill "To further protect the first day of the week as a day of rest in the District of Columbia." Sent to Committee on District of Columbia; not reported out of committee. C. R. 40:447

H. R. 12610, introduced by Harry L. Maynard of Virginia, January 20, 1906; a bill "To authorize the United States government to participate in the Jamestown Tercentennial Exposition." Sent to Committee on Industrial Arts and Expositions; reported with amendments, with proviso, "That as a condition precedent to the appropriations herein provided for, the Jamestown Exposition Company shall contract to close exhibits and places of amusement to visitors on Sundays;" did not come to vote. C. R. 40: 1336, 5486, 5637

H. R. 16483, introduced by James W. Wadsworth of New York, March 9, 1906; a bill "Requiring certain places of business in the District of Columbia to be closed on Sunday." Passed a House vote June 11, 1906, but not reported by Senate Committee. C. R. 40:2268, 3655, 7464, 8268- 71: 8307.

H. R. 16556, introduced by J. Thomas Heflin of Alabama, March 12, 1906; a bill "Prohibiting labor on buildings, and so forth, in the District of Columbia on the Sabbath day." Status not reported out of committee. C. R. 40: 3711.

S. 5825, introduced by John W. Daniel of Virginia, April 23, 1906; a bill "To authorize the United States government to participate in the Tercentennial Exposition," with proviso, "That as a condition precedent to the payment of the appropriations herein provided for, the Jamestown Exposition Company shall contract to close exhibits and places of amusements to visitors on Sundays." Sent to select Committee on Industrial Expositions; reported with amendment but not brought to vote. C. R. 40:7589.

H. R. 19844, introduced June 29, 1906, a United States Sundry Civil bill, appropriating two hundred fifty thousand dollars to the Jamestown Tercentennial Exposition. House and Senate agreed to bill with following proviso: "That as a condition precedent to the payment of this appropriation in aid of said exposition, the Jamestown Exposition Company shall agree to close the grounds of said exposition to visitors on Sunday during the period of said exposition." C. R. 40:9673-4

59th Congress – Second Session: 1906 – 1907

S. Res. 215, introduced by Elmer J. Burkett, of Nebraska, January 9, 1907; a bill directing "That the Postmaster – General be directed to inform the Senate by what authority post offices are required to be kept open on Sunday together with the regulation of Sunday opening, as to the extent of the business that may be transacted, and also what the provisions are for clerical help, and whether postal clerks and carriers are required to work more than six days per week." Considered and agreed to. C. R. 41:804.

60ᵗʰ Congress – First Session: 1907 – 1908

H. R. 327, introduced by O. M. James of Kentucky, December 2, 1907, a bill "To restore the inscription 'In God We Trust' upon the coins of the United States of America." Sent to Committee on Coinage, Weights, and Measures; not reported out of committee. C. R. 42: 18.

H. R. 353, introduced by Morris Sheppard of Texas, December 2, 1907; a bill "Requiring the motto 'In God We Trust' to be inscribed on all forms of moneys hereafter issued by the United States." Sent to Committee on Coins, Weights, and Measures; not reported out of committee. C. R. 42: 19.

H. R. 4897, introduced by Amos L. Allen of Maine, December 5, 1907, a bill "To further protect the first day of the week as a day of rest in the District of Columbia." Sent to Committee on District of Columbia; not reported out of committee. C. R. 42 : 186.

H. R. 4929, introduced by J. Thomas Heflin of Alabama, December 5, 1907; a bill "Prohibiting labor in buildings, and so forth, in the District of Columbia on the Sabbath day." Sent to Committee on District of Columbia; not reported out of committee. C. R. 42: 186.

S. 1519, introduced by Bioes Penrose of Pennsylvania, December 9, 1907; a bill "To prevent Sunday banking in post-offices in the handling of money-orders and registered letters." Sent to Committee on Post-Offices and Post-Roads; not reported out of committee. C. R. 42.209.

H. R. 11295, introduced by J. Hampton Moore of Pennsylvania, December 21, 1907; a bill "Authorizing the continuance of the inscription of a motto "In God We Trust" on the gold and silver coins of the United States." Sent to Committee on Coinage, Weights, and Measures; not reported out of committee. C. R. 42:467·

H. R. 13471, introduced by Robert Lamar of Missouri, January, 13, 1908; a bill "Prohibiting work in the District of Columbia on the first day of the week, commonly called Sunday." to Committee on District of Columbia; not reported. C. R. 42.666.

H. R. 13648, introduced by Joseph J. Beale of Pennsylvania, January 14, 1908, a bill "Requiring the motto 'In God We Trust' to be inscribed on all coins of money hereafter issued by the United States, as formerly." Sent to Committee on oil Coinage, Weights, and Measures; not reported out of committee. C. R. 42: 706.

S. 3940, introduced by Joseph F. Johnston of Alabama, January 14, 1908; a bill "Requiring certain places of business in the District of Columbia to be closed on Sunday." Sent to Committee on District of Columbia; hearing on bill before Senate subcommittee, April 15, 1908; amended and reintroduced by Mr. Johnston, May 1, 1908, as S. 3940, with Calendar No. 605 [report No. 596] attached; reported favorably; passed Senate May 15, 1908; introduced in House May 16, 1908; hearing on bill before House District Committee, February 15, 1909; not reported by House Committee. C. R. 42:676, 5514, 6314, 6434

H. R. 15239, introduced by John W. Langley of Kentucky, January 27, 1908; a bill "Requiring certain places of business in the District of Columbia to be closed on Sunday." Sent to Committee on District of Columbia; not reported out of committee. C. R. 42: 1166.

H. R. 15439, introduced by Ira W. Wood of New Jersey, January 28, 1908; a bill "Providing for the restoration of the motto 'In God We Trust' on certain denominations of the gold and silver coins of the United States." Sent to Committee on Coinage, Weights, and Measures; not reported out of committee. C. R. 42: 1257.

H. R. 16079, introduced by James McKinney of Illinois, February 3, 1908; a bill "Providing for the restoration of the motto

'In God We Trust' on certain denominations of the gold and silver coins of the United States." Sent to Committee on Coinage, Weights, and Measures; not reported out of committee. C. R. 43: 1505.

H. R. 17144, introduced by Martin D. Foster of Illinois, February 14, 1908; a bill "Providing for the restoration of the motto 'In God We Trust' on certain denominations of the gold and silver coins of the United States." Sent to Committee an Coinage, Weights, and Measures; not reported out of committee. C. R. 42: 2051.

H. R. 17296, introduced by William B. McKinney of Illinois, February 17, 1908, a bill "Providing for the restoration of the motto 'In God We Trust' on certain denominations of the gold and silver coins of the United States." Sent to Committee on Coinage, Weights, and Measures; reported favorably passed House March 16: referred to Senate Committee on Finance March 17; reported favorably; passed Senate May 13. C. R. 42 : 6189.

H. R. 19965, introduced by James Hay of Virginia, March 27, 1908; a bill "For the proper observance of Sunday as a day of rest in the District of Columbia." Sent to Committee oil District of Columbia; not reported out of committee. C. R. 42 : 40, 58.

S. 6535, introduced by Joseph F. Johnston of Alabama, April 7, 1908; a bill "For the proper observance of Sunday as a day of rest in the District of Columbia"(first section did not mention Sunday, or first day of week, and so prohibited labor on all days). Sent to Committee on all District of Columbia; hearing on this and the original S. bill No. 3940 before it was remodeled, before Senate subcommittee February 15, 1909; not reported out of committee. C. R. 42: 418.

S. 6853, Jacob H. Gallinger of New Hampshire, April 28, 1908; a bill "To amend act licensing billiard and pool tables in the District of Columbia, requiring that all such places shall be closed during the entire twenty four hours of each and every Sunday. Sent to Committee on Dist. of Columbia; not reported out of committee. C. R. 42:5324.

61ˢᵗ Congress – First Session: 1908 – 1909

H. R. Res. 17, introduced by Morris Sheppard of Texas, March 18, 1909; a bill "Proposing an amendment to the Constitution of the United States, so that it shall contain a recognition of God, and it shall begin with the words 'In the name of God.'" to Committee on Judiciary; hearing granted National Reformers before subcommittee, April 11, 1910; not reported out of committee. C. R. 44 :105.

S. 404, introduced by Joseph F. Johnston of Alabama, March 22, 1909; a bill "For the proper observance of Sunday as a day of rest in the District of Columbia." Sent to Committee on District of Columbia; not reported out of committee. C. R. 44: 135.

61ˢᵗ Congress – Second Session: 1909– 1910

H. R. 13876, introduced by Leonidas F. Livingston of Georgia, December 10, 1909; a bill "Requiring certain places of business in the District of Columbia to be closed on Sunday." Sent to Committee on District of Columbia; not reported out of committee. C. R. 45 :91.

H. R. 14619, introduced by J. Thomas Heflin of Alabama, December 14, 1909; a bill "Prohibiting labor on buildings, and so forth, in the District of Columbia on the Sabbath day." Sent to Committee on District of Columbia; adversely reported on by District Commissioners to House District Committee; not reported out of committee. C. R. 45 :135.

S. 404. Calendar No. 75, report No. 81, reintroduced by Joseph F. Johnston of Alabama, January 17, 1910, "For the proper observance of Sunday as a day of rest in the District of Columbia."

; to Committee on District of Columbia; reported favorably by Senate Committee; amended and passed Senate January 27, 1910; introduced in House January 28, 1910; hearing before House Committee on District of Columbia March 8 and 16, 1910; not reported out of committee. C. R. 45 : 681, 762, 921, 970, 1020-26, 1077-78, 1180.

NOTE: A bill to make lawful what is already not lawful:

H. R. 21475, introduced by Harry M. Coudrey of Missouri, February 21, 1910;a bill "Declaring it to be lawful to play harmless athletics and sports in the District of Columbia on the first day of the week, commonly called Sunday." Sent to the Committee on District of Columbia; not reported out of committee. C. R. 45:2234

H. R. 26462, introduced by William S. Bennet of New York, June I, 1910; a bill "Providing a weekly day of rest for certain post-office clerks and carriers." Sent to Committee on Post-Offices and Post-Roads; not reported out of committee. C. R. 45:7444·

62ⁿᵈ Congress – First Session: 1911– 1912:

S. 237, introduced by Joseph F. Johnston of Alabama, April 6, 1911; "A Bill for the Proper Observance of Sunday as a Day of Rest in the District of Columbia." Sent to Committee on District of Columbia; favorably reported by committee, but failed of passage in Senate. C. R. 47:105.

H. J. Res. 93, introduce by I. S. Pepper of Iowa, May 9, 1911; a bill "For adopting the decalogue and Jesus' rule as standard measure for laws and regulations of the government of the United States." Sent to Committee on Rules; not reported out of committee. C. R. 47: 1175.

H. R. 9433, introduced by James R. Mann of Illinois, May 16, 1911; "A Bill for the Observance of Sunday in Post Offices." Bill not passed. C. R. 47:1259.

H. R. 14690, introduced by J. Thomas Heflin of Alabama, December 6, 1911; a bill "Prohibiting labor on buildings, etc., in the District of Columbia on the Sabbath Day." Not reported out of committee. C. R. 48:59.

H. R. 21279, amended by Mr. Mann to provide "That hereafter post offices [of the first and second classes] shall not be opened on Sundays for the purpose of delivering mail to the public." Passed; approved, August 24, 1912, and became effective in post offices September 1, 1912. C. R. 48:4883. (See U. S. Stat., vol. 37, part 1, p. 543.)

H. R. 25682, introduced by William S. Howard of Georgia, July 10, 1912; a bill "To punish violations of the Lord's Day in the District of Columbia, and for other purposes." Sent to Committee on District of Columbia; not reported out of committee. C. R. 48:8881.

63rd Congress – First Session: 1913 – 1913:

S. 752, introduced by Joseph F. Johnston of Alabama, April 12, 1913; a bill "For the proper observance of Sunday as a day of rest in the District of Columbia." Sent to Committee on District of Columbia; not reported out of committee. C. R. 50:161.

H. R. 7826, introduced by Edward Keating of Colorado, August 27, 1913; a bill "To provide for the closing of barber shops in the District of Columbia on Sunday." Sent to Committee on District of Columbia; not reported out of committee. C. R. 50:3827.

H. R. 9674, introduced by J. Thomas Heflin of Alabama, December 2, 1913; a bill "Prohibiting labor on buildings, etc., in The District of Columbia on the Sabbath Day." Sent to Committee on District of Columbia; not passed out of committee. C. R. 51:92.

S. 5124, introduced by James E. Martine of New Jersey (for William Hughes), April 1, 1914; a bill "To grant all employees in the District of Columbia one day of rest in each seven days of employment." Bill not passed. C. R. 5136097.

S. 7047, Introduced by John D. Works of California, December 22, 1914; a bill "To provide for the closing of-barber shops in the District of Columbia on Sunday." Bill not passed. C. R. 52:490.

64th Congress – First Session: 1915 – 1916

H. R. 111, introduced Frank Buchanan of Illinois, December 6, 1915; a bill "To grant all employees in the District of Columbia one day of rest in each seven days of employment."
Status not reported out of committee. C. R. 53:16.

H. R. 652, introduced by Edward Keating of Colorado, December 6, 1915; a bill "To provide for the closing of barbershops in the District of Columbia on Sunday." Bill not passed. C. R. 53:28.

S. 645, introduced by John D. Works of California, December 7, 1915; a bill "To provide for the closing of barbershops in the District of Columbia on Sunday." Bill not passed. C. R. 53:84.

S. 5677, introduced by Wesley L. Jones of Washington, April 20, 1916; a bill "For the proper observance of Sunday as a day of rest in the District of Columbia." Bill not passed. C. R. 53:6476.

65th Congress – First Session: 1917 – 1917

H. R. 128, introduced by Edward Keating of Colorado, April 2, 1917; a bill "To provide for the closing of barbershops in the District of Columbia on Sunday." Bill not passed. C. R. 553124.

S. 2260, introduced by Smith of Maryland, May 11, 1917; a bill "To protect the Lord's Day, commonly called Sunday, from desecration and to secure its observance as a day of rest in the District of Columbia." Bill not passed. C. R. 55:2085.

S. 3162, introduced by Jones of Washington, December 11, 1917; a bill "For the proper observance of Sunday as a day of rest in the District of Columbia." Bill not passed. C. R. 56:114.

66th Congress – First Session: 1919– 1920

S. 635, introduced by Wesley L. Jones of Washington, May 23, 1919; a bill "For the proper observance of Sunday as a day of rest in the District of Columbia." Bill not passed. C. R. 58:151.

H. R. 12504, introduced by Henry W. Temple of Pennsylvania, February 13, 1920; a bill "To protect the Lord's Day, commonly called Sunday, and to secure its observance as a day of rest in the District of Columbia." Bill not passed. C. R. 59:2880.

67th Congress – First Session: 1921 – 1922

H. R. 4388, introduced by Fredrick N. Zihlman of Maryland, April 19, 1921; a bill "To promote the public health by providing for one day of rest in seven for employees in certain employments." Sent to Committee on District of Columbia: bill not passed. C. R. 61:461.

S. 1948, introduced by Henry L. Myers of Montana, June 2, 1921; a bill "To regulate the conducting of business in the District of Columbia on Sunday." Bill not passed. C. R. 61:2003.

H. R. 9753. "To secure Sunday as a day of rest in the District of Columbia." Fitzgerald of Ohio, January 5, 1922; bill not passed. C. R. 62:860.

68ᵗʰ Congress – First Session: 1923 – 1924

S. 3218, introduced by Wesley L. Jones of Washington, May 2, 1924;a bill "To secure Sunday as a day of rest in the District of Columbia and for other purposes." Bill not passed. C. R. 65:7666.

H. R. 12448, introduced by William C. Lankford of Georgia, February 28, 1925; a bill "To secure Sunday as a day of rest in the District of Columbia, and for other purposes." Bill not passed. C. R. 66:7666.

69ᵗʰ Congress – First Session: 1925 – 1926

H. R. 7179, introduced by William C. Lankford of Georgia, January 8, 1926; a bill "To secure Sunday as a day of rest in the District of Columbia, and for other purposes." Bill not passed. C. R. 67:1732.

H. R. 7822. "To provide for the closing of barbershops in the District of Columbia on Sunday." Keller of Minnesota, January 16, 1926; Bill not passed. C. R. 67:2268.

H. R. 10123, introduced by Charles G. Edwards of Georgia, March 8, 1926; a bill "To prohibit . . . amusements on Sunday in the District of Columbia." Bill not passed. C. R. 67:5256.

H. R. 10311, introduced by William C. Lankford of Georgia, March 13, 1926; a bill "To secure Sunday as a day of rest in the District of Columbia, and for other purposes." Bill not passed. C. R. 67:5587.

S. 4167, introduced by William J. Harris of Georgia, May 4, 1926; a bill "To enforce conformity to State laws on Sunday observance at Government military reservations." Bill not passed. C. R. 67:8655.

S. 4821, introduced by Royal S. Copeland of New York, December 14, 1926; a bill "To provide for the closing of barbershops in the District of Columbia on Sunday." Bill not passed. C. R. 68:419.

70ᵗʰ Congress – First Session: 1927 – 1928

H. R. 78, introduced by William C. Lankford of Georgia, December 5, 1927; a bill "To secure Sunday as a clay of rest in the District of Columbia, and for other purposes." Bill not passed. C. R. 69:20.

S. 2212, introduced by Royal S. Copeland of New York, November 21, 1929; a bill "To provide for the closing of barbershops in the District of Columbia on Sunday." Sent to Committee on District of Columbia, bill not passed. C. R. 71:5862.

H. R. 8767, introduced by William C. Lankford of Georgia, January 17, 1930;a bill "To prohibit the showing on Sunday of films transported in interstate commerce, and to prohibit on Sunday shows, performances, and exhibitions by theatrical troupes traveling in interstate commerce and for other purposes." Sent to Committee on Interstate and Foreign Commerce; bill not passed. C. R. 72:1843.

H. R. 16153, introduced by Gale H. Stalker of New York, January 14, 1931; a bill "To provide for the closing of barbershops on Sunday in the District of Columbia." Sent to Committee on District of Columbia; bill not passed. C. R. 74:2193.

S. 6077, introduced by Royal S. Copeland of New York, February 6, 1931; a bill "Providing for the closing of barbershops on Sunday in the District of Columbia." Sent to Committee on District of Columbia; bill not passed. C. R. 74:4121.

72ⁿᵈ Congress – First Session: 1931 – 1932

S. 1202, introduced by Royal S. Copeland of New York, December 9, 1931; a bill "Providing for the closing of barbershops on Sunday in the District of Columbia." Sent to Committee on District of Columbia; not passed. C. R. 75:205.

H. R. 8092, introduced by Gale H. Stalker of New York, January 20, 1932; a bill "Providing for the closing of barbershops on Sunday in the District of Columbia." Amended to "one day in seven." May 20, 1932. Sent to Committee on District of Columbia; bill not passed. C. R. 75:2379.

H. R. 8759, introduced by Thomas R. Amlie of Wisconsin, February 2, 1932; a bill "To prohibit commercial advertising by means of radio on Sunday." Sent to Committee on Merchant Marine, Radio, and Fisheries; bill not passed. C. R. 75:3294.

S. 4023, introduced by Royal S. Copeland of New York, March 10, 1932; a bill "Providing for the closing of barbershops one day in every seven in the District of Columbia." Sent to Committee on District of Columbia; bill not passed. C. R. 75:5628.

75ᵗʰ Congress – First Session: 1937 – 1937

H. R. 3291, introduced by James L. Quinn of Pennsylvania, January 19, 1937; a bill "To regulate barbers in the District of Columbia, and for other purposes." (Contained Sunday- closing clause.) Sent to Committee on District of Columbia; not passed. C. R. 81:313.

S. 1270, introduced by Royal S. Copeland of New York, February 1, 1937; a bill "To regulate barbers in the District of Columbia, and for other purposes." (Contained Sunday-closing clause.) Sent to Committee on District of Columbia; bill not passed. C. R. 81:610.

H. J. Res. 226, introduced by Dewey Short of Missouri, February 16, 1937; a bill "To close bowling alleys on Sunday in the District of Columbia." Sent to Committee on District of Columbia; bill not passed. C. R. 81: 1264.

H. R. 7085, introduced by James L. Quinn of Pennsylvania, May 17, 1937;a bill "To regulate barbers in the District of Columbia, and for other purposes." Bill passed both Houses of Congress and became a law. Approved June 7, 1938.

When - H. R. 3291 failed of passage, H. R. 7085, which provides only for one day of rest in seven without specifying a particular day, was introduced and passed. C. R. 81:47 16, 4742. (See U. S. Stat., vol. 52, part 1, p. 623, chap. 322, sec. 14.)

H. J. Res. 519, introduced by Dickstein of New York, November 25, 1937; a bill "To declare certain papers, pamphlets, books, pictures, and writings nonmailable, to provide a penalty for mailing same, and for other purposes – Writings of any kind . . . intended to cause racial or religious hatred or bigotry or intolerance." Sent to Committee on Post Office and Post Roads; not reported out of committee. C. R. 82:379.

76ᵗʰ Congress – First Session: 1939 – 1939

H. R. 3517, introduced by William H. Larrabee of Indiana, January 31, 1939; a bill "To promote the general welfare through the appropriation of funds to assist the States and Territories in providing more effective programs of public education." (Note) "Not to prohibit any State making any of these funds available, if it wishes, to children attending nonpublic schools." Sent to Committee on Education; not reported out of committee. C. R. 84:980.

H. J. Res. 228 [Reintroduced as H. J. Res. 65 in 77th Congress], introduced by Dickstein of New York, March 24, 1939; a bill "To declare certain papers, pamphlets, books, pictures, and writings nonmailable, to provide a penalty for mailing same, and for other purposes." Sent to Committee on Post Offices and Post Roads; not reported out of committee. C. R. 84:3280.

H. R. 5732, introduced by William H. Sutphin of New Jersey, April 12, 1939; a bill "Designating Good Friday in each year a legal holiday – To be dedicated to prayer for social and religious tolerance." Sent to Committee on Judiciary; not reported out of committee. C. R. 84:,4177.

77ᵗʰ Congress – First Session: 1941 – 1942

H. J. Res. 65 [Same as H. J. Res. 228 in 76th Congress], introduced by Dickstein of New York, January 16, 1941; a bill "To declare certain papers, pamphlets, books, pictures, and writings nonmailable, to provide a penalty for mailing same, and for other purposes – Writings of any kind designed or adapted or intended to cause racial or religious hatred or bigotry or intolerance, or to, directly or indirectly, incite to racial or religious hatred or bigotry or intolerance." Sent to Committee on Post Offices and Post Roads; not reported out of committee. C. R. 87:183.

S. 983, introduced by Robert R. Reynolds of North Carolina, February 26, 1941;a bill "To amend the act to regulate barbers in the District of Columbia, and for other purposes, giving barbers a right of referendum to choose the day all barbershops shall be closed in the District of Columbia." Sent to Committee on District of Columbia; not reported out of committee. C. R. 87:1405.

H. R. 3852, introduced by William T. Schulte of Indiana, March 6, 1941; a bill "To amend the act to regulate barbers in the District of Columbia, and for other purposes, containing a clause giving barbers a right of referendum to choose the day all barbershops shall be closed in the District of Columbia." Sent to Committee on District of Columbia; not reported out of committee. C. R. 87: 1945.

H. R. 5444, introduced by William T. Schulte of Indiana, July 30, 1941; a bill "To amend the act to regulate barbers in the District of Columbia, and for other purposes, containing clause giving barbers right to choose day all barber shops shall close in the District of Columbia." Sent to Committee on District of Columbia. Amended to include exemption for those who observe another day than the barbers may choose. Passed House. Amended in Senate and passed; returned to House and placed on consent calendar. Objection raised. Returned to Senate. Bill not passed. C. R. 87:6488.

78ᵗʰ Congress – First Session: 1943 – 1943

H. R. 2328 [Reintroduced under same number with 2d section in 79th Congress], introduced by Walter A. Lynch of New York, March 29, 1943; a bill "To declare certain papers, pamphlets, books, pictures, and writings nonmailable, to provide a penalty for mailing same, and for other purposes – Writings of any kind, containing any defamatory and false statements which tend to expose persons designated, identified, or characterized therein by race or religion, any of whom reside in the United States, to hatred, contempt, ridicule, or obloquy, or tend to cause such persons to be shunned or avoided, or to be injured in their business or occupation." Sent to Committee on the Post Office and Post Roads; not reported out of committee. C. R. 89:2670.

S. 1700 [Reintroduced Jan. 6. 1945 as S. 16, 79th Congress], introduced by Patrick A. McCarran of Nevada, February 7, 1944; a bill "To amend the District of Columbia Barber Act – Barbers to vote on a day for all to close shops. Exemption from majority choice for one making a showing made to the Board that the designated closing day conflicts with the tenets of his religion: And provided further, that his establishments shall be closed on the Sabbath of his particular religion." Sent to Committee on District of Columbia; not reported out of committee. C. R. 1276.

S. J. Res. 139, introduced by Harry Flood Byrd of Virginia and Arthur Capper of Kansas, June 22, 1944 and Patrick A. McCarran of Nevada, February 7, 1944; a bill "Designating period from Thanksgiving Day to Christmas of each year for Nation – wide Bible reading," Ending Clause: "in order that 'in God we trust' as an expression of our national life may hold new and vital meaning for all our citizens." Sent to Committee on Judiciary; reported with amendment (S. Rept. 1231); passed Senate, preamble rejected. C. R. 90:6460, 8482, 9431.

H. J. Res. 301 [see also H. J. Res. 3021, introduced by Jerry Voorhis of California. June 23, 1944; a bill "Designating the period from Thanksgiving Day to Christmas of each year for Nation-wide Bible reading." Same as H. J. Res. 139, with omission of: "in order that 'in God we trust' as an expression of our national life may hold new and vital meaning for all our citizens." Sent to Committee on Judiciary; not reported out of committee. C. R. 9036680.

H. J. Res. 302 [same as H. J. Res. 301 of same date], introduced by Donald H. McLean of New Jersey, June 23, 1944; sent to Committee on Judiciary; not reported out of committee. C. R. 90:6680.

79th Congress – First Session: 1945 – 1945

S. 16, introduced by Patrick A. McCarran of Nevada, January 6, 1945; a bill "To amend the District of Columbia Barber Act." – Compulsory closing on Sabbath of choice. Sent to Committee on District of Columbia; not reported out of committee. C. R. 91:77.

H. R. 2328 [See 78th Congress, same Bill No.], introduced by Walter A. Lynch of New York, February 23, 1945; a bill "To amend title 18, Criminal Code, to declare certain papers, pamphlets, books, pictures, and writings nonmailable – Writings of any kind, containing any defamatory and false statements which tend to expose persons designated, identified, or characterized therein by race or religion, any of whom reside in the United States, to hatred, contempt, ridicule, or obloquy or tend to cause such persons to be shunned or avoided or to be injured in their business or occupation." Sent to Committee on Post Offices and Post Roads; not reported out of committee. C. R. 91:1401.

S. 717, introduced by James M. Mead of New York and George D. Aiken of Vermont, March 8, 1945; a bill "To authorize the appropriation of funds to assist the States in more adequately financing education – Includes provision for aid for nonpublic schools." Sent to Committee on Education and Labor; not reported out of committee. C. R. 91: 1887.

S. J. Res. 46, introduced by Arthur Capper of Kansas, March 12, 1945; a bill "To provide for the use of the words 'Observe Sunday' in the cancellation of United States mail." Sent to Committee on Post Offices and Post Roads; not reported out of committee. C. R. 91:1998.

H. J. Res. 120, introduced by Jerry Voorhis of California, March 13, 1945; a bill "Designating period from Thanksgiving Day to Christmas of each year for Nation-wide Bible reading – in order that 'in God we trust' as an expression of our national life may hold new and vital meaning for all our citizens." Sent to Committee on the Judiciary; not reported out of committee. C. R. 91:2165.

80th Congress – First Session: 1947 – 1947

H. R. 156, introduced by Richard J. Welch of California, January 3, 1947; a bill "To authorize the appropriation of funds in order to assist in reducing the inequalities of educational opportunities in elementary and secondary schools – Includes provision for aid for nonpublic schools." Sent to Committee on Education and Labor; not reported out of committee. C. R.

H. R. 263, introduced by Walter A. Lynch of New York, January 3, 1947; a bill "To declare certain papers, pamphlets, books, pictures, and writings nonmailable – All papers, pamphlets, magazines, periodicals, books, pictures, and writings of any kind, containing any defamatory and false statements which tend to expose persons designated, identified, or characterized therein by race or religion, any of whom reside in the United States, to hatred, contempt, ridicule, or obloquy or tend to cause such persons to be shunned or avoided or to be injured in their business or occupation." Sent to Committee on Post Office and Civil Service; not reported out of committee. C. R.

S. 199, introduced by George D. Aiken from Vermont, January 15, 1947; a bill "To authorize the appropriation of funds to assist the States in more nearly equalizing educational opportunities among and within the States." Includes provision for aid for nonpublic schools to Committee on Labor and Public Welfare; not reported out of committee. C. R.

S. J. Res. 36, introduced by Arthur Capper of Kansas, January 20 (legislation day January 15), 1947; a bill "To provide for use of the words 'Observe Sunday' in the cancellation of the United States mail." Sent to Committee on Civil Service; not reported out of committee. C. R.

S. 472, introduced by Robert A. Taft of Ohio, January 31, 1947; a bill "To authorize the appropriation of funds to assist the States and Territories in financing a minimum foundation education, and for other purposes. Included is a provision for aid for non-public schools." Sent to Committee on Labor and Public Welfare; not reported out of committee. C. R.

H. R. 1981, introduced by Landsdale G. Sasscer of Maryland, February 17, 1947; a bill "Declaring Good Friday in each year a legal holiday." Sent to Committee on Judiciary; not reported out of committee. C. R.

The Nicene Creed

Primarily concerned with defining the nature of the three persons comprising the Trinity as one of the most important foundations of the church, this version is used by many main stream churches in the United States and other English-speaking countries.

> We believe in one God, the Father, the Almighty, maker of heaven and earth, of all that is seen and unseen.
>
> We believe in one Lord, Jesus Christ, the only Son of God, eternally begotten of the Father, God from God, light from light, true God from true God, begotten, not made, one in Being with the Father. For us and for our salvation he came down from heaven, by the power of the Holy Spirit he was born of the Virgin Mary and became truly human.
>
> For our sake he was crucified under Pontius Pilate; he suffered, died and was buried. On the third day he rose again in fulfillment of the Scriptures; he ascended into heaven and is seated at the right hand of the Father. He will come again in glory to judge the living and the dead, and his kingdom will have no end.
>
> We believe in the Holy Spirit, the Lord, the giver of life, who proceeds from the Father [and the Son]. Who with the Father and the Son is worshiped and glorified. Who has spoken through the prophets. We believe in one holy catholic and apostolic Church. We acknowledge one baptism for the forgiveness of sins. We look for the resurrection of the dead, and the life of the world to come. Amen.

NOTE: The English Version of the Nicene Creed provided above is based on the version in the 1662 Anglican Book of Common Prayer and has a few updates, made by consensus (who actually made them was not specified) for greater clarity in the general usage of modern English. There are several variations in the English translations of the Nicene Creed that are used by different Churches. Even the various Orthodox Communions in America, the English language varies slightly due to different wording being selected in the translation from the original Greek. There is still some disagreement at the beginning of each expression of belief over whether the person reciting the creed is speaking in the first person singular. (A version created in 1975 that was included in the 1979 Episcopal Church [United States] *Book of Common Prayer* included the line 'For us men and for our salvation'. The word 'men' was omitted in this version.)

CPSIA information can be obtained
at www.ICGtesting.com
Printed in the USA
BVHW03s1818150318
510692BV00001B/52/P

9 781948 653596